PANEL ONE:

COMIC BOOK SCRIPTS BY TOP WRITERS

PANEL ONE:

COMIC BOOK SCRIPTS BY TOP WRITERS

EDITED BY NAT GERTLER

About Comics

Thousand Oaks, California, USA

PANEL ONE:
COMIC BOOK SCRIPTS BY TOP WRITERS

Edited by Nat Gertler

Published by About Comics
Thousand Oaks, California

Softcover ISBN: 0-9716338-0-0

First Printing, February 2002
Seccond Printing, October 2004
Third Printing, February 2009

Printed in Canada

CONTENTS

ACKNOWLEDGEMENTS

Obviously, large thanks are due to all the fine folks who contributed their scripts to this project. Without them, this book would be a lot thinner. Thanks are also due to Batton Lash (creator of *Supernatural Law*) and Chris Schaff (of *Diamond Comics*), whose encouragement got me to switch from thinking of this project as "something that someone oughta do" to "something that I'm gonna do."

Thanks also to Vijaya Iyer *(Cartoon Books)* Carol Platt *(Marvel)* and Gail Stanley *(View Askew)* for their help in getting some of these scripts through and cleared. A round of applause goes to Marvel Comics for being generous above and beyond any reasonable call of duty. All of the answers and advice given by Rory Root *(Comic Relief)*, Brian Hibbs *(Comix Experience)*, Jackie Estrada *(Exhibit A Press)*, and Olga Pereira, Patrick Jodoin, & Angelo Messina *(Quebecor)* were helpful and greatly appreciated. If I've left anyone off, it's due to failing memory and not due to a lack of appreciation for the helpfulness!

And last but certainly not least, big thanks to The Lovely Lara Gertler, for putting up with me spending time and ravaging our bank account to publish this project.

INTRODUCTION

When anyone asks me how I write comics, I lie to them. I tell them that I write a script that's like a TV or movie script.

Actually, the differences between a comic book script and a TV, film, or dramatic script are huge and fundamental. All of those other scripts are meant to be read by dozens of people. They include the minimum possible information and keep it all carefully organized, so that each of the actors, directors, and support staff can quickly locate the information that pertains to them. The art is primarily in the dialogue; beyond that, those scripts are fairly mechanical documents.

A comics script is a personal note written to one person, the artist. Oh, it may be designed to hold up to the scrutiny of a comic book editor, and it may have some notes for the letterer (often a separate specialist, now generally adding the text via computers.) The comics writer is not just giving instructions to the artist; he is transferring a vision.

When people who are familiar with other scripts ask me about formatting comic book scripts, I tell them the truth, but they don't seem to believe me. The truth is that there is no standard format for comic book scripts. Flip through this book, and you'll see that the script layout varies from writer to writer. Certainly, Kurt Busiek's script looks little like Marv Wolfman's undialogued plot, and neither look like Jeff Smith's drawn storyboards.

If you take a closer look, you'll find that even the nature of what's being written various tremendously. Some panel descriptions have richly detailed descriptions of the visuals for the panels, while others are just brief descriptions of the actions taking place. Still other panel descriptions serve more to build the emotional context of the story in the mind of the artist, leaving it up to the artist to visually capture that feeling. These variances don't just occur from writer to writer; one writer's scripts can vary widely depending on the nature of the story being told and the artist who will be illustrating the script.

The nature of the artist involved is very important. Some artists thrive on trying to capture exactly a carefully described moment, while others want to exercise their storytelling capabilities to flesh out brief descriptions. Some love researching specific buildings, clothes, and props, while others feel it gets in the way of their imagination. Making an artist happy should not be the writer's primary job, but writing toward the artist's strengths and comforts should produce better comics. I envy those writers who are in enough demand that they can refuse to write a script until an artist has been picked.

Many of you reading this intend to write comics. While many styles of script are presented here, if you take one thing away from this book, I hope that it's not a choice of a single style. I hope, rather, that it's sense of freedom in how you approach the script. Don't lock yourself into one style that will fit all projects.

— Nat Gertler, February 2001

Long before Neil Gaiman established himself as a New York Times best-selling fantasy author, and even before his esteemed *Sandman* series became a fixture in comic shops, he was given the opportunity to take over the writing on *Miracleman*. Following in the huge footsteps of Alan Moore is a difficult prospect at best, but Neil managed to maintain the tone of Moore's work while giving it a voice all his own.

The first line in Neil's script – "this is the climbers story we've been talking about for years" – reveals something important about comic scripts: often, they are not the beginning of the process. Story concepts may be formed in conversations with the artist, either through casual conversation or deliberate planning. This gives both parties some thinking time, and allows each of them to raise questions, concerns, and suggestions toward making this a better story and a better creative experience.

Similarly, the writing process doesn't end when the script leaves the writer's word processor. It may be subject to an editor's enhancement (or meddling, depending on one's point of view). The artist may have some inspiration as well, leading to discussions with the writer or editor, or may simply implementation without discussion. Artists frequently feel free to change the pacing by altering the number of panels or the flow of the dialog through the panels.

– Nat Gertler, December 2001

MIRACLEMAN # 17, Second Story.

Neil Gaiman, for Mark Buckingham.

THIS IS THE CLIMBERS STORY WE'VE BEEN TALKING ABOUT FOR YEARS -- THE FIRST STORY I EVER THOUGHT OF WHEN TALKING TO ALAN ABOUT THE MIRACLEMAN WORLD, TWO, THREE YEARS AGO. HAVING SAID THAT, I ONLY REALISED WHAT IT WAS ABOUT WHEN I GOT TO THE VERY END. I SUPPOSE THAT'S ALWAYS THE WAY...

OK. THIS IS THE FIRST REAL STORY IN HERE -- 16 PAGES LONG. (THE LAST COUPLE OF PAGES WILL BE TAKEN UP WITH A TWO PAGE ONGOING SECTION CALLED RETRIEVAL).

EACH PANEL IS VERTICAL, FROM THE TOP OF THE PAGE TO THE BOTTOM.

THE STORY ACTUALLY STARTS ON PAGE 7, BUT IF NO-ONE MINDS, I'LL NUMBER THE PAGES FROM 1 TO 16.

PAGE 1 PANEL 1

FIRST PANEL IS A BLACK STRIP DOWN THE PAGE, WITH, REVERSED OUT, THE STORY TITLE ON IT. I DON'T SEE ANY NEED TO REPEAT THE CREDITS FOR INDIVIDUAL STORIES, BUT IF ANYONE HAS ANY VIOLENT DISAGREEMENT WITH THIS, THEN THEY CAN TALK TO ME ABOUT IT. THE TITLE SHOULD BE LETTERED VERTICALLY, WITH THE CAPTION AT THE BOTTOM OF THE PAGE.

Title: A Prayer and Hope...

caption: Date: August 3rd, 1987.

Page 1 panel 2

DAYLIGHT. OUTSIDE. IN THE FOREGROUND IS A SMALL, MALE FIGURE WITH HIS BACK TO US. HE'S GOT A BACKPACK ON, AND HAS PUT HIS HANDS ON HIS HIPS, AND IS LOOKING UPWARDS, AT THE PYRAMID. THE SIDES OF IT ARE BLACK GRANITE, WITH OCCASIONAL WINDOWS AND DOORS, IN DIFFERENT ARCHITECTURAL STYLES. IT TOWERS ABOVE HIM, VANISHES INTO THE CLOUDS WHICH MASK ITS UPPER 2/3RDS FROM US.

Caption: There are some things that are just too big. You can't fit them into your head -- they stop at the eyes, and won't go in.

Page 1 panel 3

OK, WE'VE GOT CLOSER IN. THE FIGURE OF OUR NARRATOR IS A LITTLE SMALLER THOUGH. THE PYRAMID FILLS MOST OF THE PANEL. AT THE BOTTOM WE CAN SEE A DOOR -- SOMETHING FAIRLY IMPRESSIVE, WITH DORIC COLUMNS AND ALL THAT. USE THE BRITISH MUSEUM FRONTAGE AS YOUR MODEL FOR THE DOORWAY. THE NARRATOR IS WALKING TOWARDS IT. ONE CAPTION AT THE TOP, TWO AT THE BOTTOM.

caption: You can see them, but you never believe them, no matter how familiar they become.

caption: You think about them too hard, you meet your mind coming back at you.

caption: Going up.

Page 2 panel 1

OK. THREE PANELS ON THIS PAGE. TWO THIN ONES SANDWICHING A LARGER. FIRST PANEL IS A LONG SHOT. A YOUNG WOMAN (I'LL DESCRIBE HER NEXT PANEL) SITS AT A DESK, THAT'S A RECTANGULAR BLOCK OF GLASS, OR DIAMOND, OR OBSIDIAN. THERE'S AN OLD-FASHIONED BAKELITE RADIO ON ONE CORNER OF THE DESK. WE'RE INSIDE THE PYRAMID NOW, SO THE LIGHT IS ARTIFICIAL. HUGE PALM-LIKE FERNS, PROBABLY RECONSTRUCTED PREHISTORIC PLANTS, DECORATE THE ROOM. BUT HAVING SAID THAT, IT COVERS 64 SQUARE MILES (I THINK THAT'S RIGHT. 8 BY 8.) SO TRY TO GIVE A FEELING OF SPACE IN THE BACKGROUND, OF A SMALL AREA OF A HUGE ROOM. THERE'S A COMPUTER SCREEN AND A KEYBOARD ACTUALLY SET IN THE LUCITE BLOCK.WE MIGHT BE ABLE TO SEE A LITTLE OF THE NARRATOR -- A HAND OR SOMETHING.

FOR THE RADIO WORD BALLOON, I LIKE THE IDEA OF NOT DOING JAGGED WORD BALLOONS, INSTEAD DOING SORT OF DAVE SIM KIND OF BALLOONS, NOT ROUND BUT SORT OF DROOPING AT THE EDGES. A FUNKY KIND OF FEEL.

Radio: ...nothing's gonna touch you in those golden years..

Go-ow-ow-ow-ow Golden years Wa Wa Wa Golden...

Page 2 panel 2

LARGER PANEL IN THE MIDDLE OF THE PAGE. THE RECEPTIONIST IS LOOKING UP AT US. SHE'S SMILING. SHE'S A BLEACHED BLONDE, WEARING A BLACK LATEX, BODY-HUGGING DRESS, BARE ARMS AND SHOULDERS. PALE FACE, DARK RED LIPS. OUR SHADOW FALLS ACROSS THE DESK. JUST BEHIND HER SHOULD BE A PHOTOGRAPH OF MIRACLEMAN, HEAD AND SHOULDER MOVIE-STAR-LIKE, SIGNED.

Receptionist: Hi. You're here to pray?

Narrator: Yes. I... I've never done this before...

Receptionist: Mm hmm. Few of us have. You've brought all the equipment on
the list? And food?

Narrator: Yes.

Page 2 panel 3

LONG SHOT, TWO TINY FIGURES, THE NARRATOR AND THE SECRETARY, WALKING AWAY FROM US. AGAIN, GO FOR THE FEELING OF SPACE, HERE, LIMITLESS SPACE. AS IF THE RECEPTIONIST HAS ABOUT QUARTER OF A SQUARE MILE OF SPACE TO HERSELF. FERN FRONDS AGAIN. POSSIBLY A FEW PIGEONS ARE FLUTTERING ABOUT.

Receptionist: You're lucky. There are three people already waiting to pray.

Four's the minimum number we allow. Safety.

narrator: We?

Receptionist: Sure. They don't make rules.

Page 3 panel 1

OK, FOUR PANELS ON THIS PAGE. THE FIRST THREE PANELS SHARE A COMMON BACKGROUND, A HUGE STAIRCASE SWEEPING DOWN BEHIND THEM. WE CAN SEE THAT IT LEADS TO THE NEXT FLOOR UP, THROUGH A HUGE OPENING IN THE FLOOR ABOVE US. IT HAS NO VISIBLE MEANS OF SUPPORT, IE, ONLY THE TREADS OF THE STEPS, NOTHING HOLDING THEM UP.

NOW -- A BRIEF ESSAY ON INTERNAL ARCHITECTURE. AS WE CAN SEE FROM JOHN'S BITS, THE CENTRAL 'WELL' OF THE PYRAMID IS HUGE, AND DESIGNED TO BE FLOWN UP AND DOWN. ALL AROUND THE SIDES ARE A CIRCULAR MULTIPLICITY OF ENVIRONMENTS. YOU WALK UP TO THE NEXT FLOOR, THEN YOU WALK ROUND THE INSIDE OF THE PYRAMID UNTIL YOU GET TO SOME STAIRS, THEN YOU DO IT AGAIN. SOMETIMES YOU GO THROUGH ONE ENVIRONMENT, SOMETIMES THROUGH TWENTY OR THIRTY, IN ORDER TO GET TO THE NEXT FLOOR UP. GO ALWAYS FOR A FEELING OF ARCHITECTURAL STYLES IN THEIR HUNDREDS, BUT ALWAYS THE FEELING THAT THIS STUFF WAS DESIGNED BY PEOPLE FOR WHOM BEAUTY ACTUALLY MATTERS, AND IS IMPORTANT.

THE FIRST PANEL SHOWS PEOPLE -- A COUPLE OF THEM SITTING ON THE FLOOR, ONE STANDING. THEY ARE:

A BLACK WOMAN, GWEN. IN HER LATE THIRTIES. NOT HUGELY PHYSICALLY ATTRACTIVE.

A SMALL OLD ORIENTAL MAN -- TAIPEK. HE HAS A POUCH SLUNG OVER HIS SHOULDER AT ALL TIMES, IN ADDITION TO ANY OTHER BACKPACKS ETC HE HAS. IT HANGS AS IF IT HAS SOMETHING HEAVY AND MAYBE GUN-SIZED IN IT.

AN ASIAN YOUTH -- SLIGHTLY PUDGY, WITH A LITTLE MOUSTACHE. CAIRO.

THEY ARE LOOKING TOWARDS US. THEY EACH HAVE LARGE BACKPACKS AND CLIMBING BOOTS.

Caption: I meet my fellow pilgrims at the base camp. I have nothing to say to
                  them, and they have nothing to say to me.

Caption: I introduce myself.

Page 3 panel 2

CLOSE UP (ALTHOUGH THE BACKGROUND REMAINS CONSTANT) OF THE BLACK WOMAN.

Gwen: Hello.

Page 3 panel 3

OK, THEY ARE FURTHER AWAY FROM US, NOW, ALL FOUR OF THEM, AND WALKING TOWARD THE STAIRS. THEY HAVE THEIR BACKS TO US, AND ARE ABOUT TWENTY FEET AWAY FROM US.

caption: There's a sick feeling in my chest as we walk towards the steps, and my head
                  begins to pound.

                  The hairs on the back of my neck prickle and rise.

caption: Why?

Page 3 panel 4

THEY ARE MUCH SMALLER, AND THEY HAVE BEGUN TO CLIMB THE STAIRS AWAY FROM US.

caption: Fear.

caption: Sheer, stark terror. And hope.

caption: Going up.

Page 4 panel 1

OKAY MARK, I'M GOING TO ABANDON THE HORIZONTAL GRID IN MY MIND NOW. IF YOU WANT TO STICK TO IT THAT'S FINE AND UP TO YOU.

WE SEE A BACKPACK -- THESE ARE BIG THINGS, SMALLER THAN HITCHHIKER'S RUCKSACKS, BUT FAIRLY HEFTY, BEING LOWERED TO THE FLOOR.

cap: At evening we stop for food. We have been climbing the central staircase for many hours.

cap: My lungs ache, as do my calf muscles.

Page 4 panel 2

LOOKING AT THEIR FACES AS THEY COME TOWARDS US. THEY'VE BEEN SWEATING. THE ONLY ONE IN FAIRLY GOOD SHAPE, AT LEAST UNRUFFLED, IS THE OLD CHINESE GUY. THEY LOOK SHATTERED. CAIRO HAS PULLED OFF HIS TEE SHIRT AND TIED IT AROUND HIS WAIST, REVEALING PIERCED NIPPLES. OUR NARRATOR IS HALF OFF-PANEL.

cap: We have gone through a hall filled with world war one biplanes; another hall filled with musical instruments.

Page 4 panel 3

LARGE PANEL. THE ROOM THEY'RE IN: A HUGE HALL, THAT GOES OFF INTO THE DISTANCE. THEY'VE COME OFF AT THE TOP OF THE STAIRWAY, AND WE CAN SEE IT, OFF IN THE DISTANCE, BEGINNING AGAIN (THIS IS LIKE THOSE DEPARTMENT STORES THAT MAKE YOU GO WALKING THROUGH EACH FLOOR TO GET TO THE NEXT ESCALATOR). THE ROOM IS FILLED WITH DINOSAURS OF VARIOUS SIZES AND SHAPES AND MATERIALS -- LET YOUR IMAGINATION RUN WILD HERE MARK. WE CAN SEE THEM, SMALL, WALKING, LOOKING UP AT THE THINGS AROUND THEM.

caption: The place where we stop contains nothing but dinosaurs. Skeletons of stone and bone and plastic. Tiny plastic models and huge animatronic reconstructions.

Page 4 panel 4

THE NARRATOR, SITTING DOWN, AMONGST THE OTHERS, EATING SANDWICHES. HE'S BLONDE, TALL AND THIN, IN HIS EARLY THIRTIES.

cap: Below a neon brontosaurus we sit and unwrap our food.

cap: The oriental, Taipek, eats something that smells sickly strange, like rotten honey.

Page 4 panel 5

CLOSE UP ON TAIPEK, THIS OLD CHINESE FACE, GRINNING TO HIMSELF, LICKING HIS FINGERS.

cap;   He offers me some, but I refuse.

Page 4 panel 6

WE ARE LOOKING AT CAIRO, THE ASIAN YOUTH. HE'S HOLDING SOME FOOD, EATING HAPPILY. HE'S LOOKED UP AT THEM, IS TALKING.

Cairo: I wonder what He'll be like.

Page 5 panel 1

CAIRO IS STILL TALKING. WE'VE PULLED BACK A WAY, SO WE CAN SEE THE WHOLE GROUP OF THEM, SITTING UNDERNEATH THE BONES OF THE NEON BRONTOSAURUS SKELETON, GLOWING IN RED AND BLUE AND YELLOW. WE CAN'T SEE THE WHOLE SKELETON OF COURSE, BECAUSE IT'S TOO BIG TO FIT IN HERE, AND WE DO WANT TO BE ABLE TO SEE ALL OF THEM. LARGISH PANEL, COVERS THE WHOLE OF THE TOP TIER.

Cairo: The children in my village are afflicted by a disease, that our doctors cannot identify.
         They are wasting, and dying. So thin and dry and sad.

         I volunteered to come to pray for him to cure them. I <u>know</u> he will say
         yes.

Page 5 panel 2

NEXT TIER: SMALL, SQUARE PANEL. CAIRO IS TALKING AGAIN. HIS HEAD TIPPED ON ONE SIDE, ASKING A QUESTION.

cairo: What are <u>your</u> prayers?

Page 5 panel 3

LONG PANEL, COVERING THE REST OF THE TIER, WITH THIN PANEL BORDER LINES BREAKING IT UP INTO THREE PANELS. WE ARE LOOKING AT THE OTHER THREE CLIMBERS : FIRST PANEL SHOWS TAIPEK, THE ORIENTAL. HE IS LOOKING DOWNWARDS.

No dialogue.

Page 5 panel 4

NEXT PANEL, SHOWS OUR NARRATOR. HE'S STARING AT US.

Caption: Hope...

Page 5 panel 5

GWEN, THE BLACK WOMAN, IS LOOKING AT US. SHE'S TALKING.

Miracleman 17 -- Climbers.
Page 6

Gwen: It's late. We'll sleep here and climb again at dawn.

Page 5 panel 6

BOTTOM TIER. TWO PANELS -- BOTH BLACK.

cap: During the night I am woken by the sounds of copulation. The brontosaurus has ceased to glow, and in the darkness I cannot tell who is doing what to who.

cap: Gwen and Cairo?

cap: Gwen and Taipek?

cap: Taipek and Cairo?

cap: All of them?

Page 5 panel 7

BLACK PANEL.

cap: Feeling more alone than before, I wait in silence until they grunt and thrust their way to eventual silence, and, after a while, I drift back to sleep.

cap: I dream of climbing stairs.

Page 6 panel 1

EXTREME CLOSE-UP ON THE NARRATOR'S FACE. HE LOOKS LIKE HE'S IN PAIN. EYES FIXED STRAIGHT AHEAD OF HIM.

cap: I ache all over.

Page 6 panel 2

PULL BACK A WAY. WE'RE LOOKING DOWN STAIRS AT THE FOUR PEOPLE, CLIMBING TOWARDS US. THE STAIRS BEHIND THEM STRETCH BACK AS FAR AS WE CAN SEE, DOWN A LONG WAY, APPARENTLY INTO A FOREST AT THE BOTTOM. THEY ARE CLIMBING LIKE EXHAUSTED MACHINES.

cap: The rhythms of the climb begin to imprint themselves on my consciousness.

cap: Step after step after step, hour after hour, until we reach the next floor.

Page 6 panel 3

OKAY, MOVE DOWN ABOUT 180 DEGREES, SO WE'RE LOOKING UP AT THEM WALKING IN FRONT OF US, HEADING UPWARDS. THE NEXT FLOOR IS A WAY ABOVE THEM. POSSIBLY HANG HUNDREDS OF CHANDELIERS FROM THE CEILING, THE BOTTOM OF THE NEXT FLOOR IF WE CAN SEE THEM. UP TO YOU, REALLY.

cap: Then we walk around the inside of this tower of miracles, through hall after hall filled with oddments and delights of every shape and kind, until we reach the bottom of the next rung of stairs.

cap: And up.

Page 6 panel 4

THEY ARE WADING THROUGH TWO OR THREE FEET OF SNOW. THEY AREN'T REALLY
DRESSED FOR IT, ALTHOUGH THEY'VE ALL TAKEN GLOVES AND SWEATERS OUT OF THEIR
BACKPACKS -- THEY AREN'T ALLOWED TO PUT ON THEIR INSULATED GEAR UNTIL THEY GO
OUTSIDE THE PYRAMID. THEY ARE HUGGING THEMSELVES AS THEY WALK, THEY LOOK
MISERABLE AND COLD. THEIR BREATH STEAMS ON THE AIR. IT'S A SORT OF ARCTIC
DREAMWORLD, DIAMOND-SHARP AND SNOW-SCUMBLED.

cap: Walking up the stairs we don't talk. We don't have the energy, or the air.

cap: Walking the halls we don't talk either. We don't have anything to say.

cap: Gwen sings, from time to time.

Page 6 panel 5

WE ARE LOOKING AT A POLAR BEAR, A WAY ABOVE THEM, STARING DOWN. THIS IS MUCH
MORE A POLAR BEAR STUDY THAN IT IS ANYTHING ELSE. WE CAN SEE THEM TRUDGING
ALONG, FIFTY FEET BELOW US AND THE BEAR.

Gwen (Italics): Husha little baby, don't you say a word,
                                 Momma's gonna buy you a mocking bird.

Page 6 panel 6

THE SNOW FLURRIES UP, OBSCURING OUR VIEW, REDUCING THE PEOPLE TO LITTLE DOTS OF
WHITE.

Gwen (italics): And if the mocking bird don't sing,
                                 Momma's gonna buy you a diamond ring...

cap: Song.

cap: Stairs.

cap: Climbing.

Page 7

MARK -- I'M NOT GOING TO GIVE YOU COMPLETE PANEL BY PANEL BREAKDOWNS OF THIS
PAGE. BASICALLY BECAUSE IT'S ALL SET AMIDST A HALL OF MIRRORS, AND THE WAY I SEE IT,
IT'S JUST A MASS OF FRACTURED IMAGES, OF PANELS LYING ACROSS EACH OTHER, ALL OF
THEM SHAPED LIKE MIRRORS, OR LIKE BROKEN BITS OF GLASS. HAVE A SEQUENCE OF MAIN
IMAGES, BUT FILL THE LITTLE SPACES WITH TWO OR THREE IMAGES THAT REPEAT,
REVERSED BACK AND FORWARDS, LIKE MIRROR IMAGES.

I SUSPECT THE INITIAL IMAGE IS A LONG, ESTABLISHING SHOT. THE HALL OF MIRRORS,
SMALL, AND FOUR TINY FIGURES SILHOUETTED AGAINST A BANK OF BLANK MIRRORS.

Miracleman 17 -- Climbers.
Page 8

cap: I don't know how long we spent on the Hundred and fiftieth floor, in the mirror halls.

OKAY -- FROM HERE ON OUT THIS PAGE IS UP TO YOU, REALLY MARK. SHATTERED, JUMBLED IMAGES.

cap: We must have walked for miles, looking for a way up, or a way out, finding only mirrors.

cap: Regular mirrors, row after row of them.

cap: Distorting mirrors, that made us look fat, or thin, or twisted.

cap: And other mirrors.

cap: Taipek said he saw an angel in one of them.

cap: I didn't see any angels.

cap: In one mirror I saw myself naked.

cap: In another I was looking out at myself, but I was holding up a piece of paper.

[IT SAYS <u>HELLO</u>, BUT WRITTEN BACKWARDS, IN MIRROR WRITING.]

cap: After a while Cairo began to giggle.

Page 8 panel 1
THREE PANELS ON THIS PAGE. FIRST PANEL -- THE INSIDE OF THE PYRAMID: WE CAN SEE THE FOUR PEOPLE STANDING BY AN OPEN WINDOW. BESIDE THEM IS A PILE, A ROUGH PYRAMID OF BUBBLE-HELMETS. THEY PROBABLY JUST LOOK LIKE A HEAP OF TRANSPARENT BEACH BALLS FROM HERE. THE WINDOW OPENS STRAIGHT OUT ONTO THE OUTSIDE OF THE PYRAMID -- IT'S AS MUCH DOOR AS IT IS WINDOW. THEY ARE OPENING THEIR BACK PACKS -- POSSIBLY ONE OF THEM IS ACTUALLY CLIMBING INTO OVERALLS, ONE PIECE INSULATED CLOTHES (COVER HANDS). THEY'RE MIRACLE TECHNOLOGY STUFF-- A THIN, WARMING INSULATOR, AND SHOULD HAVE THE MM LOGO OVER THE BREAST, SMALL, WHERE THE ALLIGATOR IS ON THOSE YUPPIE THINGS.

cap: Half way up, as we had been warned, the stairs stop.

cap: It's cold out there. We count our blessings.

cap: Lightweight Oxygen helmets, one piece bubbles; light-weight, heated clothing. Part of their benison to all of us.

Page 8 panel 2

ONE OF THEM, WEARING A BUBBLE HELMET, HAS GONE OUT OF THE DOOR/WINDOW -- THERE'S A LEDGE OF SOME KIND. THE OTHERS ARE PUTTING ON THEIR BUBBLE HELMETS, TAKING THEM FIRST FROM THE PILE.

Cap: Don't think. Just do it. Hope.

cap: Cairo is the first one out.

Page 8 panel 3

BIG PANEL -- 2/3 OF THE PAGE. LONG SHOT OF A PORTION OF THE PYRAMID FROM OUTSIDE. THERE ARE CLOUDS BELOW AND A WAY ABOVE. WE CAN SEE THE FOUR PEOPLE -- TINY LITTLE DOTS STANDING ON THE BASE OF A SCULPTURE OF SOME KIND. WE CAN SEE A TINY PATCH OF SKY, PERHAPS, BUT BASICALLY WE'RE JUST GIVING PEOPLE AN IDEA OF THE MINDBOGGLING SCALE. WE'RE ABOUT THREE MILES HIGH, AND WE HAVE AS FAR AGAIN TO GO. AND WE'RE LOOKING AT A COMPARATIVELY SMALL PORTION OF THE OUTSIDE, AND EVEN THAT REDUCES HUMAN BEINGS TO TINY BUBBLE-HELMETED SPECKS. TWO WORD BALLOONS -- BOTH OF THEM GO DOWN TO THE SAME LITTLE FIGURES, LONG BALLOONS TAILS, POSSIBLY A LITTLE ANGULAR.

Cairo: <u>Oh.</u> My friends. It is <u>such</u> a long way down.
                He. He. He.

Cairo: He.
                He he he.
                He.

Caption: Cairo had been giggling solidly for two days, perhaps even three. I had
                lost track of time. Lost track of all except the imperative to pray, the
                drive upwards.

Cap: Lost track of everything except hope.

Page 9 panel 1

SEVEN PANEL PAGE, MARK -- THREE ON TOP, ONE ALONG, THREE BELOW. WE'RE LOOKING AT A PROJECTION FROM THE RIGHT-HAND SIDE -- SOMETHING JUTTING FROM THE FABRIC OF THE PYRAMID. A RIGHT ARM HAS REACHED UP FROM BELOW, HAND HAS GRABBED HOLD OF THE PROJECTION.

No dialogue.

Page 9 panel 2

OKAY-- EXACTLY THE SAME CAMERA POSITION, SAME SHOT, BUT THE NARRATOR'S PULLING HIMSELF UP. HE'S CENTRE SHOT. WE CAN SEE HIM IN PROFILE, STARING UPWARDS. HIS RIGHT HAND HOLDS THE PROJECTION, HIS LEFT HAND REACHES UPWARDS TO ANOTHER JUTTING HANDHOLD, JUST ABOVE THE TOP OF THE PAGE.

No dialogue.

PAGE 9 PANEL 3

SAME SHOT. NOW THE NARRATOR'S BOOT IS RESTING ON THE LEDGE (THE OVERALLS GO UNDER THE BOOTS, BUT THEY HAVE SOCK-BOOTIE BITS) AND A HAND IS REACHING UP FROM BELOW, WAITING FOR HIM TO PULL HIMSELF UP FURTHER.

No dialogue.

Page 9 panel 4

Miracleman 17 -- Climbers.
Page 10

LONG SHOT ACROSS THE PAGE. THREE OF THEM ARE STANDING TOGETHER, IN A GROUP, BLACK SILHOUETTES, THE OTHER IS JUST SITTING ON A STATUE OR SOMETHING. INCIDENTALLY, THE BUBBLE HELMETS DON'T HAVE BULKY AIR SUPPLIES. SOMETHING VERY COMPACT, I SUSPECT. AND THEY'VE ABANDONED THEIR FOOD SUPPLIES.

cap: After three hours of climbing we lost him for good.

seated figure (cairo)   I will stop here.

Page 9 panel 5

BOTTOM TIER -- THREE PANELS. CAIRO GRINNING OUT AT US, THROUGH THE HELMET BUBBLE, EYES WIDE, PINPOINT PUPILS. HE HAS A GOLD TOOTH, UPPER FRONT.

Cairo: I do not need to climb any more. You see, I understand it all now.

              I am Him. I am a miracle.

              To think I was so blind.

Page 9 panel 6

PULL BACK ABOUT TEN FEET. HE'S SITTING ON THE STATUE, TALKING TO US. WE CAN SEE A BOOT CLIMBING ABOVE HIM, ENTERING FROM THE TOP OF PANEL. ONE OF THE OTHER CLIMBERS HEADING UPWARDS.

Cairo: I myself can save my town. I will fly to them, whoosh, and say, look at me, it is Cairo.
              I'm back!

              All along I was he, I was the Miracle God, and not one of you silly
              people knew it.

Page 9 panel 7

PULL BACK EVEN FURTHER, TO SEE THEM CLIMBING UP THE SIDE OF THE BUILDING AS HE SITS SADLY AND FORLORNLY ON THE HEAD OF SOME JEWELLED AND FABULOUS MONSTER, A BEAUTIFUL GARGOYLE FOUR MILES HIGH.

cairo: Oh how we must laugh. I can fly, so how foolish I was to climb all this way.
              Whoosh! He. He. He.

              Look up, silly people! Look up!

Page 10

ONE PAGE PICTURE, WITH FOUR SECTIONS OF IT SQUARED OFF INTO PANELS, IF YOU SEE WHAT I MEAN. THE WHOLE IS A SECTION OF THE SIDE OF THE PYRAMID, SO THE LEFT SIDE OF THE PAGE IS BASICALLY SKY, THE RIGHT HALF IS BASICALLY PYRAMID. POSSIBLY DISTORT THINGS A LITTLE LIKE A SET OF ANDY WARHOL POLAROIDS, SO WE'RE LOOKING STRAIGHT UP TOWARDS THE TOP OF THE PAGE AND STRAIGHT DOWN TOWARDS THE BOTTOM -- SEE WHAT YOU THINK, REALLY.

Page 10 panel 1

TOP LEFT PANEL. THREE NAKED LITTLE BABIES, ONE MALE, TWO FEMALE (ONE WHITE, ONE LIGHT BLACK, ONE CHINESE/EURASIAN), ARE FLOATING IN THE AIR. GO OUT OF YOUR WAY TO MAKE THEM CUTE, WITHOUT ACTUALLY GOING CARTOONY OR CHOCOLATE BOX -- THESE BOBBING LITTLE CHERUBS. THEY ARE A COUPLE OF MONTHS OLD, ONE FLOATS ON ITS BACK, EXAMINING ITS TOES, THE OTHER TWO HOVER LOOKING DOWN TOWARDS OUR CLIMBERS, GRAVE LITTLE EXPRESSIONS ON THEIR BABY FACES.

Baby 1: Hello.

You know, there _are_ meant to be four of you.

Baby 2 (lower case): four.
of.
You.

OVER ON THE RIGHT HAND SIDE OF THE PAGE, OUTSIDE OF THE PANEL BORDER, WE GET A CAPTION.

cap: There are 'rest-stops' on the way. Every half-mile, or so. Places where you can take off
your air helmet, use the toilets, and drink water.

Page 10 panel 2

THIS PANEL IS NEXT TIER DOWN, ON THE RIGHT, WE CAN SEE A SORT OF CAVE OPENING, AND OUR THREE PEOPLE, SANS HELMETS, SITTING AND STANDING. TAIPEK STANDS IN THE DOORWAY, TALKING TO THE BABIES. POSSIBLY WE CAN SEE THE GLOW OF A FORCE-FIELD, OR, FAILING THAT, A GLASS SHEET THAT COVERS THE CAVE ENTRANCE.

Taipek: We _were_ four, but one of us went mad, and we had to leave him behind.

CAPTION OVER ON THE LEFT, WHERE NOTHING'S HAPPENING.

cap: We were long out of food. Hungry, now, and light-headed. But that is the correct way
to approach a god, having fasted, and undergone travail.

Page 10 panel 3

OK, OVER ON THE LEFT, NEXT TIER DOWN-ISH, WE'RE LOOKING AT THE BABIES. ONE JUST SITTING IN SPACE LOOKING UP AT OUR PEOPLE ON THE RIGHT, IN PANEL 2, ONE UPSIDE DOWN, ONE LOOKING DOWN AND AWAY.

Baby 1: Miracledog found a body, on a ledge on the 30th floor.

I expect _that_ was your friend.

Baby 2 (lower case):   was.

your.
friend.

Page 10 panel 4

THREE TINY DOTS, THE BABIES ARE ON THEIR WAY DOWN, HEADING TOWARDS LONDON. AS IF WE'RE NOW A HUNDRED FEET ABOVE THEM.

No dialogue.

Page 11

OKAY -- FIVE PANELS ARRANGED A LITTLE IRREGULARLY, BUT BASICALLY GETTING BIGGER, THEN SMALLER AGAIN. LONG, NARROW, VERTICAL PANELS. NOT COVERING ALL THE PAGE -- WHERE THE PAGE IS BANK, WE SEE OCCASIONAL HIGH THIN CLOUDS.

Page 11 panel 1
WE SEE THE NARRATOR. HE'S NOW BEARDED -- WHAT FOR ME IS ABOUT A WEEK AND A HALF'S BEARD, BUT I THINK IT'S A BIT LONGER FOR SOME OTHER PEOPLE -- AND A LITTLE DIRTY. HE'S ALSO THINNER THAN BEFORE. IN REASONABLE CLOSE UP.

cap: I trained for six months before coming here, on quarry walls, on tall buildings.

Page 11 panel 2

LONG SHOT -- THE THREE OF THEM CLIMBING, SILHOUETTED AGAINST THE PYRAMID FACE. SORT OF LIKE THE CLASSIC RADIO TIMES-TYPE SHOT OF ROCK-CLIMBERS, SILHOUETTED AGAINST THE OLD MAN OF HOY, ONLY THE SIDE IS COVERED WITH STATUARY, WITH BEAUTY, WITH GARGOYLES.

cap: It's not a hard climb. Don't let anyone ever tell you it's a hard climb. It's not a hard climb.

cap: To talk now we needed to touch helmets. I wished I could hear Gwen singing.

Page 11 panel 3

REALLY LONG SHOT. PULL BACK EVEN FURTHER, SO WE CAN SEE THE SHAPE OF THE PYRAMID, SEE THEY'RE GETTING NEAR TO THE TOP. ALTERNATELY. DO THIS AS A FLASHBACK SHOT, PROBABLY OF THE NARRATOR AND GWEN KISSING, JUST HEADS IN SHOT AT THE BOTTOM OF THE PANEL, AND THEN STACKS OF BOOKS GOING UP AND UP AROUND THEM. VERY DARK PANEL.

cap: We had made love on the library floor, in the darkness, before we began to climb the outside, and she sang the whole time.

cap: I wished that I could fly.

Page 11 panel 4

EXTREME CLOSE UP, IN PROFILE, OF THE NARRATOR.

cap: I wondered if Cairo thought he was flying, as he fell. If it felt good.

cap: If I let go I could find out.

cap: Easy.

Page 11 panel 5

VERY LONG SHOT, OF THE TOP OF THE PYRAMID. WE CAN'T SEE THE PEOPLE CLIMBING -- SMALL PANEL, LONG SHOT.

cap: Perhaps in some way our ordeal was purifying us.

cap: Cleansing us.

cap: Sanctifying us.

cap: Making us fit for his presence.

Page 12 panel 1

OKAY, MARK. LONG SHOT ACROSS THE TOP TIER. WE'RE IN THE GARDEN AT THE TOP OF THE TOWER AS IN MM 15 .-- WE'RE OFF ON THE EDGE. IN FRONT OF US IS SOME GORGEOUS ALIEN PLANT, WITH BLOSSOMS LIKE RUFF-NECKED LIZARD-HEADS. JUST BEHIND IT IS A LOW WALL -- A COUPLE OF FEET HIGH. THE NIGHT SKY SHINES BESPATTERED WITH STARS. THERE'S AN ILLUMINATION FROM BEHIND OUR VIEWPOINT, FROM THE DIAMOND CAPSTONE, THAT CASTS LIGHT AS BRIGHT AS DAY OVER THE PLANT AND THE WALL. THE WALL SHOULD APPEAR ABOUT 2 FEET HIGH, AND BE BUILT OF DRY STONE, OR NORMAL RED BRICK. A GLOVED HAND IS COMING OVER THE EDGE.

No Dialogue.

Page 12 panel 2

OK, MARK -- IF THIS WAS IN THE CINEMA WE'D JUST HAVE JERKED THE CAMERA STRAIGHT UP FIFTEEN FEET. WE'RE LOOKING DOWN, AS THE THREE CLIMBERS COME OVER THE EDGE. AND WE REALISE THAT THE DRYSTONE WALL MAY ONLY BE TWO FEET HIGH BUT IT'S THE TOP LIP OF ONE PART OF THE PYRAMID. THE WAY I SEE IT, IT'S NOT QUITE AT THE TOP, AT THE CAPSTONE, BUT THE GARDEN'S A LITTLE WAY DOWN AND TO ONE SIDE. I CAN'T (DAMMIT) FIND MY MIRACLEMAN WITH THE GARDEN STUFF IN IT OFFHAND, AND I'M NOT GOING TO RING ALAN FOR SOMETHING SO TRIVIAL, SO IF YOU CAN JUST CHECK THIS OUT, MARK... ANYWAY, WE CAN SEE, BELOW US, THE THREE CLIMBERS, AND, BELOW THEM, THE SIDE OF THE PYRAMID GOING DOWN, AND BELOW THAT, THE LIGHTS OF ENGLAND. AGAIN, ACROSS THE TIER.

No dialogue.
Page 12 panel 3

BOTTOM HALF OF THE PAGE. OKAY, NOW WE MOVE AROUND 180 DEGREES. THE THREE CLIMBERS ARE STANDING WITH THEIR BACKS TO US IN SILHOUETTE PROBABIY DIRECTLY IN FRONT OF US. HANGING IN THE SKY LIKE A GOD IS MIRACLEMAN -- ARMS AT HIS SIDES, SLIGHTLY RAISED, RATHER THAN IN CRUCIFIXION POSE. HE'S LOOKING DOWN AT THEM WITH A LITTLE INTEREST. HE WAS IN THE GARDEN, THINKING. BELOW HIM, IF WE CAN SEE IT, ARE SOME OF THE TREES JOHN DREW -- THE TREE OF WEIRD HAND-FRUIT, AND THE REST. BUT MIRACLEMAN IS THE FOCUS OF THE PANEL, WITH THE NIGHT SKY BEHIND HIM. LOSE WHATEVER ELSE YOU NEED TO MAKE SURE HE'S IMPRESSIVE AND TWINKLING. HE'S TALKING. WE CAN SEE THE BACK OF THE TOWER, OFF TO THE RIGHT, AND POSSIBLY THE MOON OVER ON THE EXTREME LEFT.

Miracleman 17 -- Climbers.
Page 14

Miracleman: There is atmosphere up here, and warmth.

                It means little to me, but certain of the plants require it.

Caption: Hope...

Page 13 panel 1

FOUR EQUAL SIZED PANELS, ONE BENEATH THE OTHER. ON THE LEFT ARE CLUSTERED THE THREE CLIMBERS -- GWEN, THE NARRATOR, AND TAIPEK. TAIPEK IS REACHING INTO THE POUCH AROUND HIS WAIST, (REMEMBER THAT?), FUMBLING FOR SOMETHING. MIRACLEMAN IS OVER ON THE RIGHT OF PANEL, SETTLING TOWARD THE GROUND, LIGHT AS A GLITTERING FEATHER. GWEN AND THE NARRATOR ARE JUST REMOVING THEIR HELMETS. TAIPEK'S LEFT HIS ON.

Miracleman: Well, my pilgrims?

                What have you come to me for?

Page 13 panel 2

YOU CAN MOVE AROUND ON THIS IF YOU LIKE BUT THE WAY I IMAGINE IT IS SAME SHOT, SAME ANGLE. TAIPEK, ARM EXTENDED, IS SHOOTING A GUN AT MIRACLEMAN. NO PYROTECHNICS; LIKE A VERY HIGH SPEED PHOTO, SO WE CAN SEE A LITTLE PUFF OF SMOKE FROM THE MUZZLE. POSSIBLY A BULLET JUST BOUNCING OFF THE TINKERBELL EFFECT, WHICH TWINKLES A LITTLE MORE HEAVILY IN THAT POINT. MIRACLEMAN LOOKS GRAVELY INTERESTED, THERE SEEMS NO REAL CHANGE IN HIS EXPRESSION OR FEELINGS. TAIPEK IS STILL WEARING HIS BUBBLE HELMET. MIRACLEMAN HAS STOPPED A FEW FEET FROM THE GROUND.

Taipek: Death.

Page 13 panel 3

NEXT PANEL DOWN. TAIPEK HAS LOWERED THE GUN, HESITANTLY, NERVOUSLY. THE OTHER TWO ARE JUST FROZEN INTO POSITION, THEY DON'T KNOW WHETHER THEY SHOULD BE LOOKING AT MIRACLEMAN OR AT TAIPEK, SO INSTEAD THEY'RE JUST -- NOT FROZEN -- EDGING AWAY SLIGHTLY. MIRACLEMAN HAS STOPPED TWINKLING.

No dialogue.

Page 13 panel 4

SAME SHOT, POSSIBLY CLOSE IN ON TAIPEK AND THE PILGRIMS A LITTLE. TAIPEK HAS PUT THE GUN TO HIS FACE MASK, NEXT TO WHERE HIS MOUTH IS INSIDE, AND IS FIRING IT. THE FRONT OF THE MASK HAS SHATTERED. THE BACK OF HIS HEAD IS BLOWING OPEN, LEAVING A BLOODY MESS ON THE INSIDE BACK OF THE GOLDFISH BOWL HELMET. NOW HAVING DESCRIBED IT LIKE THAT, I DON'T SEE IT AS VERY GORY OR REVOLTINGLY DEPICTED. THIS IS A MAN KILLING HIMSELF, AND THAT'S WHAT HAPPENS, BUT TRY TO REDUCE THE SHOCK VALUE AS MUCH AS POSSIBLE, SO IT CARRIES EMOTIONAL IMPORT, BUT NOT REVULSION. EVERYONE IS LOOKING AT HIM. HE'S STILL STANDING.

No dialogue.

Page 14

OKAY, MARK. WE'RE ONTO A SIX PANEL GRID FOR THE NEXT TWO PAGES AS FAR AS I CAN TELL. FEEL FREE TO PLAY WITH IT, BUT I'LL WRITE IT AS SIX EQUAL PANELS PER PAGE.

Page 14 panel 1

MIRACLEMAN, HEAD AND SHOULDERS. WE'RE LOOKING UP AT HIM FROM BELOW. HE'S TOTALLY UNMOVED BY THIS. ASKING, WITH MILD INTEREST.

MM: And are your prayers also this abrupt?

Page 14 panel 1 A

EXTRA PANEL HERE -- I THINK THAT LAST LINE SHOULD BE OFF ON ITS OWN, REALLY. HALF-SIZED PANEL. EXTEND THE NEXT PANEL INTO THIS ONE -- SO WE'RE LOOKING AT TAIPEK'S FEET.

caption: I stood there, stunned, gasping in the strangely scented air. I had climbed with
            Taipek for --

caption: -- How long?--

caption: And now this.

Page 14 panel 2

WE'RE LOOKING DOWN AT THE CRUMPLED BODY OF TAIPEK, A RED AND SPATTERY MESS ON THE INSIDE OF THE BUBBLE. WE CAN'T SEE HIS FACE. STRANGE FLOWERS ALL AROUND.

caption: It seemed a long way to go for a shot and a suicide; for a futile gesture that
            only two other human beings would see.

caption: And him, of course.

Page 14 panel 3

NARRATOR'S VIEWPOINT. WE'RE LOOKING AT GWEN FROM THE SIDE. SHE'S LOOKING UP, SLIGHTLY, AT MIRACLEMAN, OFF. AGAIN, HEAD SHOP.

Gwen: No.

            No, they're not. I -- we -- we didn't know he was going to do that.

MM: So?

            Tell me your reason for coming here?

Page 14 panel 4

LOOKING DOWN FROM MIRACLEMAN'S VIEWPOINT AT GWEN, LOOKING SMALL AND LONELY, LIKE A SUPPLICANT, SHE'S TELLING US HER DEEPEST WISH, HER MOST HEARTFELT DESIRE.

Gwen: I want to be an <u>artist.</u> And I can't draw, or paint.

But I have these pictures, in my head. The way I see the world. But I just can't make my <u>hands</u>... my <u>fingers</u>...

Page 14 panel 5

PULL BACK A WAY, SO WE CAN SEE OUR NARRATOR LOOKING AT GWEN, HIS HEAD TURNED, LOOKING NERVOUSLY.

Gwen: I've tried <u>so</u> hard.

Gwen: I don't know if you can help me. But I had to ask.

Gwen: Can you do it?

Page 14 panel 6

LOOKING UP AT MIRACLEMAN AGAIN. HE'S THINKING.

No dialogue.

Page 15 panel 1

SAME SHOT AS THE LAST ONE, BUT HE'S -- NOT ACTUALLY SMILING, BUT HE LOOKS LIKE HE'S COME TO A DECISION, AND IN A DISTANT SORT OF WAY, HE'S A LITTLE PLEASED WITH HIMSELF.

Miracleman: Yes. Yes, I can. You are correct: each of you should have the right to art. <u>Yes.</u>

I will see what I can do.

And <u>you</u>?

Page 15 panel 2

THE NARRATOR'S HEAD, AT THE BOTTOM OF THE PANEL, LOOKING DOWN WARDS, LOOKING UPSET.

Narrator: My daughter, <u>Hope.</u> She was hurt in London, in the battle with your adversary. <u>Brain damage.</u>

She has been in a coma for two years. They're getting ready to pull the plug.

Can't you <u>save</u> her? Give her a new <u>body</u>? Get her <u>back</u> for me?

Page 15 panel 3

WE'RE LOOKING AT MIRACLEMAN -- A FULL BODY SHOT. HE'S FLOATING IN FRONT OF US, ARMS FOLDED.

MM: No.

Page 15 panel 4

THE NARRATOR LOOKS UPSET -- REALLY UPSET. HE'S HURT, AND DESPERATE.

Man: <u>No?</u>

                <u>Why not?</u>

Page 15 panel 5

WE ARE LOOKING AT MIRACLEMAN, HIS BACK TO US, DRIFTING UPWARDS AND AWAY FROM US, TOWARDS THE DIAMOND CAPSTONE.

No dialogue.

Page 15 panel 6

WE'RE LOOKING AT THE NARRATOR. HE'S CRYING, SHOUTING AT THE RECEDING GOD.

Man: <u>Dammit</u>! You're going to make this woman into an artist and you won't save my daughter's life?

                What kind of sense is <u>that</u>?

Page 16

OVER THE PAGE. LAST PAGE...

Page 16 panel 1

PULL BACK FOR A LONG SHOT. TWO STANDING FIGURES: ONE CRUMPLED IN THE FLOWERS AT HIS FEET. GWEN HAS PUT HER ARM ON HIS SHOULDER, AS WELL AS SHE CAN TRYING TO COMFORT HIM WITHOUT GETTING TOO CLOSE. MIRACLEMAN'S GONE -- THERE'S A LIGHT SHINING FROM THE CAPSTONE.

Gwen: It's just a question of relative values, I suppose.

                What's important changes from where you're looking.

                Come on. We've got a <u>long</u> way to go.

Page 16 panel 2

THE NARRATOR, LOOKING DOWN AT THE MESS THAT USED TO BE TAIPEK. HE'S LIFTING UP HIS BUBBLE HELMET.

Miracleman 17 -- Climbers.

Page 18

cap: There are some things that are just too big. You can't fit them into your head -- they stick in
         the mind, and won't go in..

Page 16 panel 3

HE'S PUTTING ON HIS HELMET.

cap: You never believe them, no matter how familiar they become.

Page 16 panel 4

THROUGH THE BUBBLE HELMET, WE'RE LOOKING AT HIS FACE. LIPS PRESSED TOGETHER.
FACE DRAWN AND TIRED AND THIN. EYES DARK-RIMMED AND POUCHY.

cap: You think about them too hard, you see a little girl's dead eyes staring up at you.

Page 16 panel 5

PULL BACK A WAY. WE'RE LOOKING AT TOP OF THE PYRAMID. WE CAN SEE GWEN AND THE
NARRATOR CLIMBING OVER THE LIP, OUT OF THE GARDEN, PREPARING TO HEAD OFF BACK
DOWN EIGHT MILES, TO THE SOLID GROUND. BEHIND THE PYRAMID THE STARS SHINE AS
THEY ONLY CAN WHEN THERE'S ALMOST NO AIR. THEY'RE GETTING READY TO HEAD ON
DOWN. SHE'S EXUBERANT, HE'S CAST DOWN.

cap: Hope?

cap: Going down.

END:

NOW, AS FOR THE LAYOUT OF THE ISSUE. I THINK IT WOULD WORK BEST IF THE LETTERS
PAGE COMES NEXT, AND THEN AFTER THAT THE TWO PAGES OF RETRIEVAL. SO RETRIEVAL
IS SEPARATED FROM THE BODY OF THE ISSUE BY THE LETTERS EACH TIME, AND SO IT
OCCURS ON TWO FACING PAGES. SO LETTERS FOR ONE OR THREE PAGES, THEN RETRIEVAL.
THEN WE CAN ALL GO HOME...

Hope you all like it. Let me know if there's any problems...

best,

Neil.

There are several ways to write comics. The full script is the most accepted way and I still do most of my work full script. A full script breaks the story down page by page and panel by panel. It gives a complete scene description for every panel as well as all the captions, dialogue and sound effects. The problem with full scripts comes when an artist doesn't draw everything asked for. Often a major story telling point is accidentally eliminated or ignored. This could cause a ripple effect down the line that will blow the story's climax.

Unfortunately, once you write a full script the story is out of the writer's hands. If the artist didn't follow your script, short of the editor sending back the page for corrections (which, due to ever-encroaching deadlines doesn't happen all that often) your story will most likely make no sense. Of course the readers won't blame the artist – they'll assume the writer didn't do his job.

To compensate for a poor art you find yourself writing an "artist-proof" script. That is you write dialogue and captions that are more expository than you would prefer just to make sure your story will be understood no matter who draws it. This forces occasionally awkward captions and stilted dialogue. You're concentrating more on telling your plot than developing your story through your characters.

Plot style differs from writer to writer. Some writers give a page or two overview of the story and assume the artist will fill in the rest. Most of us however write very complete plots, breaking down the book on a page by page basis – to aid the artist in structuring the story – and then we write a long paragraph or two describing every action on the page, the motivation of the characters and sample dialogue. Sometimes we'll even put /-slash marks between sentences to indicate panel breaks.

I did all my Marvel work and much of my DC work plot style. When you're working with someone who understands story telling, there is nothing better.

Plot style allows the artist to 'play' with the descriptions, to, one hopes, come up with a more powerful way of illustrating what you, the writer, want to say. The artist, if they understand the intricacies of story telling, will pace out the material properly. They'll know who to focus the drawing on, and they'll give the page a cinematic, dynamism that you might not get otherwise. By nature the artist thinks visually and the writer thinks conceptually. Comics are a hybrid of the two. When you work script style the writer is telling the artist what to do. When you work plot style, writer and artist are a team.

Once the artist has drawn the page the writer gets it back to write in the dialogue and indicate balloon placement. If the story telling is good, the writer can eliminate a lot of exposition and spend his time writing better character driven dialogue. I've found this to work wonderfully when I worked with artists like Gene Colan on *Dracula* or George Perez on *The New Teen Titans*. Their art was so good a reader can figure out much the story even before the dialogue is put in. That means the writer can spend their time creating better characters and building mood.

Writer and artist are working as a unit to tell a better graphic story instead of the art merely servicing the writer or the writer having to explain the art. When story and art mesh as one the result is a better comic for everyone. Neither the artist nor the writer should be the star. The story should be all that's important.

When doing work plot style, should the artist not tell the story well, you can adjust the dialogue to explain what should have been in the art. Unlike in full scripts, you can fill in all those holes that were left out.

The down side of plot style writing is that not every artist knows how to tell a story visually. They might draw beautifully, but comics is not about gallery art, it's about telling stories. Still, when working with the right artist I find writing a comic story plot style makes my writing better, my dialogue stronger and more natural, and I have more room to play with the emotions of the characters.

Working full-script is best if you're working with an artist who might not be a good story-teller or when you're working with an artist you've not worked with before. It's also good for artists who feel more comfortable having all the information in front of them. Writing a full script is also best when writing short stories where every panel counts, humor stories where rhythm is king, and detective stories where every detail may be some important clue that simply can't be left out.

I enjoy writing scripts as well as plot-style comics. Writing full scripts lets me be in total charge of the pacing and structure But, if the truth can be told, I don't think I've ever written a script that's as good as the best of my plot-style comics. The finished art inspires me and therefore inspires my dialogue.

– Marv Wolfman 4/12/01

Marv Wolfman has been a Senior Editor at DC Comics and the Editor-in-Chief at Marvel. Among his many co-creations are the 1980s sales sensation The New Teen Titans *and the vampire slayer Blade. His miniseries* Crisis on Infinite Earths *was voted the second-best comic story of the century. He is co-writer of the upcoming* ElfQuest *movie.*

MARV WOLFMAN

THE MAN CALLED A•X #5

Shawn, I've tried to plot this with far fewer panels throughout. To do so, however, I did this pretty much page by page so I could see how much is on each page. Let me know if this is better. At least I'm hoping it is.

Also, this is very much a character story with little action. So please do as much as you can to avoid this being head shots talking.

Also, this story will be first person narrated by Liz's son, Jack. Leave room atop some of the panels for captions.

"FROM THE PAST THE FUTURE!"

1:    FULL PAGE SPLASH: Dusk over Bedlam. Liz's kid, <u>JACK</u> (Original series issue #2, page 15. Also, Shawn, Jack's Dad, <u>DAN</u> appears on this page and Dan will show up at the end of this issue so check it out or I'll fax it to you.) is watching his friends (kids his own age) play baseball on a park diamond. Jack is behind the high wire fence, holding onto the fence, looking sad. It's obvious he wants to play but they won't let him. Note, I repeat this scene twice again (in different locations, but essentially it's the same scene of Jack trying to get into someplace but he's not allowed. So check out the full plot and see if you can draw the angle of how Jack is looking at the scene the same for all three situations. Scene two is at a farm when he's trying to get past a fence. And scene three is at a hospital trying to get back into a room. Anyway, everyone around Jack is having fun, the players, the kids in the bleachers, etc. A kid is sliding into home, kicking up dirt, so we get a nice shot of Jack. Leave room for the logo, title and credits. We see lots of kids' bikes leaning against the fence.

2:    Jack watches sadly, removed from the others, as the kids hoist the base runner up on their shoulders, celebrating his home-run. Pull back to see a few mothers noticing Jack, alone, looking miserable. They're gossiping about how weird that kid is. After all, their mother is a tramp and his father is, well, you know. Jack hears this, tears in his eyes as they continue. Finally, he turns on them and curses them. Go to hell. How do you know what my mother is? She's a reporter for the Bedlam Gazette. She's a good person. He stalks off with his bike (he can ride it or walk it--your choice) tears in his eyes as the mothers look horrified but they continue to gossip. I hear tell she doesn't even speak to her own son. Imagine that. The tramp!

3:    Evening. Jack is alone on the streets. He's in tears; everything around him is frightening. He pulls back into a doorwell as a leather-clad guy on a motorcycle tears by him, almost running him over. Two Silicon Enforcers on hovercraft, sirens blaring, are whipping around buildings, pursuing the cycle, firing. Jack watches in terror from inside a closed store door area as the cycle spins out of control and skids into the store Jack hides in. The guy goes smashing through the window. A second later the cops are there, on the ground, lasers drawn. One is pulling the dead culprit by the neck from the window. He's a bloody mess, glass shards everywhere, etc. The cop says you picked the wrong store in the wrong town to rob, you idiot. That place was owned by one of the biggest crimelords in town. And nobody robs from them. Nobody. Jack is watching this all in horror.

4: Night. If you need to move some of that over to this page do so. Jack runs in horror calling for his mom. Cut to him on the fire escape outside her open window. He's climbing through it. As he wipes the tears from his eyes he looks around the apartment, sees the couch with a few nice <u>pillows</u> on it, photos of her Mom in the Marines, sees the A•IX belt buckle on a table, looks at it confused as it's sitting on a photo of the dead A•IX. He also sees the photo of Liz and him we've seen before. Final shot is of him asleep in the space under Liz's desk. He's curled up, looking bad, and in his sleep he's calling for his mom. His head is on a small pillow from the couch. We can see the front door in the BG past the table.

5: Same angle looking up at the front door in the BG. The door opens suddenly. He awakens, but he stays quiet as AX walks in, A•8 slumped over his shoulder. Liz is behind. Jack watches in horror as AX tosses the unconscious A8 onto the floor. Liz and AX hunker over A8. He watches in terror, hands clamped over his mouth so he doesn't speak as AX pulls open A8's face as if it's hinged somewhat or can come off. Up to you. Liz looks down into the cavity filled with a human brain but with computer parts attached to it. As AX looks in it he notices the picture of Liz and Jack on the table. AX asks if Liz called her son after he called her last issue. Jack, listening from under the table, pays attention now.

6: Liz says no. It wouldn't be good. He wouldn't understand. Shawn, keep showing Jack listening, reacting. She says after the war she and Dan didn't get along like they did before the war. We have a two-panel flashback to a dance club. Liz is dressed as sexily as possible, dancing with some guy. Through the crowd we see Dan staring with hate in his eyes coming at them. In the present Liz says she felt different. Changed in some ways. She can't explain. She needed to prove she was still a woman. Dan...didn't understand, and Liz says she didn't blame him. She pushed him further than she had any right to, but she had to explore who she was. She had to prove herself by going out with other guys. To prove she was attractive. Jack is listening. Horrified.

7: Flashback: Liz is in bed with some guy as Dan breaks in to the room. He smashes the guy with a lamp then slaps Liz down. In the present Liz says she got pregnant that night. With Dan. Jack was born 9 months later and she says she didn't want him. As she says we stay on Jack. Jack begins to cry, but we can see he's keeping it in. As we focus on Jack we HEAR the off panel Liz say she didn't want a kid. She hated him, and didn't want anything to do with him. Jack is in tears here. Jack is listening, trying to keep it all in. We go into flashback. She says she left them both and began to drink. We see her at a bar, drunk like crazy, half naked, a guy pawing her.

8:     We see another flashback of her, naked, in the alleyway, shadows playing on her so we don't see anything. We see a final picture of her in detox, Doctors filling out forms while she's strapped to her hospital bed, screaming bloody murder for a drink. her hair matted, horrible. Back in the present Jack sees Liz look up at AX and say she'd been drunk for a full year till she was sent to detox. And, Liz says, Jack knew how bad it was. Knew about all the guys I'd go to bed with to get a drink. How can I face him now. He's got to hate me. He's got to despise this person who gave birth to him then ran away. And Jack is crying as his mom says this.

9:     Large pic. AX awkwardly holds Liz as she's crying in his arms. If possible, show this past Jack, under the table, crying but not having anyone to hug. Maybe he's hugging his small pillow. AX looks at her and says he's searching for his family because he doesn't know if he has one. She needs to find her family because she knows she does have one. He turns and says he's got to work on A8. She asks if he wants something to drink...coffee, she says. She hasn't had a drink in months although by all rights she should have. AX says no as he reaches in to A8's head and touches something. Suddenly, A8 jerks up.

10:    Jack watches in terror as A8, face off, slams at AX who smashes through some furniture, etc. Liz grabs her gun and fires, but A8 whirls around and slams Liz back. Jack is still watching, so keep the focus on him.

11:    More of this until AX slams A8 down to the ground and snaps the robots neck. A8s neck is now askew from his body. Jack watches as AX says that was motor impulses. What do we do? Liz says she called around to her friends who were in the Marines with her. She knows someone who may be able to help. AX grabs the broken A8 and takes him with them. Last panel: we see Jack scurrying down the fire escape. Below he can see AX toss A8 into Liz's waiting car. Liz entering from the driver's side.

12:    Night in Bedlam. Liz's car is driving through the city. Pull back to Jack following on his bike. PUSH IN on Jack, in tears, frightened. He calls out Mom? Mom? What's going on? As many or as few panels as you want here, Shawn. Just play him up as a kid who has no idea what his mom is up to. We pull back to see him riding over some great Bridge somewhere (not the Silicon Span). Final panel shows we're on a farm but there's a wire fence surrounding it. A KEEP OUT PRIVATE PROPERTY SIGN on the fence. Liz's car parked outside farmhouse. Next to it is a barn. We can see a TINY figure of AX carrying A8 and Liz heading toward some man in front of the barn who's calling them to the barn. The lights are on. This farmhouse is in the middle of the state outside Bedlam. IF you can show Jack on his bike outside the fence, staring in, just as he did on page one at the baseball game. He's always on the outside looking in. Whether with his friends or his mother.

13:    Cut to a small inset shot of Bradbury in his wetroom. He's speaking to someone over his computer. Cut to a large picture of some underground lab/storage facility.

We see Hundreds of A•9s and A•Xs, standing unconscious, being loaded, by technicians pushing carts, onto trucks and a large airplane. Armed guards are everywhere. On a large view screen over the scene we see Bradbury saying they're moving the Assassins into position. He will now alert the Cadre.

14: Back to the farm. We see Jack squeezing through a small torn part of the fence. Cut to inside the barn by the farmhouse. It's set up with lots of science equipment. We see the farmer now, his name is SKUZZY. Early-30s, long hair, beard, scraggly. Tiny 'Granny glasses' looking very off-kilter. He's hunkered over the unconscious and fully opened up A8 who is lying on a dirty table filled with equipment, radios, TVs, VCR parts, etc. This is a weird place to say the least. A8 is completely opened revealing his insides; body parts mixed with mechanics. Skuzzy is working on A8 with a screwdriver and some other device. AX and Liz watch. Skuzzy talks about a zillion things -- his mind is everywhere at once. In a large panel, the largest on the page, Skuzzy removes part of a mechanical chest cavity from A8. Pull back to see Jack, outside the barn, watching. A rake near him on the ground. Skuzzy is impressed. This is very futuristic technology. He didn't think anything like this existed yet. But then, he says, the Government doesn't want any of us to know what is really going on in the world. Do you know the entire Russian coup was faked. The Commies are still in control, but now they're receiving Big American bucks to help them out of their financial hellhole. Skuzzy is into this kind of rambling paranoid conversation. He also happens to be a brilliant scientist. Suddenly, as Jack watches, a hand grabs him from behind, over his mouth. This is R-Mor's hand.

15: We now see R-Mor moving away from him and into the barn. Jack's tied up, gagged, and can't do anything but he rolls over to the rake and begins cutting at the ropes around his arm with the rake tines. Inside the barn, R-Mor moves silently behind the crew, hiding behind a wall-sized computer, as Skuzzy is using a soldering iron on A8's brain. Skuzzy says this thing had some brain damage recently. Liz tells AX that happened when they blew up Mercy Island. Skuzzy says it restructured his memories, returned some to him. Liz turns to AX and says that's why he wanted answers. He was remembering. Close on AX as she says this.

16: More of that as AX, thinking, brooding. As AX thinks and we keep on him, we hear the OS Skuzzy say he's fix up this model. On Skuzzy we see him soldering up A8s head. Good as new. A8'll answer to them now. Fixed all the defects, etc. AX turns to Skuzzy and in a powerful shot says take me apart. Let me remember. I want to know who I am. I want to know what I was about. I want to know what happened. Note to Shawn. As he says this show a one panel reaction from R-Mor. She's interested in this.

17-19: Pull back to see Jack running in and calling to his Mom (who reacts with shock when she sees him) that they've been followed by some armored guy. AX whirls and fires into the barn as R-Mor jumps out of hiding, weapons ready. AX fires again as R-Mor dodges the blast and fires back, blasting AX. Note, Shawn, during the first I want Liz somehow hit. Jack should see it and race to her.

Phone (███) ███-████ • (███) ███-████ • Email ██████@████████

Otherwise, the gist of the battle is AX assumes R-Mor is the enemy and is trying to get her. She leaps, jumps, etc. while trying to avoid being grabbed. AX tries to smash R-Mor but she keeps out of his path. She manages to flip him into Liz, putting her down, then she blasts AX back. As Jack runs to Liz R-Mor does a jumping kick into AX knocking him back down. She turns to Skuzzy, who just watches, and tells him to make sure the A8 robot won't turn on them. She flips up and out of the barn. As AX runs outside to find her, she's gone. Back with Jack. He's cradling his mom, crying, saying someone has to help her. Please...help her. Shawn, play on this for many panels. Liz looks at him, tries to talk to him, but can't. He shouts he loves her. He loves her. Please love him. She starts to say something but slumps unconscious. As Jack cries over her Skuzzy and AX stare at each other.

20:    Bedlam General Hospital. Seen in issue #2. It's night. Skuzzy and Jack are outside in the waiting room as the Doctor enters. Tired, worn. Jack runs to him. How is she? How's my mom? The Doctor says she's suffered some contusions, nothing more. She'll be find. Jack runs and says he has to speak to her. In Liz's room AX climbs in the window. Liz looks up at him and says she should be out tomorrow. Was that my son, or was I dreaming. AX says that was him. And he loves you. Liz says she heard that. Despite everything he loves me. I don't even deserve that but he loves me. I thought I hated him, AX, she says. But it wasn't him I hated. I hated what happened to me and he represented that. I always knew better, though. I knew I loved him because sometimes at night I'd come in and look at him and he was such an angel I'd sit and watch him and cry. Shawn, you may want to mix this scene with a flashback of a younger Liz watching her baby son in the crib. Also, show at least one scene of Jack running through the corridors.

21:    Liz lifts her hand and AX takes it. She says she wants him to know she was wrong. She does love him. She wants to make it up to him. She wants to try to be better. Wants to become the mother she wasn't. If only she has a chance. Just then Jack enters. They stare at each other, Liz in bed, Jack across the room. AX watches and steps outside the window, on the hospital's fifth story ledge. Inside, they stare. Jack is in tears. Liz lifts a hand and says Jack...come here. Please. Jack slowly begins to walk to her. Shawn, play this up with lots of panels of him slowly walking. Drag this out as much as you can. She's waiting for him. Her hands up for him. he's coming closer.

22:    He's almost by her when the door to her room opens and DAN, her ex-husband comes in. Dan grabs Jack by the arm and says there's a court order keeping her from you. She'll never hurt you again, Jack. Dan pulls him out of the room and tells Liz never to try to speak to her son again. Outside, in the corridor a shot of Jack looking back at the door to his mother's room. Set it up like the scenes with Jack at the baseball fence and the fence around the farm. Staring at what's there but unable to get to it. Final panel, as large as you can make it: AX holds a crying Liz, still in her bed, buried in AX's arms and crying.

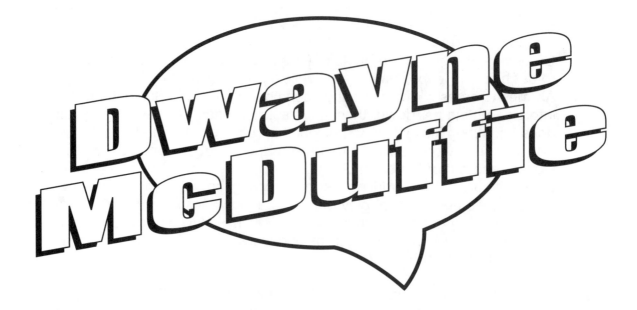

Dwayne McDuffie

A confession: If I'd had my way, *Deathlok* #5 is not the script I would have chosen to include in this volume. For one thing, I'd only written a handful of comics at this point in my career, so I'm not very good yet. For another, it's the conclusion to a four part story arc, consequently I'm often speaking in shorthand to an artist (the esteemed Denys Cowan) who, unlike you, has had 66 pages to get used to decoding "Dwayne-speak" (my own personal language that contains words like "Kirbyesque," which I would have sworn was in the OED). I'd actually intended to offer my script for *Icon* #42, which has the benefits of being a complete story with no super-heroics and a much better-written piece. Unfortunately, contractual entanglements prevented me from reproducing it here (although if you want to compare and contrast, *Icon* #42 is posted over at www.dwaynemcduffie.com, where you're welcome to give it a look). The good news is that the fine folks at Marvel Comics were kind enough to cut through the red tape and allow Nat to reproduce one of my Marvel super-hero scripts. Perhaps *Deathlok* #5, with numerous examples of my early rough edges will prove more instructional than my later, more polished work.

Deathlok #5 is written "full-script" and not as a "Marvel-style" plot. I used to write in both formats but have increasingly come to prefer full-script. The more information the artist has about what's in my head, the better he can do his job. If you compare the script to the finished comic, you'll note that Denys felt free to alter my panel breakdowns and shot descriptions whenever he had a better idea. Still, to get what you want on the finished page, it's the writer's responsibility to communicate their ideas clearly. If you don't set a pace, don't get angry when the artist doesn't create one for you.

You'll note from this script that I believe in plot recaps, every issue <u>is</u> someone's first, damn it! I also believe in clearly introducing characters the first time they appear, even though this doesn't always lend itself to naturalistic dialog, Reader. Speaking of dialog, I use way too much of it in this script. Over the years, I've learned my lesson, cutting back on dialog ping-ponging between characters (that stuff works great in sit-coms or buddy movies but it takes too much precious space in a comic). Somewhere along the line, I also discovered that my beloved monologues work best in pages, not panels.

Looking back, I do see some potential in my early work. I delivered plenty of the Marvel-style,

"Hoo-Ha Action" that both the readers and my editors expected but I also managed to sneak in something of myself, Humanistic values somewhat at odds with the conceit of vigilante fiction. For those of you going mainstream, it's your own individual qualities that will separate your work from the run-of-the-mill. Don't be afraid to be yourself, it's the most valuable thing in your writing toolbox.

– Dwayne McDuffie
January 12, 2002
Orlando, Florida

Dwayne McDuffie is the co-creator and owner of Milestone Media, Inc., the most successful black-owned comic book company in history. He's been a writer and/or editor for Marvel Comics, Milestone Media, DC Comics, Harvey Comics, Archie Comics, Valiant/Acclaim Comics, and several other companies he's either forgotten about or an ashamed to admit to. Dwayne continues to keep his hand in comics while working on the TV versions of Justice League *and* Static Shock.

DEATHLOK #5

"Deus Ex Machina"

Dwayne McDuffie
Script for 22 Pages
First Draft, 12-1-90
REVISED, 3-29-91

Page 1

ART NOTE, the first two pages are RECAP, framed as a handwritten letter to Tracy. The panels "float" on top of the letter, the letter's text runs underneath everything, including the gutters. Please use a standard panel grid and a muted color palate. Thanks.

Panel 1

    Symbolic FLASHBACK PANEL. MICHAEL COLLINS' head, behind an identical pose of DEATHLOK. Deathlok Caption is a letter to Tracy.

                    DEATHLOK CAPTION
            "Dear Tracy,
                I'm still trapped inside the
            Deathlok cyborg. And the most important
            thing in my life remains trying to find a
            way to become human again, to return to
            you and our son.

Panel 2

    FLASHBACK PANEL. Deathlok reacts to the Cyborg torture chamber in surprise.

                    DEATHLOK CAPTION
            "Recently though, I've been distracted. I
            have discovered that there are others
            like me, cyborgs, intelligent robots,
            other beings I can't even define. folks
            call them Cybernetters. And ~~they're~~ we're
            in trouble.

Panel 3

    FLASHBACK PANEL. MECHADOOM is disassembling FORGE's bionics, it's as horrific as we can get away with.

                    DEATHLOK CAPTION
            "A robot that calls himself Mechadoom has
            taken it upon himself capture and dissect
            as many Cybernetters as he can get his
            hands on.

Panel 4

    FLASHBACK PANEL. Mechadoom faces off with Deathlok.

1

DEATHLOK CAPTION
"I took it upon __myself__ to __stop__ him."

Page 2

Panel 1
FLASHBACK PANEL. Deathlok laying motionless against the wall, Mechadoom looming over him.

DEATHLOK CAPTION
"Or __try__ to. He beat me before I could even get a punch in.

Panel 2
FLASHBACK PANEL. The FF, X-MEN, MISTY KNIGHT and the VISION, run towards the camera.

DEATHLOK CAPTION
"And when the cavalry arrived to pull my fat out of the fire...

Panel 3
FLASHBACK PANEL. An EXPLOSION fills the panel.

DEATHLOK CAPTION
"Mechadoom killed them all.

Panel 4
FLASHBACK PANEL. Deathlok is on his feet putting his rifle together as Mechadoom watches the explosion on the screen, his back to Deathlok.

DEATHLOK CAPTION
"The lives of those heroes bought me just enough time to get back on my feet.

Page 3

SPLASH
DEATHLOK fires at MECHADOOM, who is dodging the blast. The blast trashes a number of the tentacles behind Mechadoom.

DEATHLOK CAPTION
"I'm no super hero, but this is a __promise__:

DEATHLOK CAPTION
"They __won't__ have died in vain."

2

TITLE
THE SOULS OF CYBER FOLK, PART 4
DEUS EX MACHINA

CREDITS

Dwayne McDuffie	Writer
Denys Cowan	Artist
Mike Manley	Inker
Ken Lopez	Letterer
Gregory Wright	Colorist
Tom Brevoort	Editor
Bob Budiansky	Executive Editor
Tom DeFalco	Editor-In-Chief

INDICIA

[LEAVE SPACE]

Page 4

Panel 1
The FLASHBACK is over. Tight on a resolute Deathlok's face.

DEATHLOK CAPTION
All right Computer, time to earn your keep. How do we beat this guy?

COMPUTER
(typeset Chicago)
Request for clarification. Use of maximum force permitted?

DEATHLOK CAPTION
No. He's the murderer. Not us.

COMPUTER
(typeset Chicago)
Hostile designate: "Mechadoom" does not meet this unit's working definition of "living organism." NO KILLING PARAMETER DOES NOT APPLY.

DEATHLOK CAPTION
I don't care! Do not kill Mechadoom. Shoot only to wound. Got it?

3

Panel 2
    Big panel. Deathlok fires several shots.

                    COMPUTER
                 (typeset Chicago)
Affirmative. Running.

                      SFX
ZZZRRAK

Panel 3
    Mechadoom dodges the blasts.

                    COMPUTER
                 (typeset Chicago)
Mechadoom has successfully evaded point blank weapon fire on two occasions. Reevaluating strategy.

                    MECHADOOM
I will <u>punish</u> you, cyborg.

Panel 4
    The machines on the walls and floor around Deathlok come to life. New tentacles reach out towards him.

                    MECHADOOM
This entire complex is mine to control with but a <u>thought</u>. The walls themselves rebel against you, Deathlok.

                    MECHADOOM
<u>Your</u> destruction is as certain as that of those you seek to <u>avenge</u>...

                    Page 5
Panel 1
    Back in the chamber Mechadoom blew up last issue. Debris is all over the floor, except for inside of a 25 foot diameter circle on the floor.

                    CAPTION
Moments ago, Mechadoom's fortress was invaded by an awesome assemblage of super-powered beings. Mechadoom dealt harshly with the intruders.

4

                              CAPTION
            But these heroes aren't the sort of
            problem that you can make disappear with
            an explosion.

                              CAPTION
            At least, not <u>permanently</u>...

                         INVISIBLE WOMAN
                          (not visible)
            I can't keep us invisible any longer,
            Reed. It's too much of a strain.

Panel 2
    Similar to previous. WOLVERINE, STORM, JUBILEE, MISTY
    KNIGHT, VISION and the FF (a very tired and sweaty SUE
    RICHARDS prominent) are semi-transparent, Sue had made
    them invisible, and protected them with her force field.

                              REED
            That's all right, Sue. You can drop the
            <u>invisible</u> <u>shield</u> as well. That was good
            work, you saved us all.

                              BEN
            Hey, Suzie? How come you bothered makin'
            us invisible?

                              SUE
            Mechadoom obviously saw us come in here.
            It's better if he thinks he <u>succeeded</u> in
            killing us.

Panel 3
    Favoring the Thing, who thinks that the explosion
    probably took out any monitoring devices. Wolverine isn't
    so sure. He's pointing at trouble from off-panel

                              BEN
            You couldda saved yer strength. The
            cameras probably got wiped out in the
            explosion.

                            WOLVERINE
            Good theory, Bub. But I wouldn't put any
            money on it.

                                5

                              BEN
                    Hah? Whaddaya mean?

                              BEN
                        (small letters)
              Oh.

                          Page 6
Panel 1
    Big panel. The heroes are in a circle, covering each
    others' backs. They are surrounded by LOTS of DOOMBOTS
    (Standard Doctor Doom doubles). Reed is adjusting some
    sort of high-tech, hand-held device. Misty Knight

                             MISTY
              Anybody care to offer a suggestion?

Panel 2
    Thing raises his fist. He's ready to rumble.

                             THING
              I got one. <u>Heads</u> <u>up</u>, <u>heroes</u>--

                             THING
                           (burst)
                   --IT'S CLOBBERING TIME!

Panel 3
    Wolverine pops his claws, a wicked smile on his face.

                             SFX
                  SNIKKT

                          WOLVERINE
              I like the sound of that.

                          Page 7
Panel 1
    Wolverine jams his claws through one of the Doombots'
    head.

                             SFX
                  SKRESHH

Panel 2
    The Thing punches another one into scrap.

                              BEN
              Good shot, Wolvie!. I--

                              6

                         SFX
          KRUNCHH

                         BEN
          --I just scrapped a Doombot with <u>one</u>
          shot?

Panel 3
   Thing looks at his fist in surprise.

                         BEN
          They sure don't make them like they <u>used</u>
          to.

Panel 4
   Reed stretches his way between two Doombots, who punch
   each other while trying to hit Reed.

                         REED
          You're correct, Ben. My examination of
          the Doombot that Deathlok defeated
          earlier yielded a great deal of
          information, some of which I've already
          put to use.

                         REED
          I've constructed a <u>jamming</u> <u>device</u> that
          destructively alters the Doombot's
          control frequency. As a result, these
          Doombots are slower, less agile--

Panel 5
   The Human Torch burns clean through one.

                         TORCH
          --<u>softer</u>!

                         SFX
          FOOOSSSH

                         Page 8
Panel 1
   A fast-flying Storm vaporizes a Doombot with a lightning
   bolt.

> STORM
> But _still_ dangerous. These devices were
> sufficient to capture _Forge_ and the other
> cyborgs we've come here to rescue.

Panel 2

Reed slingshots a Doombot into several others.

> REED
> Fortunately, Mechadoom's force field
> design is inferior to that of the real
> Doctor Doom.

> SFX
> SNNAPP

> SFX
> KLANNG

> REED
> _These_ force fields interfere explosively
> with one another. A safety feature shuts
> them down when they are in dangerous
> proximity.

Panel 3

Sue's force field blocks a blast from the gauntlets of
another Doombot.

> SFX
> SHRAKK

> SUE
> One thing's for certain--

Panel 4

Sue impales the Doombot with an invisible lance.

> SUE
> --_Without_ their force fields, they aren't
> _nearly_ as formidable.

> SFX
> CHOK

> SFX
> (impaled Doombot)
> SQUAWWK

8

-38-

Page 9

Panel 1
   Wolverine slashes into a Doombot's chest.

                    WOLVERINE
          Don't underestimate them, darlin'. They
          still got the numbers.

Panel 2
   The Thing is getting pounded by two doombots.

                    BEN
          Eeeyowtch! Yer tellin' me?

                    SFX
          THUMP THUDD

Panel 3
   VISION passes through a Doombot, disrupting it.

                    VISION
          By reducing my density to that of a
          wraith, I can disrupt the Doombot's
          circuitry, reducing their numerical
          advantage.

                    SFX
          SQUEE SQUAWWW

Panel 4
   JUBILEE is dodging a blast from a Doombot..

                    JUBILEE
          Sure, the Vision can trash the bad guys
          with his powers. Good for him! Fat lotta
          good my lousy powers're doin' me!

                    SFX
          shrakk

Page 10

Panel 1
   Back in Mechadoom's chamber, Deathlok is bound by
   mechanical tentacles

9

                         COMPUTER
                    (typeset Chicago)
**Attack plan within prescribed parameters
["No killing", Wounding force permitted.]
now complete.**

                    DEATHLOK CAPTION
Fat lotta good that'll do us if we can't
get loose.

                         COMPUTER
                    (typeset Chicago)
**Stress analysis of restraining devices
underway.**

                         DEATHLOK
Oh. <u>Do</u> take your time.

Panel 2
   Mechadoom's hand folds over, revealing a dangerous
   looking DRILL BIT.

                         MECHADOOM
Perhaps I can yet learn something of
value from your mechanical body—

                           SFX
                      (drill bit)
         CHOK

Panel 3
   Mechadoom thrusts the sharp, spinning bit at Deathlok's
   face..

                         MECHADOOM
--Once I've removed all of that
troublesome <u>organic</u> material.

                           SFX
                      (drill bit)
         WHIRRRRRR

Panel 4
   Tight as Deathlok moves his head out of the way.

                         DEATHLOK
   Ah, <u>computer</u>...

                            10

Panel 5
The drill bit sinks into the wall just to the side of his head.

>   COMPUTER
>   (typeset Chicago)
> **Stress analysis complete.**

>   DEATHLOK CAPTION
> Computer, you <u>do</u> understand that when I said "take your time," I was being--

>   COMPUTER
>   (typeset Chicago)
> **--"Sarchastic." Affirmative.**

>   SFX
>   (drill bit hits wall)
>   SKRIITCH

Page 11

Panel 1
   Deathlok tears free of the tentacles, punching Mechadoom in the face as he does so.

>   SFX
>   (punch)
>   KLANNG

>   DEATHLOK CAPTION
> About time you got us out of there.
> Where's our gun?

Panel 2
   Deathlok dives for the floor, reaching for his gun.

>   DEATHLOK CAPTION
> Never mind, I found it myself.

Panel 3
   Deathlok wheels on one knee, firing his gun.

>   DEATHLOK CAPTION
> Target to cripple. Take his legs out.

11

                          COMPUTER
                      (typeset Chicago)
          Targeting...

Panel 4
    The blast cuts Mechadoom's legs off.

                          COMPUTER
                      (typeset Chicago)
          **Objective accomplished. Direct hit has
          severed hostile's primary locomotive load-
          bearing limbs.**

                            SFX
                      (blast impact)
          CHOOM

Panel 5
    Mechadoom "assembles" new legs out of the substance of
    the room.

                      DEATHLOK CAPTION
          Oh, yeah? Then what do you call <u>those</u>?

                          COMPUTER
                      (typeset Chicago)
          **Mechadoom is reassembling damaged limbs
          from raw materials removed from
          surrounding machinery.**

                        Page 12
Panel 1
    Deathlok he dives aside, contorting himself to avoid four
    separate laser beams from various parts of the room..

                        MECHADOOM
          You cannot destroy me, cyborg. But I most
          assuredly can destroy <u>you</u>--

                      DEATHLOK CAPTION
          We need a new stategy, computer.

12

>   COMPUTER
>   (typeset Chicago)
> **Mechadoom is reassembling damaged limbs
> from raw materials removed from
> surrounding machinery.**

Panel 2
   Deathlok punches Mechadoom in the mouth, causing a
   splatter of Mechanical teeth. Cheaper than orthodontia.

>   MECHADOOM
>   (burst)
>   --Ueeerrgh!

>   DEATHLOK
>   You know, you got an overbite something
>   serious!

>   COMPUTER
>   (typeset Chicago)
> **TACTICAL ALERT: This unit being targeted for
> high energy laser fire. Refractive coating
> insufficient to prevent serious damage.**

Panel 3
   Big panel. Multiple image of Deathlok avoiding fire,
   firing at and destroying the laser sources one after
   another. Four shots.

>   DEATHLOK
>   Then get us out of the way. And while
>   you're at it, target and destroy the
>   laser sources.

>   COMPUTER
>   (typeset Chicago)
> **Running...**

>   SFX
>   (laser fire)
>   ZATZ ZATZ ZATZ ZATZ

>   SFX
>   (Deathlok blasts)
>   RAK ZRAK ZRAK ZRAK

COMPUTER
(typeset Chicago)
Lasers neutralized.

Page 13

Panel 1
Deathlok grapples with a now repaired Mechadoom.

DEATHLOK CAPTION
Geez! Where'd <u>he</u> come from? And <u>look</u> at him, will you? Must save a bundle on dental work.

DEATHLOK CAPTION
How're we supposed to beat this guy if he can fix himself every time we bust him up?

COMPUTER
(typeset Chicago)
Tactical scan indicates Mechadoom's primary power source is broadcast microwave. The remote power supply allows his extremely energy-intensive reconstructions.

Panel 2
Deathlok fires point blank at Mechadoom.

DEATHLOK
(burst)
Back off!

SFX
(blast)
ZZRAKK

Panel 3
Mechadoom parries the blast with a shield made from machinery that grows from the floor

DEATHLOK CAPTION
Then cut off his juice! Jam the signal.

COMPUTER
(typeset Chicago)
Option unavailable. Suggest destruction of Mechadoom's main power supply.

14

Panel 4
   Deathlok is assembling his rifle.

                        DEATHLOK
            Let's do it!

                        COMPUTER
                        (typeset Chicago)
            **Mechadoom main power supply located and
            targeted. Recommend rifle-based
            deployment of plasma grenade to maximize
            odds of total target destruction.**

Panel 5
   Deathlok puts the grenade on the end of his rifle as the
   computer targets the power source

                        SFX
                        (grenade clicks into
                        place)
            CHAK

                    Page 14
Panel 1
   Deathlok fires the rifle, discharging the Plasma grenade.

                        SFX
                        (grenade discharge)
            POOMF

Panel 2
   The Grenade flies a couple of hundred yards across the
   chamber.

                        SFX
                        (grenade in flight)
            SKREEEEEEEEE

                        COMPUTER
                        (typeset Chicago)
            Plasma grenade closing on target.

Panel 3
   Mechadoom watches in horror.

                        15

MECHADOOM
(burst)
Nooooooo!

Panel 4
  Deathlok tackles Mechadoom from behind.

DEATHLOK
Get <u>down</u>! When that thing goes--

Panel 5
  The grenade explodes, releasing energy obliterating
  everything in its range.

SFX
(explosion)
WHOOOM

COMPUTER
(typeset Chicago)
**Mechadoom primary power supply
obliterated. Reserve battery power still
available.**

Page 15

Panel 1
  Deathlok straddles Mechadoom's chest, holding his pistol
  on him.

DEATHLOK
Now. What am I supposed to do with you?

MECHADOOM
You have destroyed my main power source!
I cannot fully function without it.
<u>Please</u>! You must <u>aid</u> me!

Panel 2
  Tight on Deathlok's face.

DEATHLOK
Tell you what, Jaws. You do something for
<u>me</u>, I'll see what I can do for <u>you</u>.

Panel 3
  Deathlok watches on a view screen as The Thing smashes

16

two of the Doombots together.

> DEATHLOK
> First things first. How do we call off
> the Doom patrol?

Panel 4
Big panel. Pull back to reveal the triumphant, if
bewildered, heroes among the wreckage of dozens of former
Doombots. The undamaged ones have frozen in their tracks.

> THING
> What the heck's goin' <u>on</u> here? One second
> we're fightin' for our blamed lives, and
> the next thing you know, the Doombots are
> all standing around like somebody shut
> them off.

> REED RICHARDS
> I suspect that's precisely what happened,
> old friend. The question is <u>how</u>?

Panel 5
Tight on a resolute Storm.

> STORM
> Those answers can wait until <u>after</u> we
> have rescued our friends.

Page 16

Panel 1
All the heroes rush into the torture chamber to find a
bemused Deathlok standing among the now-repaired
cybernetters. Mechadoom is just finishing up work on
Ultron.

> DEATHLOK
> Hi, guys! What took you so long?

> THING
> You wanna start explainin' what the
> <u>blazes</u> is goin' on here?

> DEATHLOK
> Mechadoom is just finishing up repairs on
> the Cybernetters he took apart.

Panel 2

An enraged Ultron yells at Mechadoom, swearing vengeance.

> ULTRON
> Know this, creature. I will not suffer
> lightly the indignities I have been
> subjected to this day--

Panel 3
  Ultron stalks away from the others.

> ULTRON
> --Ultron will have his revenge upon you!

> DEATHLOK
> Not exactly the "forgive and forget"
> type, huh? If I were you, Mechadoom, I'd
> watch my back.

Panel 4
  Storm faces off with Deathlok, she's not happy.

> STORM
> Perhaps he should watch his front as
> well. I am not in a particularly
> forgiving mood either.

> DEATHLOK
> At least everybody's okay.

> STORM
> No thanks to him.

Panel 5
  Storm points an accusing finger at Mechadoom.
  Bushwacker's got her back.

> STORM
> What about it, Mechadoom? What shall we
> do with you?

> BUSHWACKER
> That's simple. He's too dangerous to let
> live. We off him.

Page 17

Panel 1
  Deathlok says no, positioning himself between Mechadoom
  and Storm, Wolverine, Jubilee and Forge. The others are

18

watching.

> DEATHLOK
> <u>Wrong</u> answer. Let's cool off and think
> this over for a minute.

> BUSHWACKER
> You're going to stop all of us?

Panel 2
  Favoring resolute Deathlok, he's fronting Bushwacker.

> DEATHLOK
> I'm going to try. I don't kill, or allow
> killing.

> DEATHLOK
> I'm not condoning Mechadoom's actions,
> but you've got to try and see it from his
> point of view.

Panel 3
  Deathlok explains Mechadoom's troubles, or begins to.
  Jubilee can't believe what she's hearing.

> DEATHLOK
> Everything he did, he did to escape his
> "father's" influence. Doctor Doom--

> JUBILEE
> --Oh, <u>for</u>...! You're not going to try and
> tell us he had an unhappy childhood, are
> ya?

Panel 4
  Deathlok is sheepish as he explains.

> DEATHLOK
> Well, he <u>did</u>!

Panel 5
  Misty Knight makes the case to the heroes. Favor one of
  the mutants, listening. I'm trying to implicitly connect
  the cyborgs to mutants and oppressed minorities.

> MISTY
> Mechadoom reacted violently to a world
> that defined him by a stereotype --

19

soulless machine, hideous freak,
whatever. <u>Different</u>.-- then held him to
the ridiculous limitations <u>inherent</u> in
that false definition.

MISTY
All Mechadoom really tried to do was
assimilate. But nobody would tell him
<u>how</u>. Or even <u>let</u> him.

Panel 6
Beat panel as the heroes consider the point. Favor the
freakier-looking ones.

OFF-PANEL MISTY
I suppose none of the <u>rest</u> of us have
ever felt that way...

Page 18
Panel 1
Wolverine's convinced. Storm isn't sure, but she's
wavering.

WOLVERINE
I"m with Misty on this one, 'Roro. What
do <u>you</u> say?

STORM
I say it's up to Forge. He was hurt the
most.

Panel 2
Forge looks to Deathlok. Deathlok doesn't want the
responsibility.

FORGE
Well, Deathlok saved the day, seems to me
it's <u>his</u> call.

DEATHLOK
Dandy. I don't know what we <u>should</u> do,
just what we <u>shouldn't</u>.

Panel 3
Human Torch notices that Mechadoom is getting hot.

20

                         TORCH
             Um, I hate to interrupt. But Mechadoom's
             temperature is rising fast.

                         COMPUTER
                      (typeset Chicago)
             Observation confirmed. Mechadoom reserve
             battery on overload. Detonation in
             approximately three minutes. Strongly
             reccomend rapid retreat.

Panel 4
    Favoring Deathlok as he explains. Wolverine points out
    the flaw in his suggestion.

                         DEATHLOK
             He's going to self-destruct in three
             minutes. I suggest you guys make a run
             for it.

                         WOLVERINE
             Think again, bub. This joint's
             underwater. We'd never make it out of
             here.
Panel 5
    On the FF, favoring Sue. Thing has his fist cocked.

                         THING
             I'll bust him up.

                         REED
             Ben, no! You'd just set it off
             prematurely

                         SUE
             Maybe I can contain the explosion in my
             force field.

                         REED
             Even if you weren't already exhausted, I
             doubt you could survive a blast of such--

Panel 6
    Deathlok is angry, yelling up at Mechadoom.

                            21

>   DEATHLOK
>   (burst)
> --What do you think you're <u>doing</u>?

>   MECHADOOM
> I do not wish to lose my freedom. I do
> not wish to lose my identity when I see
> Doctor Doom. If I cannot reproduce, if I
> cannot <u>live</u>, I choose <u>death</u>.

Page 19

Panel 1
   Deathlok incensed, he pushes Mechadoom.

>   DEATHLOK
> You haven't been paying <u>attention</u>, have
> you? You have <u>no</u> right to kill yourself,
> and even less right to endanger the lives
> of <u>others</u>.

Panel 2
   Favor Deathlok as Computer counts down.

>   DEATHLOK
> Let me see if I've got this straight.
> You're afraid you're alone and your life
> doesn't <u>count</u>. You're afraid of losing
> your <u>individuality</u>. You're afraid of
> <u>dying</u> and not leaving anything behind for
> the world to <u>remember</u> you by.

Panel 3
   Tighter and More heroic shot of Deathlok.

>   DEATHLOK
> You're afraid of being too <u>different</u>.
> You're afraid of being too much the <u>same</u>.
> You're <u>confused</u> and you lash out in
> anger.

Panel 4
   Big shot of Deathlok and Mechadoom.

>   DEATHLOK
> Misty's <u>right</u>. None of these feelings are
> the product of being a <u>machine</u>. I've felt

22

like you do, and so has everybody else
who's ever been alive.

> DEATHLOK
> Look <u>around</u> you. Cyber folk feel what you
> do. <u>Everybody</u> does; Male or female.
> Straight or gay. Black, white, yellow or
> brown. Homo Sapien or Homo Superior. Man
> and super-man alike.

Panel 5
  Favoring Deathlok.

> DEATHLOK
> Mechadoom, you're suffering from an
> advanced case of <u>humanity</u>. Deal with it.
> The rest of us do.

> MECHADOOM
> Human…?

> COMPUTER
> (typeset Chicago)
> **Mechadoom has aborted self-destruct cycle.**

Panel 6
  Mechadoom looks almost pleased

> MECHADOOM
> What should I do?

> SFX
> I'm sure we can work <u>something</u> out.

Page 20

Panel 1
  Time cut. Reed is reprogramming Mechadoom, he's got some
  kind of Kirby device stuck in Mechadoom's head.

> CAPTION
> Shortly…

> REED
> <u>There</u>. I've completed my alterations of
> your recognition circuits. You need never
> fear Doctor Doom again. At least, no more
> than the <u>rest</u> of us.

23

Panel 2
    Misty Knight speaks to Mechadoom.

                        MISTY
                It's actually quite impressive what we
                can accomplish when we pool our
                resources.

                        MECHADOOM
                I have been thinking along much the same
                lines, MistyKnight.

Panel 3
    Wide, Mechadoom speaks to the group. Way too much dialog,
    so leave room.

                        MECHADOOM
                I have decided to remain here, and act as
                a clearinghouse of information and
                technical support for cyborgs abd
                intelligent machines. My purpose will be
                to serve our community and work to bring
                about the day when we are fully accepted
                into society.

Panel 4
    Closer on Deathlok, summing up.

                        DEATHLOK
                That ought to keep him busy for a while.
                So. If we're all agreed, I think we're
                done here.

Panel 5
    Ultron reappears, pointing his crackling gauntlets at a
    surprised Mechadoom

                        ULTON
                        (burst)
                Not quite!

                        MECHADOOM
                Ultron?

                        Page 21
Panel 1
    Ultron blasts Mechadoom into a fireball.

24

-54-

                              SFX
              CHOOOM

Panel 2
    The heroes, Deathlok prominent, react in shock.

                         DEATHLOK
              No...!

Panel 3
    New angle reveals a pile of smoldering rubble where
    Mechadoom was.

                    OFF-PANEL DEATHLOK
              He's gone.

Panel 4
    Wolverine notices that Ultron is also gone. The heroes
    scatter, trying to find him.

                         WOLVERINE
              So's Ultron!

Panel 4
    Later, Misty walks Deathlok over to the Skycycle that
    Reed gave him back in issue 3.

                         CAPTION
              Several hours later, back at the pier...

                         DEATHLOK
              How do you suppose Ultron managed to pull
              it off? He disappeared without a trace.

                         MISTY
              Ultron's a maniac, but he's no fool. No
              way he would have tried a stunt like that
              with all those guys around if he didn't
              have his escape well-planned.

Panel 5
    As Deathlok climbs on the Cycle, Misty vows revenge on
    Ultron.

                         MISTY
              Ultron got his revenge but he'll show up
              again. And he'll pay for what he did
              today.

Page 22

Panel 1
    Tighter as Deathlok admits to his own insecurities. He's holding his copy of "The Souls Of Black Folk."

> DEATHLOK
> Lousy time to die, wasn't it? He was just learning how to be comfortable in his own skin. But for one brief moment, Mechadoom got everything anyone can ask for.

Panel 2
    Warm moment as Deathlok reads from the book to Misty.

> DEATHLOK
> (italics)
> "This then, is the end of his striving: to be a co- worker in the kingdom of culture, to escape both death and isolation, to husband and use his best powers and latent genius.... And now what I have briefly sketched in large outline let me tell again in many ways, with loving emphasis and deeper detail, that men may listen to the striving in the souls of black folk."

Panel 3
    Favoring a moved Misty as Deathlok's Skycycle rises into the night sky.

> MISTY
> Folk is folk, Michael. That striving is in everyone's soul.

> MISTY
> And you're a very good listener.

Panel 4
    Later. Long shot of Deathlok writing a letter to Tracy as he sits on the roof of Jesus' place.

> CAPTION
> Brooklyn, much later...

26

                        DEATHLOK CAPTION
        "Dear Tracy, Even though a lot of the
        cyborgs Mechadoom tortured weren't
        exactly displeased that he died, some of
        them decided to have funeral services for
        him anyway. The Fantastic Four, and some
        of the X-Men are also coming to pay their
        last respects. And so am I.

Panel 5
    Closer on Deathlok as he writes.

                        DEATHLOK CAPTION
        "It was a hard way to learn it, but
        Mechadoom taught me something. I've come
        to realize that my pretentious little
        speech wasn't entirely for his benefit.
        In a way, I was talking to myself. And
        despite what I said to Misty about having
        to live in your own skin, somehow,
        knowing that there are others like you
        validates you--

Panel 6
    Deathlok is looking up at the rising sun and allows
    himself a small , bittersweet smile.

                        DEATHLOK CAPTION
        "And makes you feel just a little less
        alone."

                        NEXT ISSUE BOX
        NEXT:

                        -30-

-57-

Jeff Smith is a full-fledged cartoonist, generally writing and drawing his own material. *Rose*, a miniseries set in the Bone continuity, is a rare case of Smith writing comics that he wasn't drawing; the series sports the lush art of Charles Vess. With Jeff's background in art and animation and his years of work on his fantasy series *Bone*, he is used to expressing himself visually. It comes as no surprise that instead of writing his script, he draws it. His "script" is really a loosely-drawn comic book.

A drawn script conveys more information than a typed script, as it contains not only the conceptual content of each panel, but suggestions for layout and visual depictions of facial emotion. If you compare this script to Vess's finished work (which show up as the first four chapters in *Rose* issue 1 and are reprinted in the *Rose* collected volume), you'll find that he usually followed those suggestions. Sometimes, however, he reworked the panel, most notably changing the scale of the image in a given panel. Even when a writer is drawing a script, the artist still gets the final say on the visuals.

Drawn scripts are not limited to artists. Some writers like scripting in this form, particularly for humor material where the visual rhythms of character placement in panels can be vital. It's not unknown for drawn scripts to be used for superhero material, but it is the exception rather than the rule.

For the new comics writer, drawing a script can be a useful learning experience. Actually trying to build the page layout can teach you things about the limitations of the page that you may have missed by writing solely in text format.

– Nat Gertler, December 2001

(Note: Jeff drew the script all the way out to the edges of 8.5" by 11" pieces of paper, often running off the page. For production reasons, his pages have been shrunk slightly for reproduction. The images have also been darkened, so that his light pencil drawings can be seen clearly.)

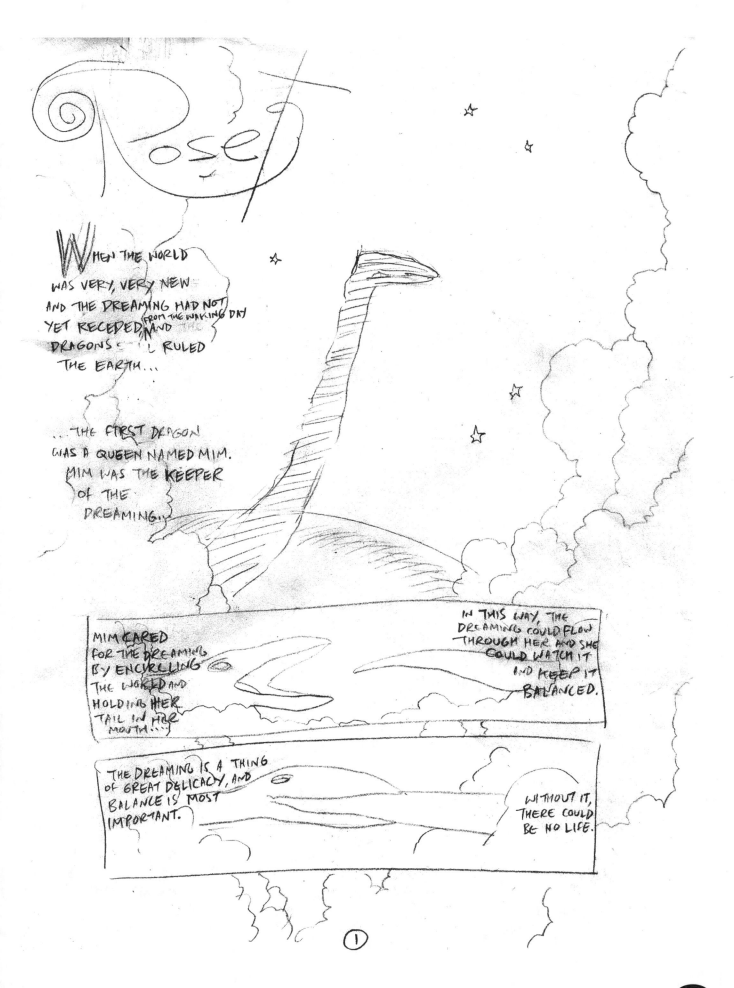

Rose

When the world was very, very new and the dreaming had not yet receded from the waking day, and dragons still ruled the earth...

...the first dragon was a queen named Mim. Mim was the KEEPER of the DREAMING...

Mim cared for the dreaming by encircling the world and holding her tail in her mouth...

In this way, the dreaming could flow through her and she could watch it and keep it BALANCED.

The dreaming is a thing of great delicacy, and balance is most important.

Without it, there could be no life.

①

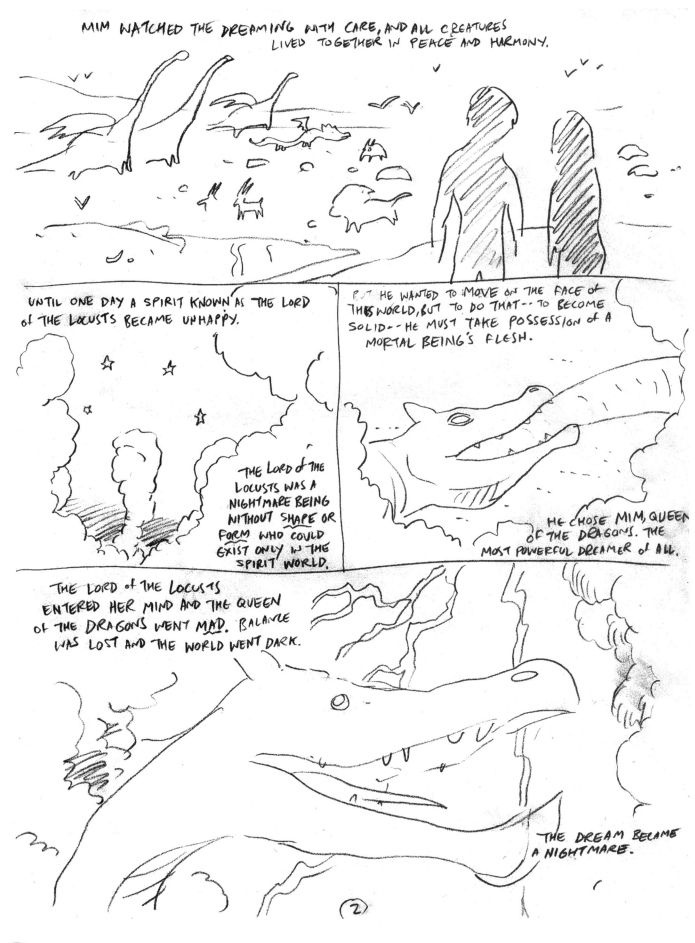

MIM WATCHED THE DREAMING WITH CARE, AND ALL CREATURES LIVED TOGETHER IN PEACE AND HARMONY.

UNTIL ONE DAY A SPIRIT KNOWN AS THE LORD OF THE LOCUSTS BECAME UNHAPPY.

THE LORD OF THE LOCUSTS WAS A NIGHTMARE BEING WITHOUT SHAPE OR FORM WHO COULD EXIST ONLY IN THE SPIRIT WORLD.

BUT HE WANTED TO MOVE ON THE FACE OF THIS WORLD, BUT TO DO THAT-- TO BECOME SOLID-- HE MUST TAKE POSSESSION OF A MORTAL BEING'S FLESH.

HE CHOSE MIM, QUEEN OF THE DRAGONS. THE MOST POWERFUL DREAMER OF ALL.

THE LORD OF THE LOCUSTS ENTERED HER MIND AND THE QUEEN OF THE DRAGONS WENT MAD. BALANCE WAS LOST AND THE WORLD WENT DARK.

THE DREAM BECAME A NIGHTMARE.

②

TO SAVE THE WORLD, ALL THE OTHER DRAGONS HAD TO MOVE AGAINST HER.

A TERRIBLE BATTLE ENSUED.

AS THE DRAGONS FOUGHT WITH THEIR MAD QUEEN, THEY CRASHED BACK AND FORTH, PUSHING UP ROCKS AND MOUNTAINS.

ON AND ON THE BATTLE WAGED, WITH MANY VALIANT DRAGONS LOSING THEIR LIVES

THE DRAGONS WERE FORCED TO TAKE DESPARATE MEASURES.

TERRIBLE DESPARMED MEASURES... FOR THEY KNEW IT WOULD BE THE END OF THEIR BELOVED MIM...

...BUT FOR THE GOOD OF THE WORLD AND TO DESTROY THEIR ENEMY THE LORD OF THE LOCUSTS...

...THEY TURNED THEIR QUEEN INTO STONE, TRAPPED THE LORD OF LOCUSTS INSIDE HER FOREVER.

LATER, THE LAND COOLED...

AND THAT IS HOW THE VALLEY WAS BORN--

ROSE! ARE YOU PAYING ATTENTION?

4

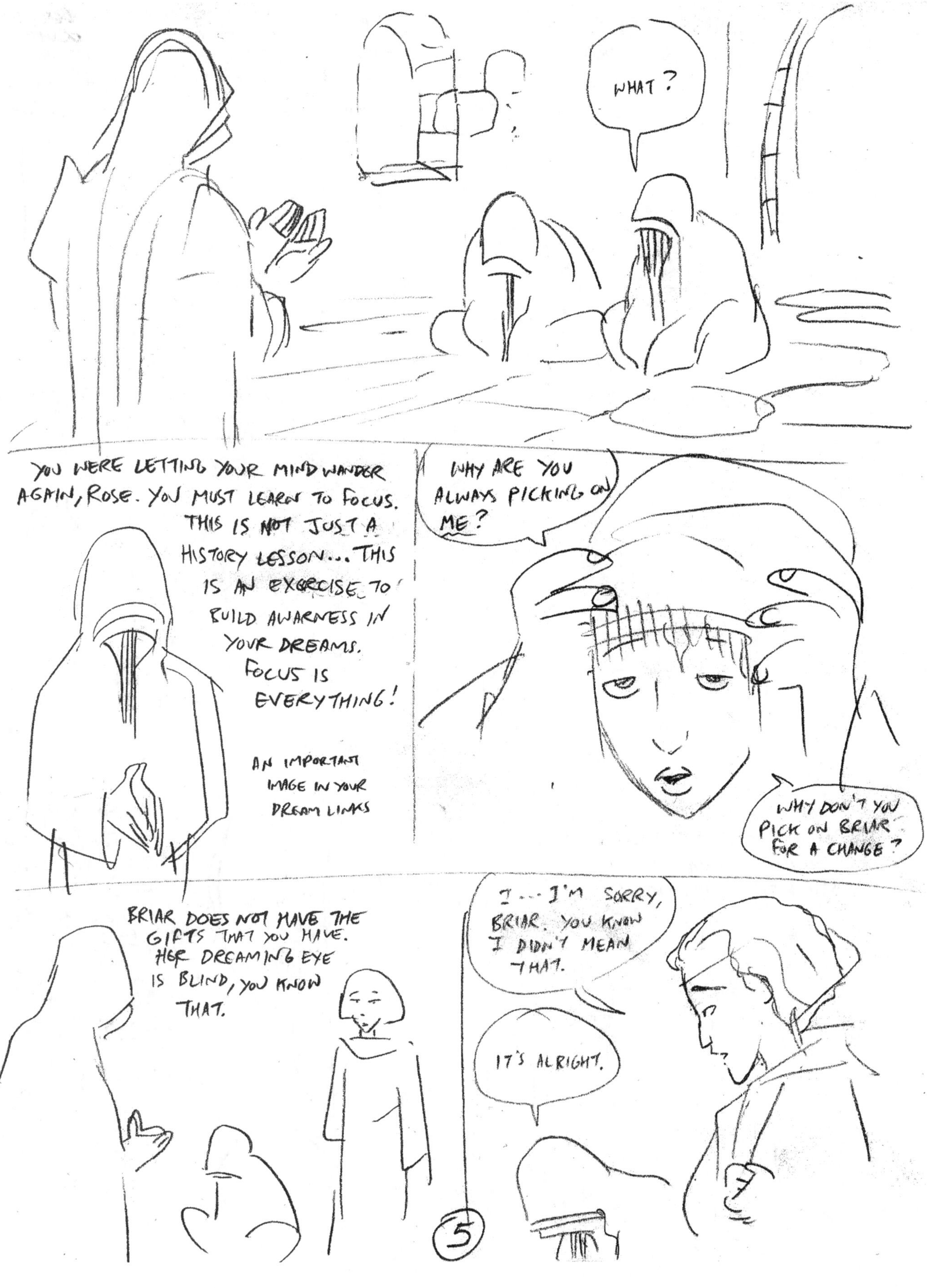
WHAT?
YOU WERE LETTING YOUR MIND WANDER AGAIN, ROSE. YOU MUST LEARN TO FOCUS. THIS IS NOT JUST A HISTORY LESSON... THIS IS AN EXERCISE TO BUILD AWARNESS IN YOUR DREAMS. FOCUS IS EVERYTHING!
AN IMPORTANT IMAGE IN YOUR DREAM LINKS
WHY ARE YOU ALWAYS PICKING ON ME?
WHY DON'T YOU PICK ON BRIAR FOR A CHANGE?
BRIAR DOES NOT HAVE THE GIFTS THAT YOU HAVE. HER DREAMING EYE IS BLIND, YOU KNOW THAT.
I... I'M SORRY, BRIAR. YOU KNOW I DIDN'T MEAN THAT.
IT'S ALRIGHT.
5

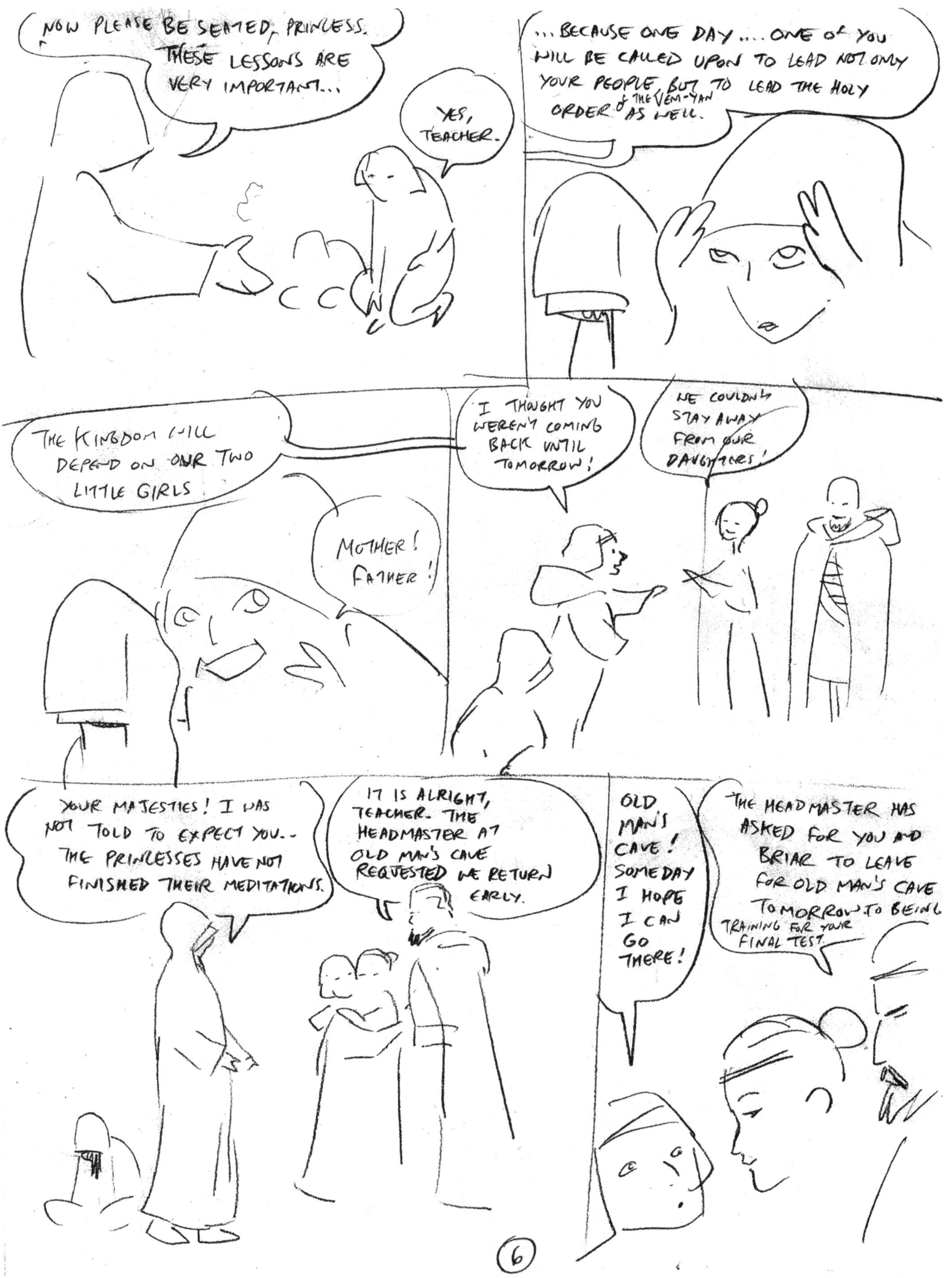
NOW PLEASE BE SEATED, PRINCESS. THESE LESSONS ARE VERY IMPORTANT...
YES, TEACHER.
...BECAUSE ONE DAY.... ONE OF YOU WILL BE CALLED UPON TO LEAD NOT ONLY YOUR PEOPLE, BUT TO LEAD THE HOLY ORDER OF THE VEM-YAN AS WELL.
THE KINGDOM WILL DEPEND ON OUR TWO LITTLE GIRLS
MOTHER! FATHER!
I THOUGHT YOU WEREN'T COMING BACK UNTIL TOMORROW!
WE COULDN'T STAY AWAY FROM OUR DAUGHTERS!
YOUR MAJESTIES! I WAS NOT TOLD TO EXPECT YOU.. THE PRINCESSES HAVE NOT FINISHED THEIR MEDITATIONS.
IT IS ALRIGHT, TEACHER. THE HEADMASTER AT OLD MAN'S CAVE REQUESTED WE RETURN EARLY.
OLD MAN'S CAVE! SOMEDAY I HOPE I CAN GO THERE!
THE HEADMASTER HAS ASKED FOR YOU AND BRIAR TO LEAVE FOR OLD MAN'S CAVE TOMORROW TO BEING TRAINING FOR YOUR FINAL TEST.
6

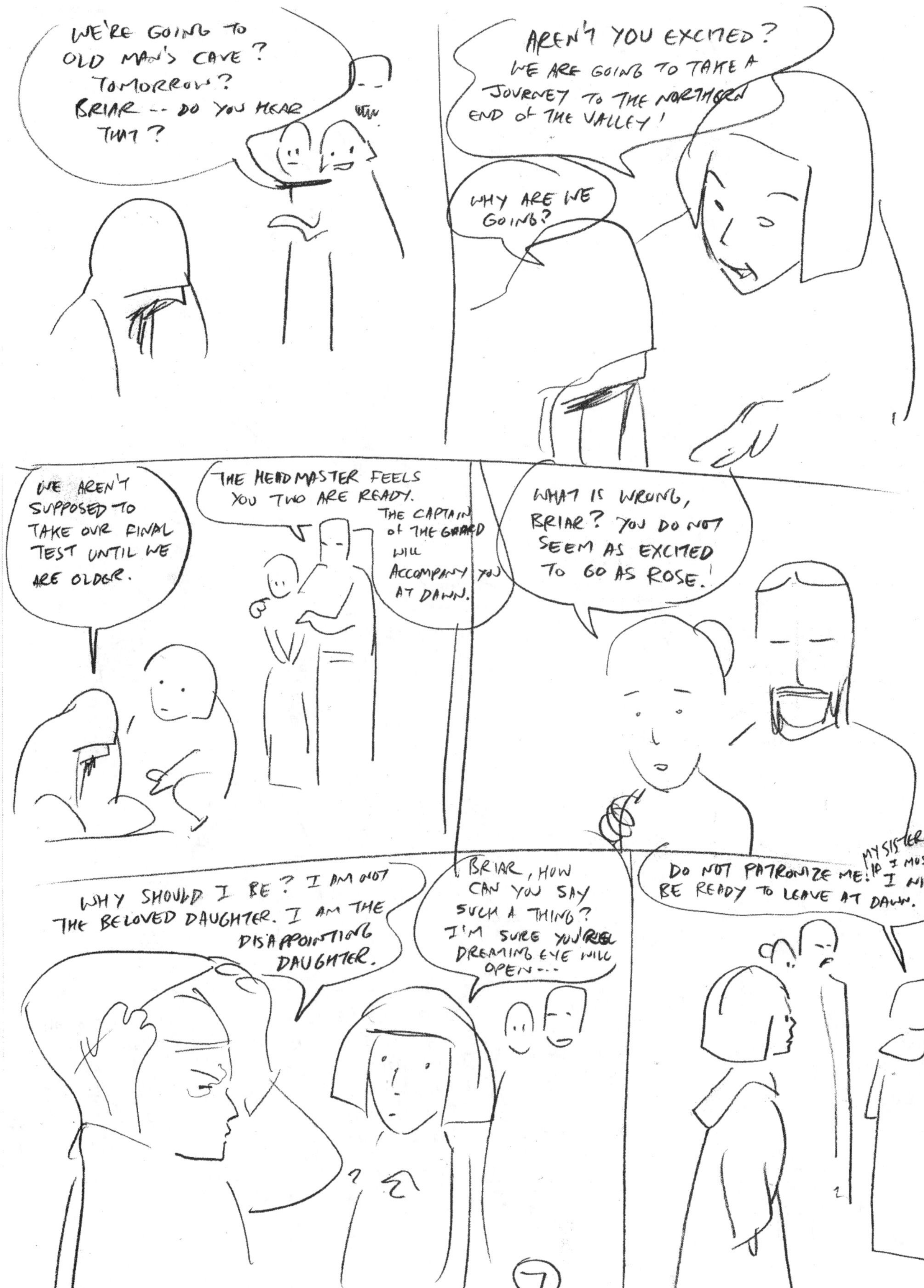
WE'RE GOING TO OLD MAN'S CAVE? TOMORROW? BRIAR -- DO YOU HEAR THAT?
AREN'T YOU EXCITED? WE ARE GOING TO TAKE A JOURNEY TO THE NORTHERN END OF THE VALLEY!
WHY ARE WE GOING?
WE AREN'T SUPPOSED TO TAKE OUR FINAL TEST UNTIL WE ARE OLDER.
THE HEADMASTER FEELS YOU TWO ARE READY.
THE CAPTAIN OF THE GUARD WILL ACCOMPANY YOU AT DAWN.
WHAT IS WRONG, BRIAR? YOU DO NOT SEEM AS EXCITED TO GO AS ROSE!
WHY SHOULD I BE? I AM NOT THE BELOVED DAUGHTER. I AM THE DISAPPOINTING DAUGHTER.
BRIAR, HOW CAN YOU SAY SUCH A THING? I'M SURE YOUR DREAMING EYE WILL OPEN...
DO NOT PATRONIZE ME! MY SISTER IF I MUST, I WILL BE READY TO LEAVE AT DAWN.

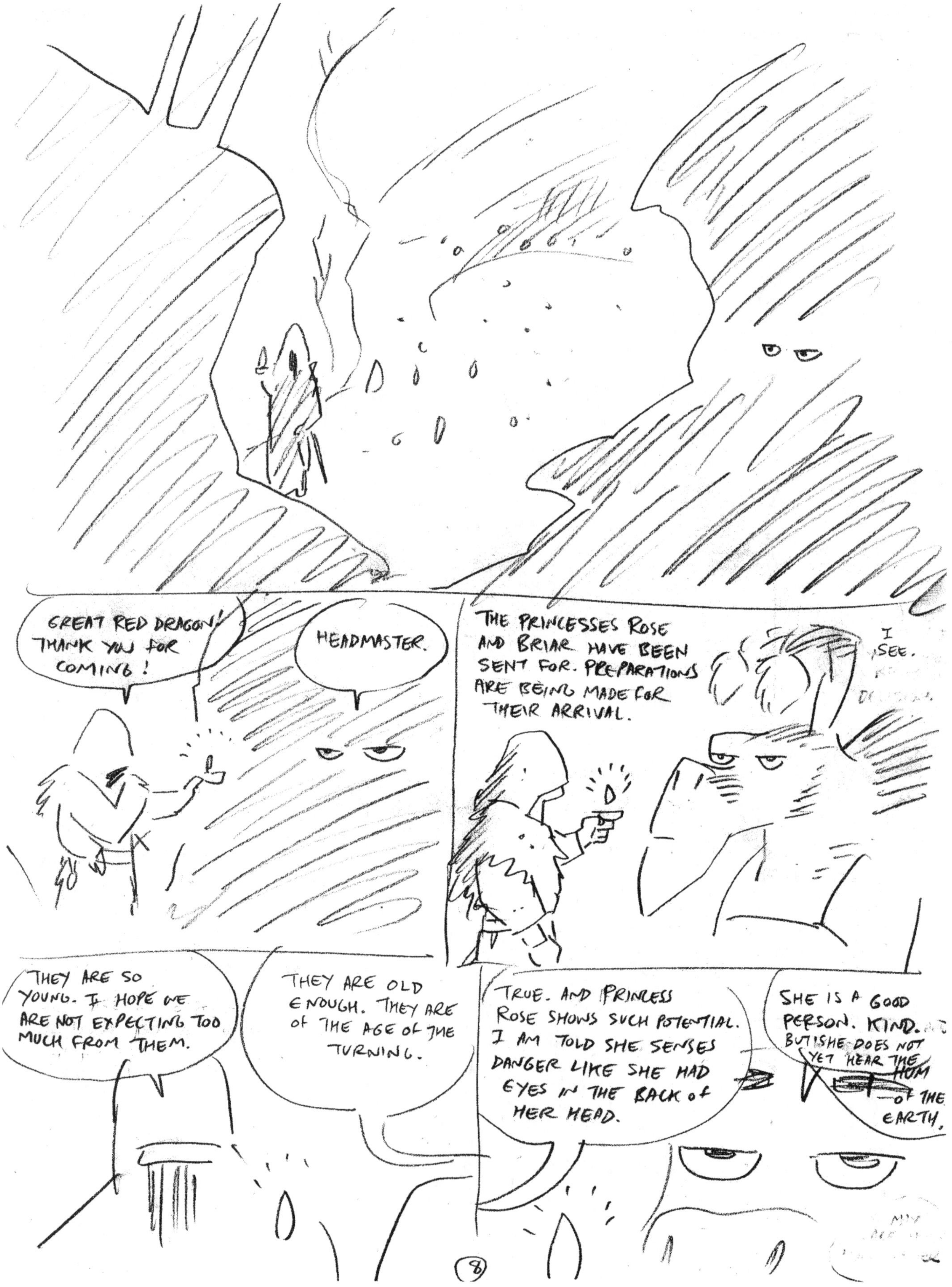
GREAT RED DRAGON! THANK YOU FOR COMING!
HEADMASTER.
THE PRINCESSES ROSE AND BRIAR HAVE BEEN SENT FOR. PREPARATIONS ARE BEING MADE FOR THEIR ARRIVAL.
I SEE.
THEY ARE SO YOUNG. I HOPE WE ARE NOT EXPECTING TOO MUCH FROM THEM.
THEY ARE OLD ENOUGH. THEY ARE OF THE AGE OF THE TURNING.
TRUE. AND PRINCESS ROSE SHOWS SUCH POTENTIAL. I AM TOLD SHE SENSES DANGER LIKE SHE HAD EYES IN THE BACK OF HER HEAD.
SHE IS A GOOD PERSON. KIND. BUT SHE DOES NOT YET HEAR THE HUM OF THE EARTH.
8

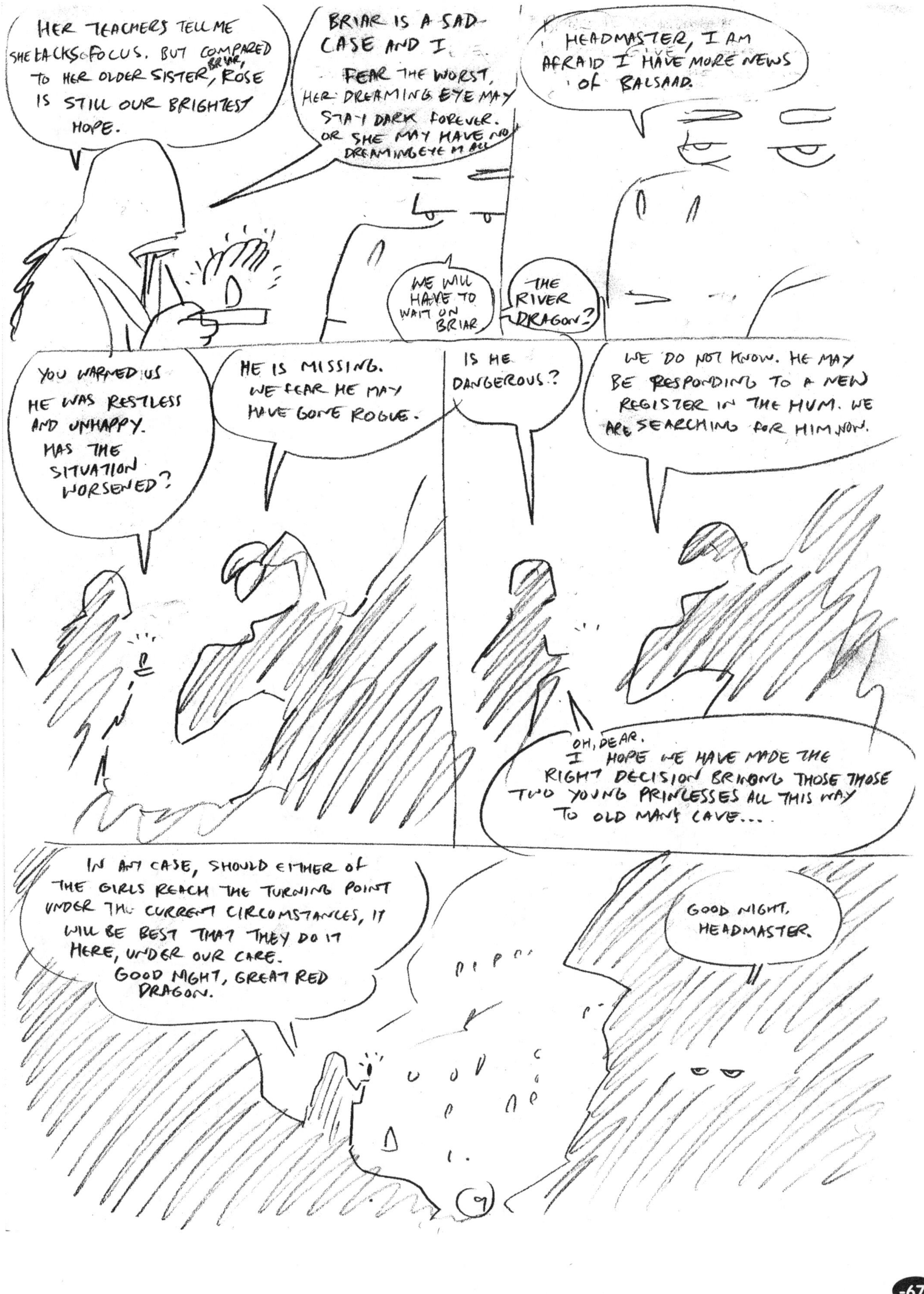

HER TEACHERS TELL ME SHE LACKS FOCUS. BUT COMPARED TO HER OLDER SISTER, BRIAR, ROSE IS STILL OUR BRIGHTEST HOPE.
BRIAR IS A SAD CASE AND I FEAR THE WORST. HER DREAMING EYE MAY STAY DARK FOREVER. OR SHE MAY HAVE NO DREAMING EYE AT ALL
WE WILL HAVE TO WAIT ON BRIAR.
HEADMASTER, I AM AFRAID I HAVE MORE NEWS OF BALSAAD.
THE RIVER DRAGON?
YOU WARNED US HE WAS RESTLESS AND UNHAPPY. HAS THE SITUATION WORSENED?
HE IS MISSING. WE FEAR HE MAY HAVE GONE ROGUE.
IS HE DANGEROUS?
WE DO NOT KNOW. HE MAY BE RESPONDING TO A NEW REGISTER IN THE HUM. WE ARE SEARCHING FOR HIM NOW.
OH, DEAR. I HOPE WE HAVE MADE THE RIGHT DECISION BRINGING THOSE THOSE TWO YOUNG PRINCESSES ALL THIS WAY TO OLD MAN'S CAVE...
IN ANY CASE, SHOULD EITHER OF THE GIRLS REACH THE TURNING POINT UNDER THE CURRENT CIRCUMSTANCES, IT WILL BE BEST THAT THEY DO IT HERE, UNDER OUR CARE. GOOD NIGHT, GREAT RED DRAGON.
GOOD NIGHT, HEADMASTER.
9

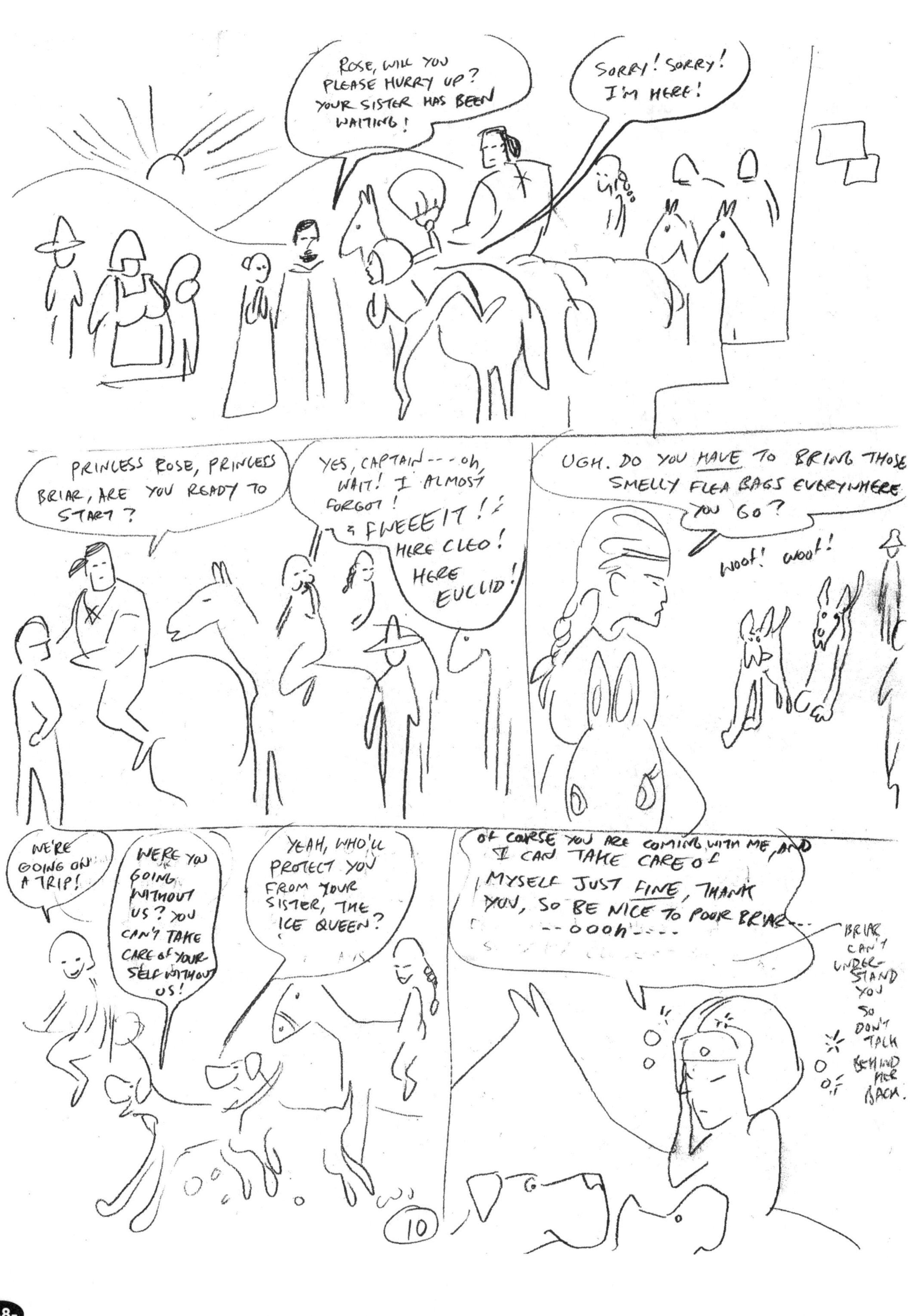
ROSE, WILL YOU PLEASE HURRY UP? YOUR SISTER HAS BEEN WAITING!
SORRY! SORRY! I'M HERE!
PRINCESS ROSE, PRINCESS BRIAR, ARE YOU READY TO START?
YES, CAPTAIN --- oh, WAIT! I ALMOST FORGOT!
FWEEEIT!!
HERE CLEO! HERE EUCLID!
UGH. DO YOU HAVE TO BRING THOSE SMELLY FLEA BAGS EVERYWHERE YOU GO?
woof! woof!
WE'RE GOING ON A TRIP!
WERE YOU GOING WITHOUT US? YOU CAN'T TAKE CARE OF YOURSELF WITHOUT US!
YEAH, WHO'LL PROTECT YOU FROM YOUR SISTER, THE ICE QUEEN?
OF COURSE YOU ARE COMING WITH ME, AND I CAN TAKE CARE OF MYSELF JUST FINE, THANK YOU, SO BE NICE TO POOR BRIAR... --oooh----
BRIAR CAN'T UNDERSTAND YOU SO DON'T TALK BEHIND HER BACK.
10

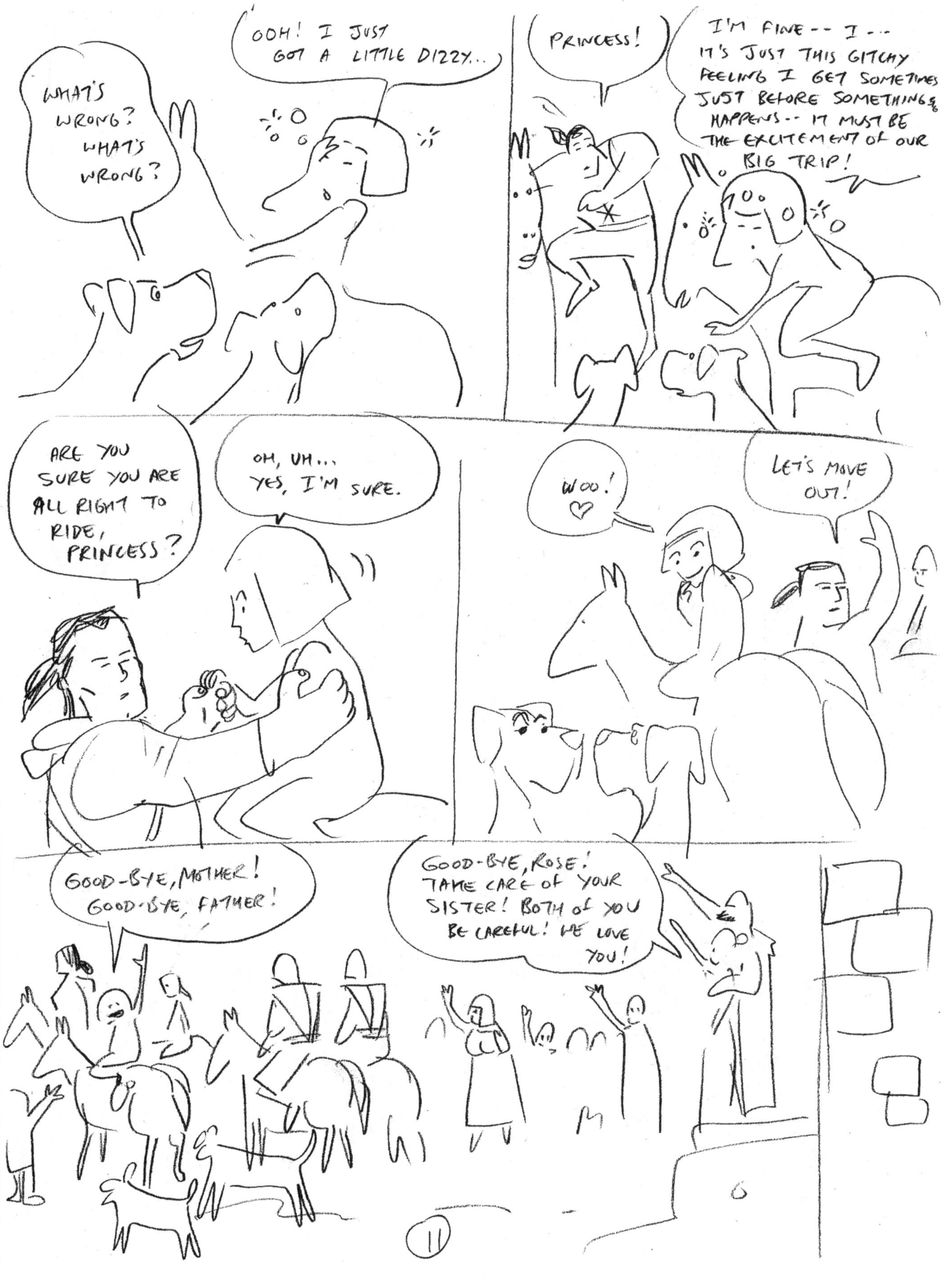
WHAT'S WRONG? WHAT'S WRONG? WHAT'S WRONG?
OOH! I JUST GOT A LITTLE DIZZY...
PRINCESS!
I'M FINE -- I -- IT'S JUST THIS GITCHY FEELING I GET SOMETIMES JUST BEFORE SOMETHING HAPPENS -- IT MUST BE THE EXCITEMENT OF OUR BIG TRIP!
ARE YOU SURE YOU ARE ALL RIGHT TO RIDE, PRINCESS?
OH, UH... YES, I'M SURE.
WOO! ♡
LET'S MOVE OUT!
GOOD-BYE, MOTHER! GOOD-BYE, FATHER!
GOOD-BYE, ROSE! TAKE CARE OF YOUR SISTER! BOTH OF YOU BE CAREFUL! WE LOVE YOU!
11

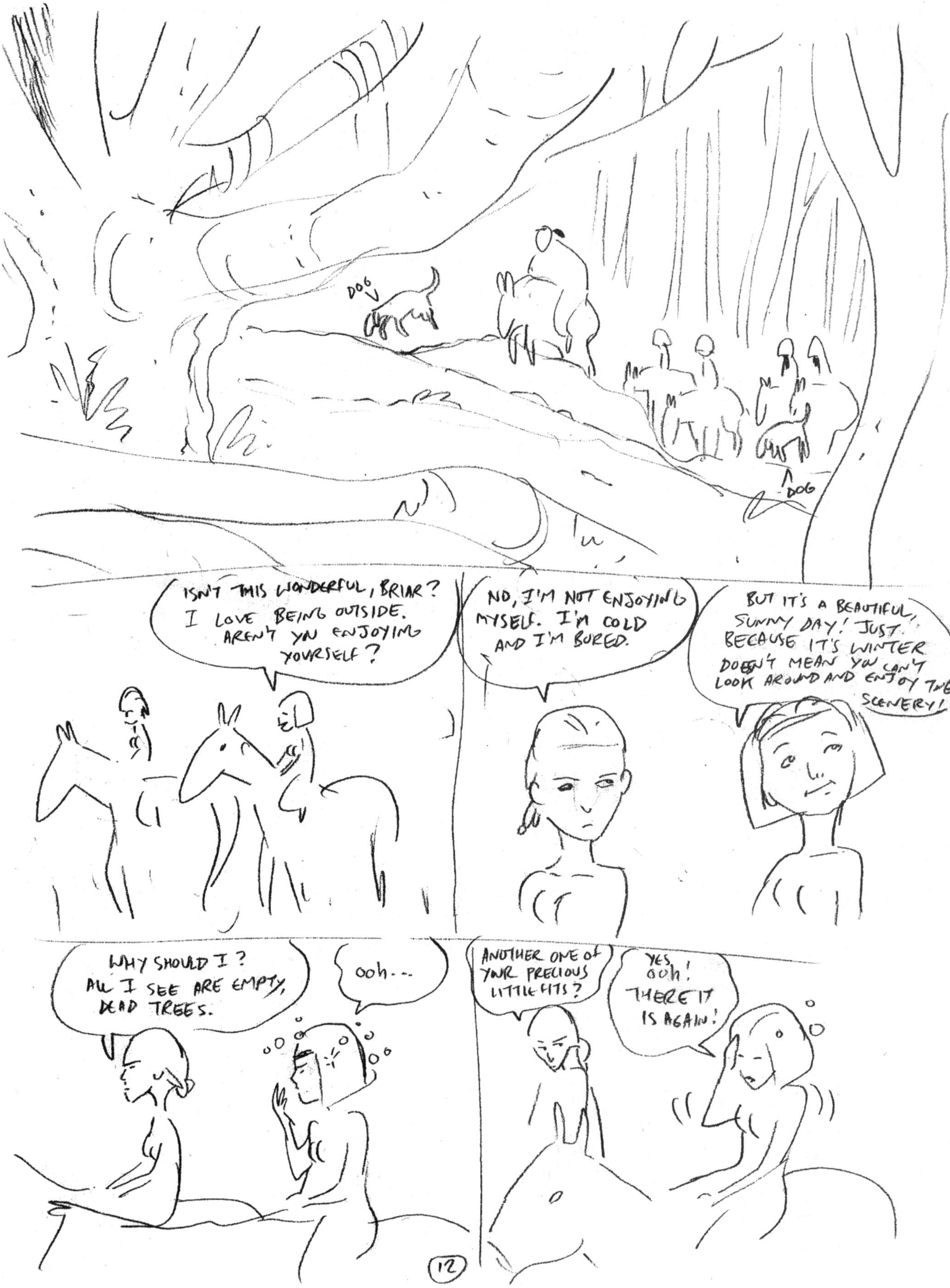

DOG
DOG
ISN'T THIS WONDERFUL, BRIAR? I LOVE BEING OUTSIDE. AREN'T YOU ENJOYING YOURSELF?
NO, I'M NOT ENJOYING MYSELF. I'M COLD AND I'M BORED.
BUT IT'S A BEAUTIFUL, SUNNY DAY! JUST BECAUSE IT'S WINTER DOESN'T MEAN YOU CAN'T LOOK AROUND AND ENJOY THE SCENERY!
WHY SHOULD I? ALL I SEE ARE EMPTY, DEAD TREES.
ooh...
ANOTHER ONE OF YOUR PRECIOUS LITTLE FITS?
YES, ooh! THERE IT IS AGAIN!
12

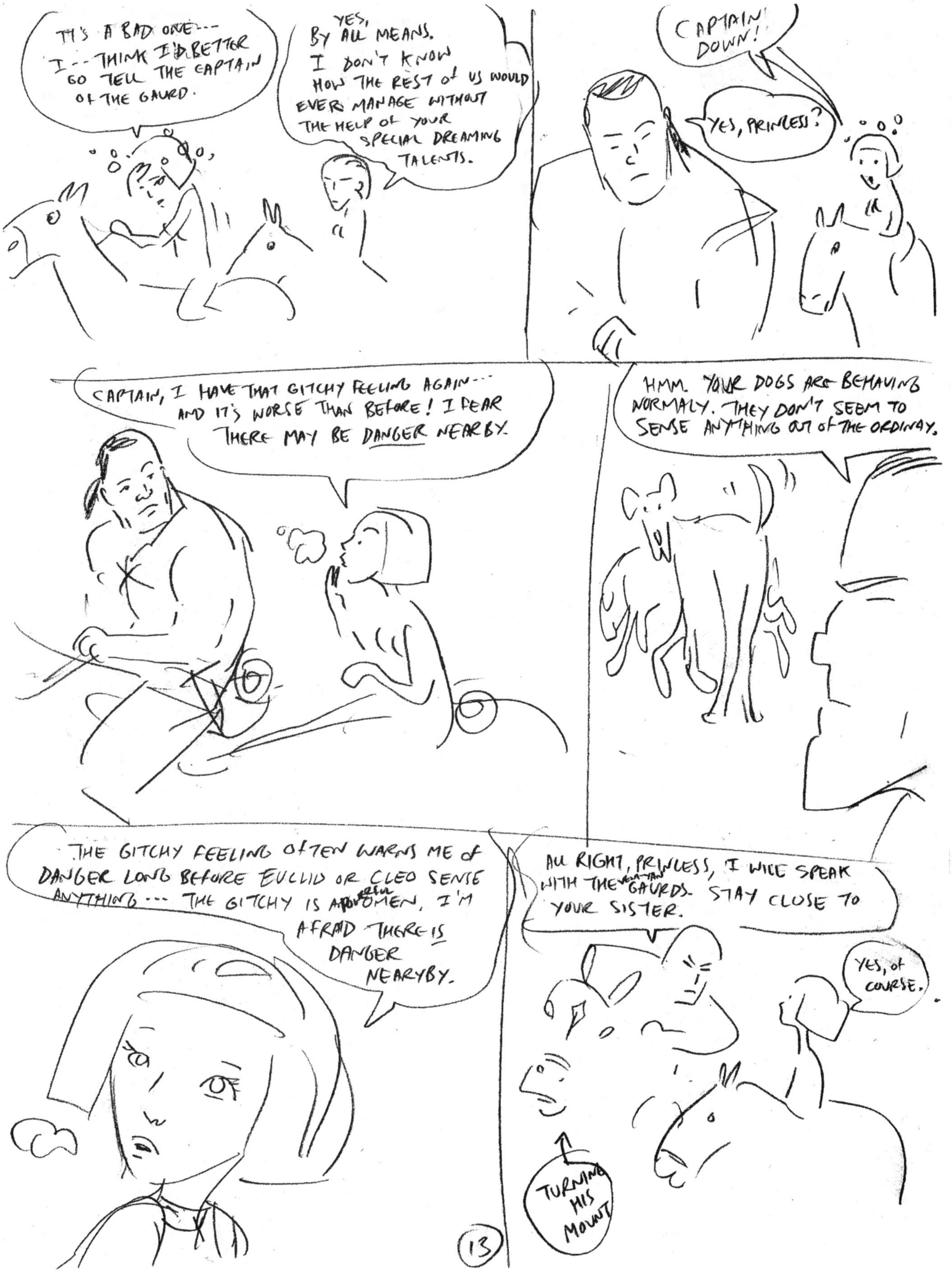

IT'S A BAD ONE... I -- THINK I'D BETTER GO TELL THE CAPTAIN OF THE GAURD.
YES, BY ALL MEANS. I DON'T KNOW HOW THE REST OF US WOULD EVER MANAGE WITHOUT THE HELP OF YOUR SPECIAL DREAMING TALENTS.
CAPTAIN DOWN!
YES, PRINCESS?
CAPTAIN, I HAVE THAT GITCHY FEELING AGAIN... AND IT'S WORSE THAN BEFORE! I FEAR THERE MAY BE DANGER NEARBY.
HMM. YOUR DOGS ARE BEHAVING NORMALY. THEY DON'T SEEM TO SENSE ANYTHING OUT OF THE ORDINAY.
THE GITCHY FEELING OFTEN WARNS ME OF DANGER LONG BEFORE EUCLID OR CLEO SENSE ANYTHING... THE GITCHY IS A OMEN, I'M AFRAID THERE IS DANGER NEARYBY.
ALL RIGHT, PRINCESS, I WILL SPEAK WITH THE GAURDS. STAY CLOSE TO YOUR SISTER.
YES, OF COURSE.
TURNING HIS MOUNT
13

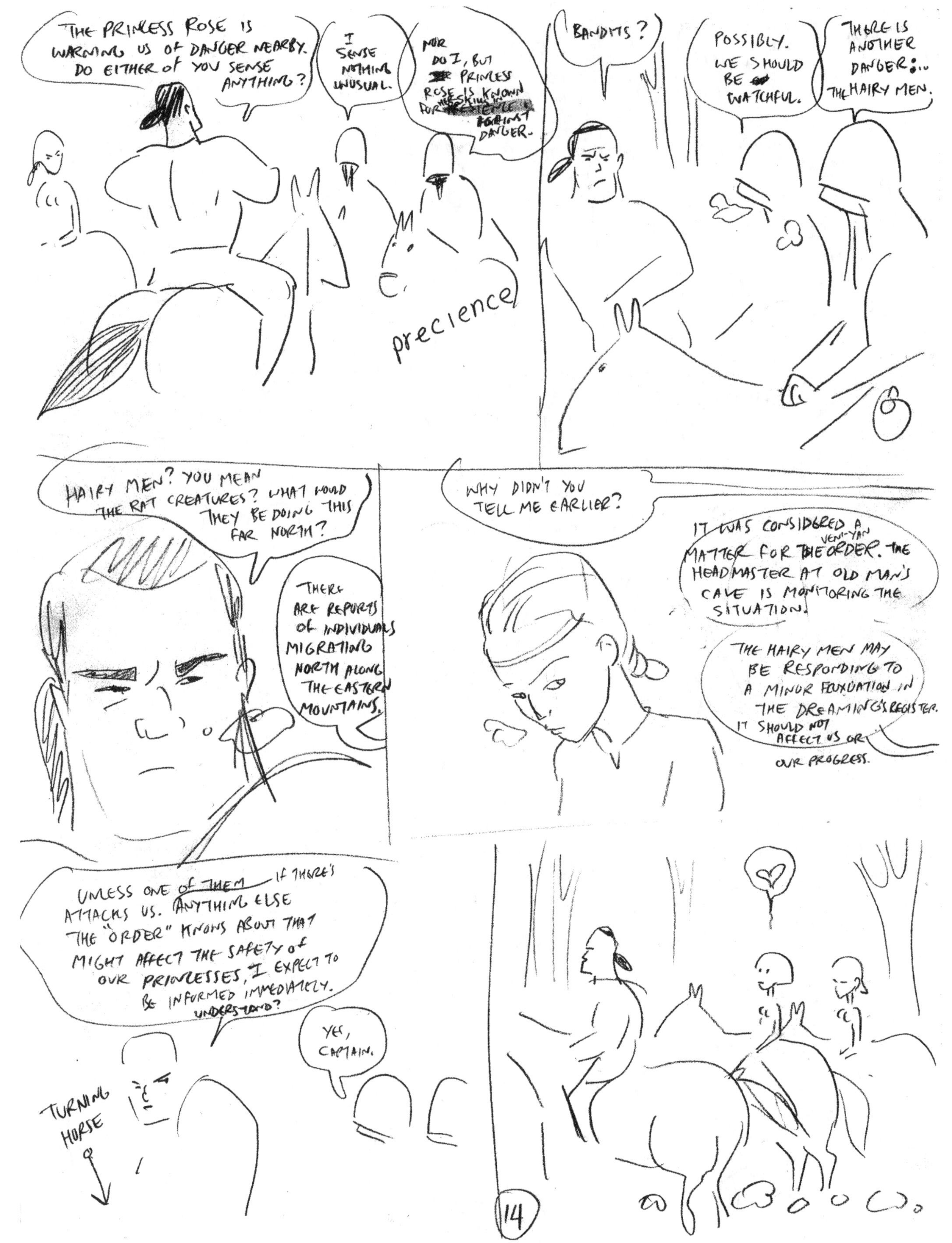
THE PRINCESS ROSE IS WARNING US OF DANGER NEARBY. DO EITHER OF YOU SENSE ANYTHING?
I SENSE NOTHING UNUSUAL.
NOR DO I, BUT PRINCESS ROSE IS KNOWN FOR HER SKILL IN AGAINST DANGER.
precience
BANDITS?
POSSIBLY. WE SHOULD BE WATCHFUL.
THERE IS ANOTHER DANGER... THE HAIRY MEN.
HAIRY MEN? YOU MEAN THE RAT CREATURES? WHAT WOULD THEY BE DOING THIS FAR NORTH?
THERE ARE REPORTS OF INDIVIDUALS MIGRATING NORTH ALONG THE EASTERN MOUNTAINS.
WHY DIDN'T YOU TELL ME EARLIER?
IT WAS CONSIDERED A MATTER FOR THE VENI-YAN ORDER. THE HEADMASTER AT OLD MAN'S CAVE IS MONITORING THE SITUATION.
THE HAIRY MEN MAY BE RESPONDING TO A MINOR FLUXUATION IN THE DREAMING'S REGISTER. IT SHOULD NOT AFFECT US OR OUR PROGRESS.
UNLESS ONE OF THEM IF THERE'S ATTACKS US. ANYTHING ELSE THE "ORDER" KNOWS ABOUT THAT MIGHT AFFECT THE SAFETY OF OUR PRINCESSES, I EXPECT TO BE INFORMED IMMEDIATELY. UNDERSTAND?
YES, CAPTAIN.
TURNING HORSE
14

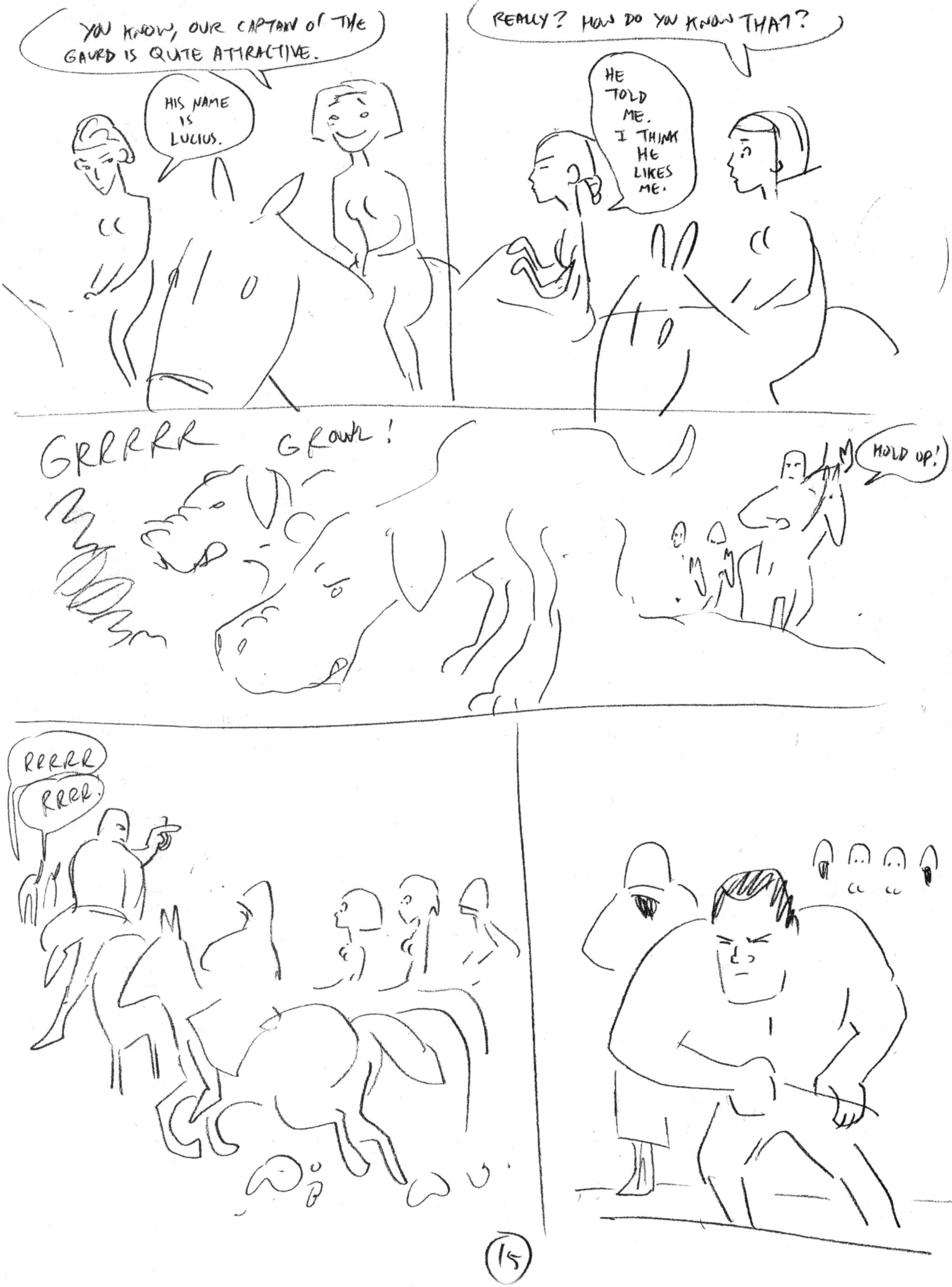
YOU KNOW, OUR CAPTAN OF THE GAURD IS QUITE ATTRACTIVE.
HIS NAME IS LUCIUS.
REALLY? HOW DO YOU KNOW THAT?
HE TOLD ME. I THINK HE LIKES ME.
GRRRRR
GROWL!
HOLD UP!
RRRRR
RRRR.
15

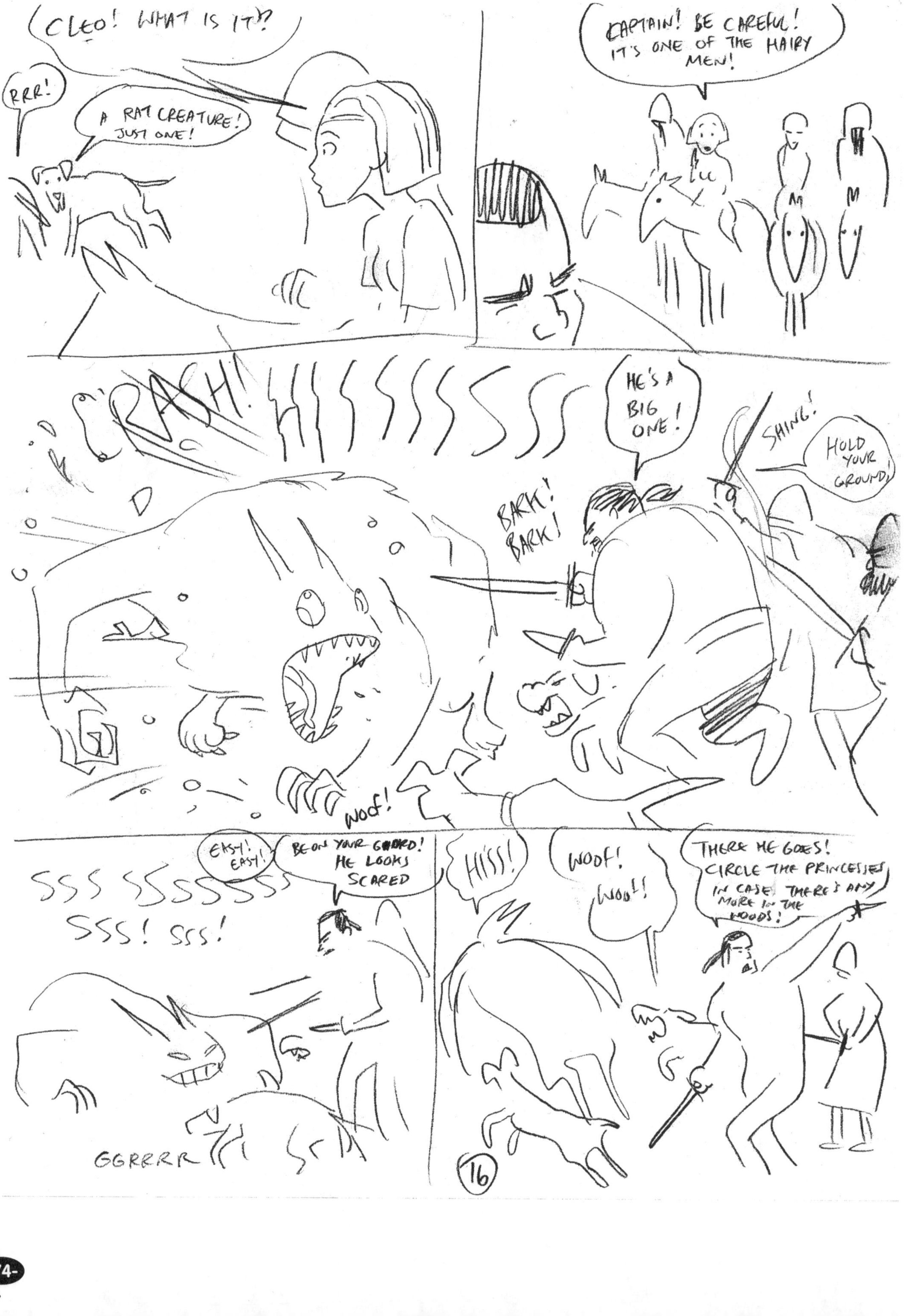
CLEO! WHAT IS IT?!
RRR!
A RAT CREATURE! JUST ONE!
CAPTAIN! BE CAREFUL! IT'S ONE OF THE HAIRY MEN!
CRASH!
HISSSSSSS
HE'S A BIG ONE!
SHING!
HOLD YOUR GROUND!
BARK! BARK!
WOOF!
SSS SSSSSSSS SSS! SSS!
EASY! EASY!
BE ON YOUR GUARD! HE LOOKS SCARED
GGRRRR
HISS!
WOOF! WOOF!
THERE HE GOES! CIRCLE THE PRINCESSES IN CASE THERE'S ANY MORE IN THE WOODS!
16

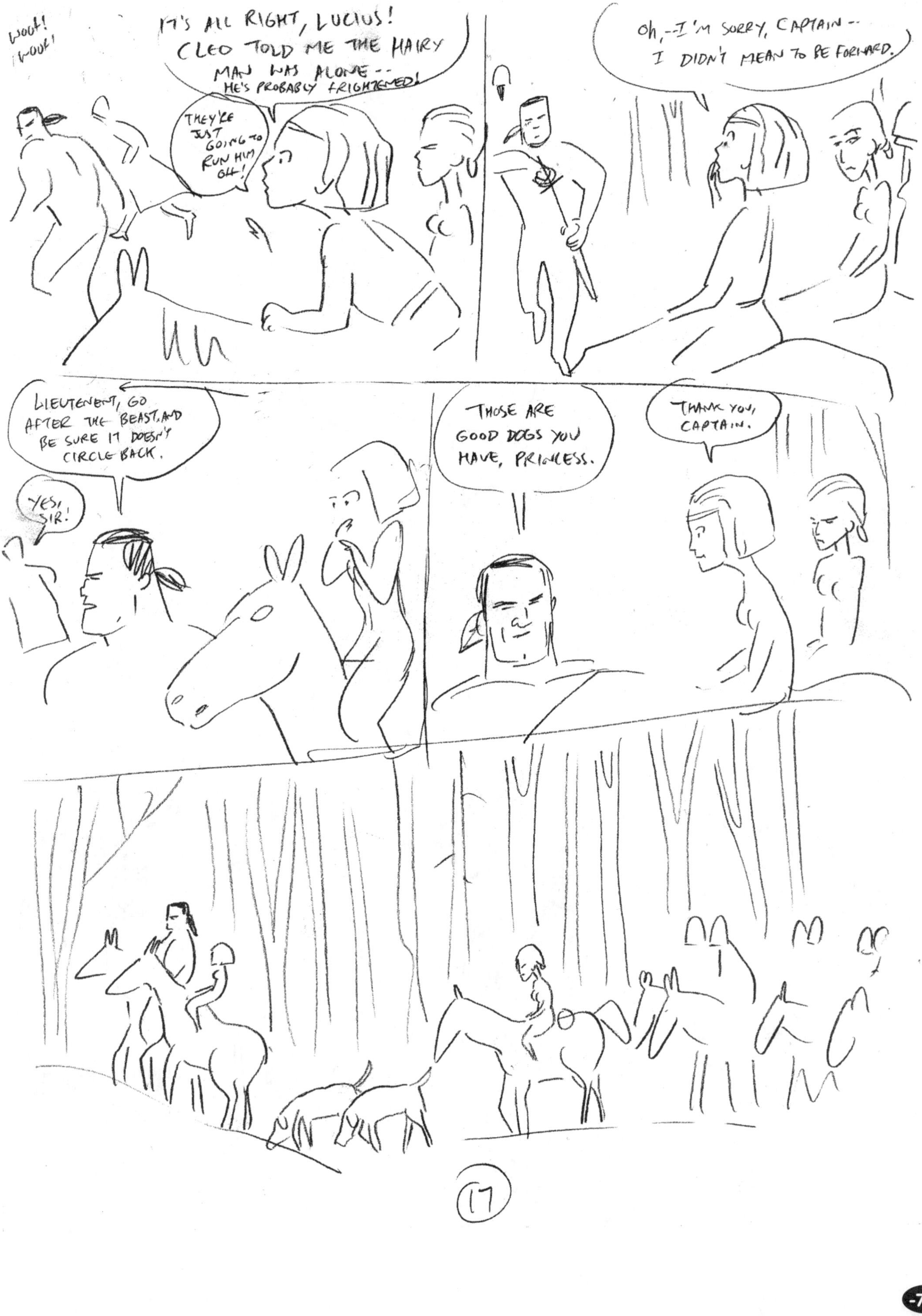
WOOF! WOOF!
IT'S ALL RIGHT, LUCIUS! CLEO TOLD ME THE HAIRY MAN WAS ALONE -- HE'S PROBABLY FRIGHTENED!
THEY'RE JUST GOING TO RUN HIM OFF!
Oh, -- I'M SORRY, CAPTAIN -- I DIDN'T MEAN TO BE FORWARD.
LIEUTENENT, GO AFTER THE BEAST, AND BE SURE IT DOESN'T CIRCLE BACK.
YES, SIR!
THOSE ARE GOOD DOGS YOU HAVE, PRINCESS.
THANK YOU, CAPTAIN.
17

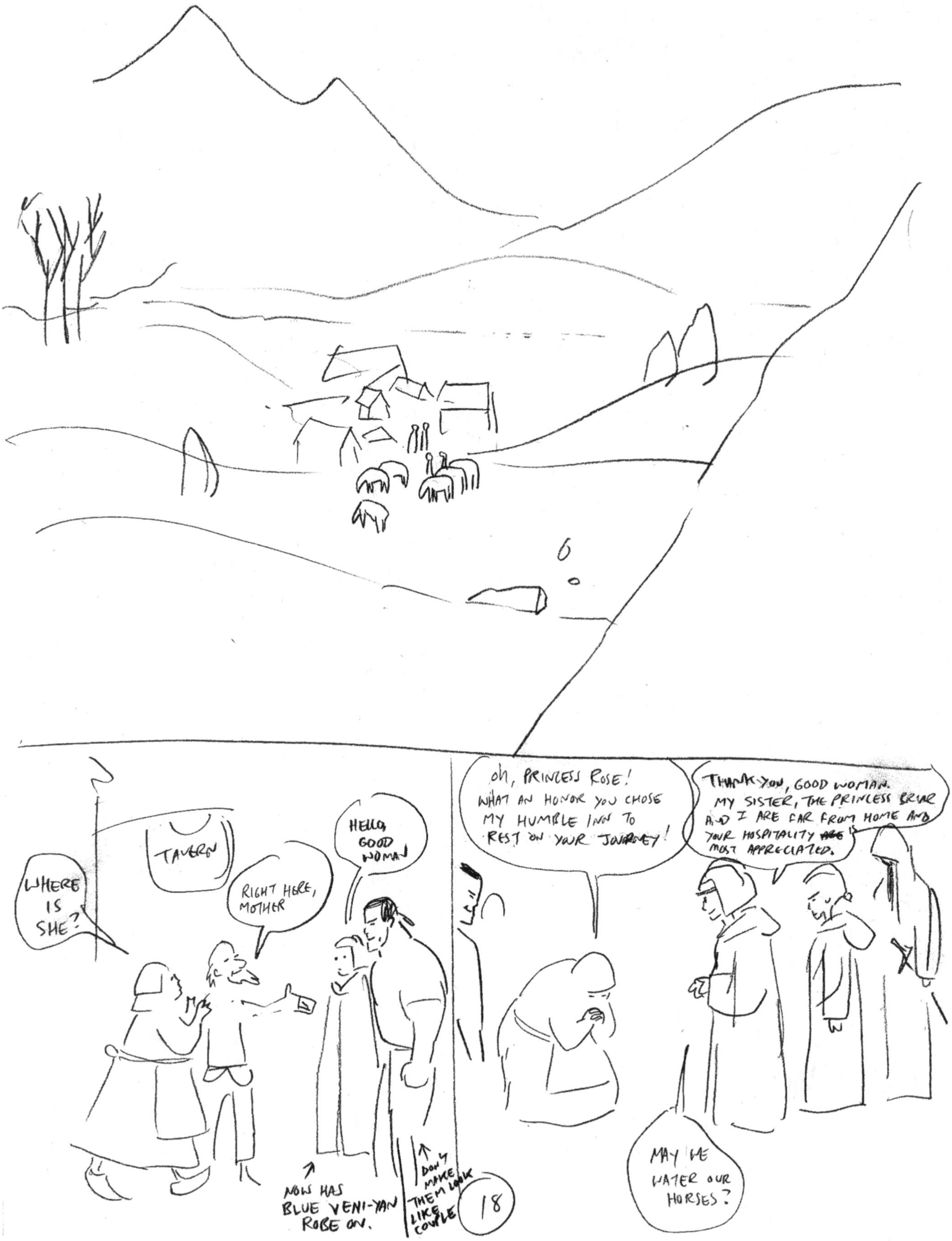
TAVERN
WHERE IS SHE?
RIGHT HERE, MOTHER
HELLO, GOOD WOMAN
NOW HAS BLUE VENI-YAN ROBE ON.
DON'T MAKE THEM LOOK LIKE COUPLE
18
Oh, PRINCESS ROSE! WHAT AN HONOR YOU CHOSE MY HUMBLE INN TO REST ON YOUR JOURNEY!
THANK YOU, GOOD WOMAN. MY SISTER, THE PRINCESS BRIAR AND I ARE FAR FROM HOME AND YOUR HOSPITALITY IS MOST APPRECIATED.
MAY WE WATER OUR HORSES?

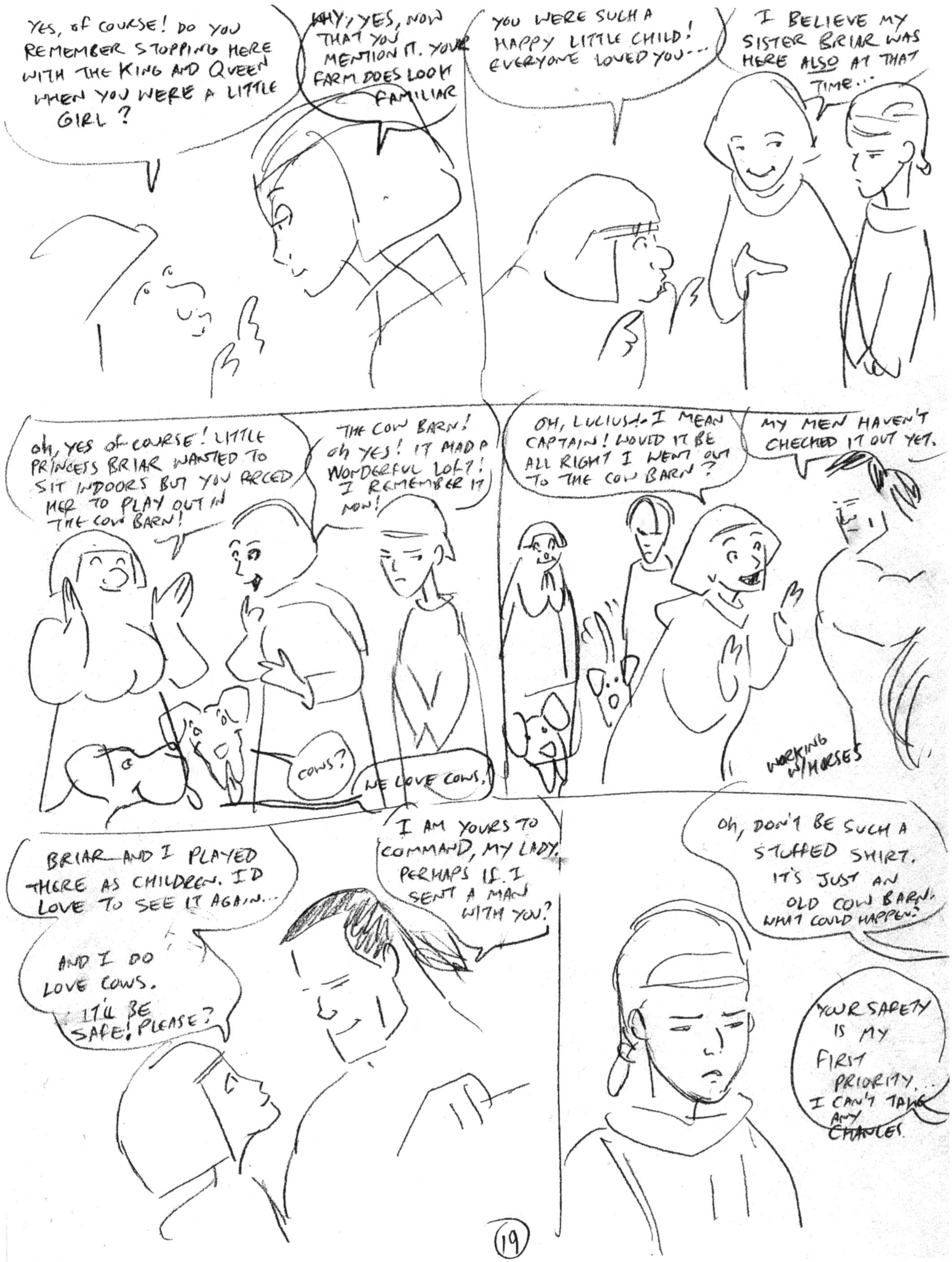
YES, OF COURSE! DO YOU REMEMBER STOPPING HERE WITH THE KING AND QUEEN WHEN YOU WERE A LITTLE GIRL?
WHY, YES, NOW THAT YOU MENTION IT. YOUR FARM DOES LOOK FAMILIAR
YOU WERE SUCH A HAPPY LITTLE CHILD! EVERYONE LOVED YOU...
I BELIEVE MY SISTER BRIAR WAS HERE ALSO AT THAT TIME...
OH, YES OF COURSE! LITTLE PRINCESS BRIAR WANTED TO SIT INDOORS BUT YOU FORCED HER TO PLAY OUT IN THE COW BARN!
THE COW BARN! OH YES! IT HAD A WONDERFUL LOFT! I REMEMBER IT NOW!
COWS?
WE LOVE COWS.
OH, LUCIUS! - I MEAN CAPTAIN! WOULD IT BE ALL RIGHT I WENT OUT TO THE COW BARN?
MY MEN HAVEN'T CHECKED IT OUT YET.
WORKING W/HORSES
BRIAR AND I PLAYED THERE AS CHILDREN. I'D LOVE TO SEE IT AGAIN...
AND I DO LOVE COWS.
IT'LL BE SAFE! PLEASE?
I AM YOURS TO COMMAND, MY LADY. PERHAPS IF I SENT A MAN WITH YOU?
OH, DON'T BE SUCH A STUFFED SHIRT. IT'S JUST AN OLD COW BARN. WHAT COULD HAPPEN?
YOUR SAFETY IS MY FIRST PRIORITY... I CAN'T TAKE ANY CHANCES.
19

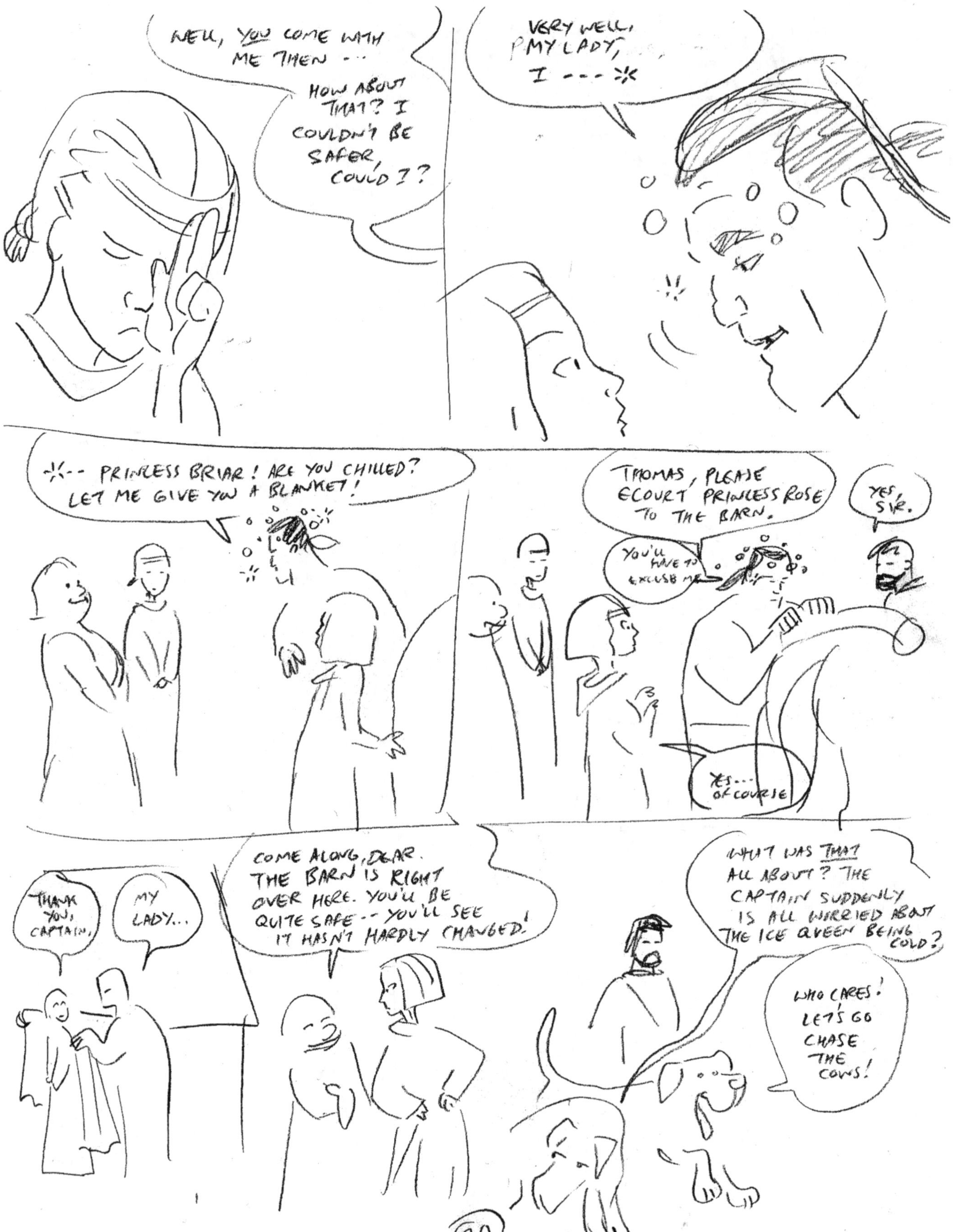

WELL, YOU COME WITH ME THEN --
HOW ABOUT THAT? I COULDN'T BE SAFER, COULD I?
VERY WELL, MY LADY, I --- *
*-- PRINCESS BRIAR! ARE YOU CHILLED? LET ME GIVE YOU A BLANKET!
THOMAS, PLEASE ECOURT PRINCESS ROSE TO THE BARN.
YES, SIR.
YOU'LL HAVE TO EXCUSE ME
YES... OF COURSE
THANK YOU, CAPTAIN,
MY LADY...
COME ALONG, DEAR. THE BARN IS RIGHT OVER HERE. YOU'LL BE QUITE SAFE -- YOU'LL SEE IT HASN'T HARDLY CHANGED!
WHAT WAS THAT ALL ABOUT? THE CAPTAIN SUDDENLY IS ALL WORRIED ABOUT THE ICE QUEEN BEING COLD?
WHO CARES! LET'S GO CHASE THE COWS!
20

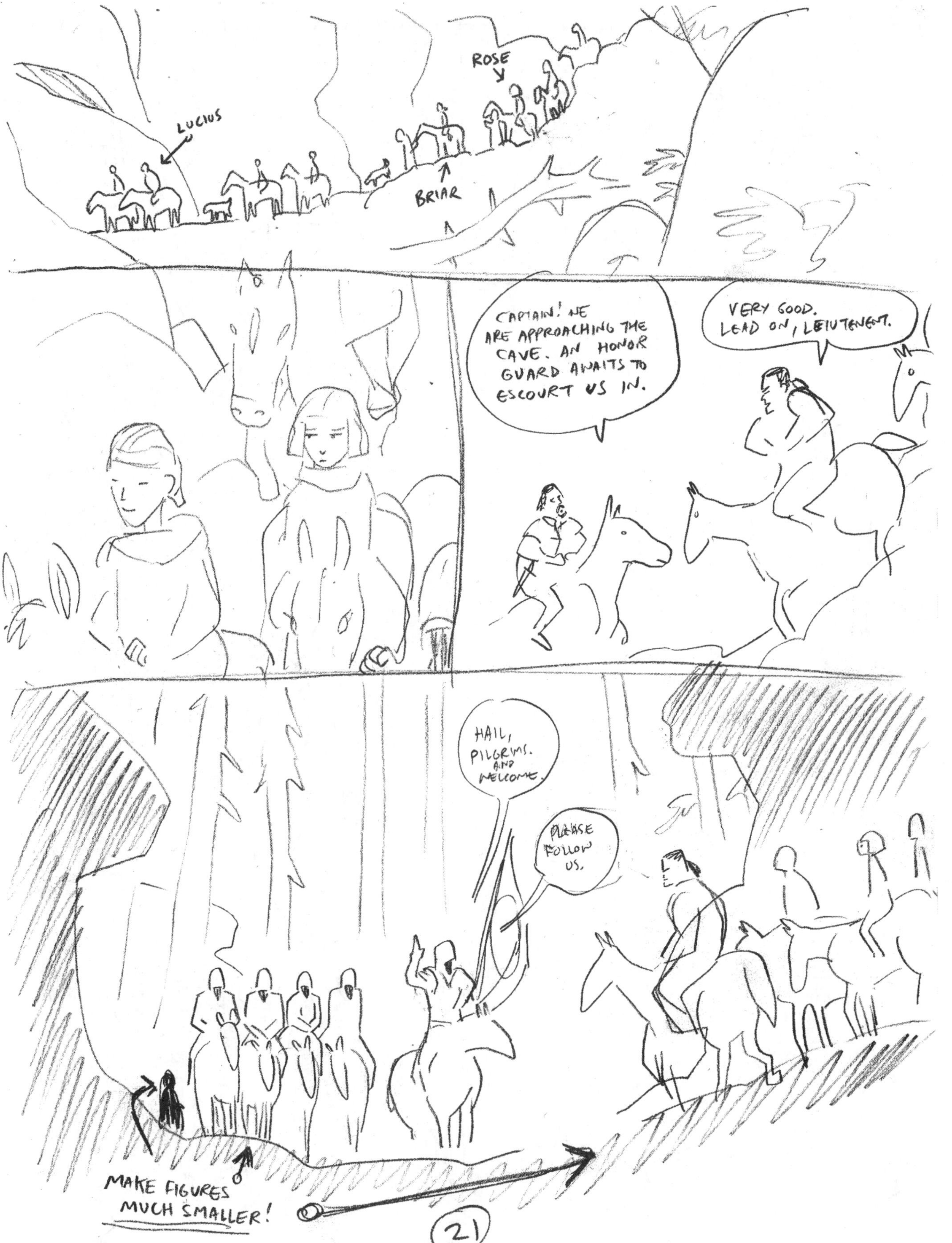
ROSE
LUCIUS
BRIAR
CAPTAIN! WE ARE APPROACHING THE CAVE. AN HONOR GUARD AWAITS TO ESCOURT US IN.
VERY GOOD. LEAD ON, LEIUTENENT.
HAIL, PILGRIMS. AND WELCOME.
PLEASE FOLLOW US.
MAKE FIGURES MUCH SMALLER!
21

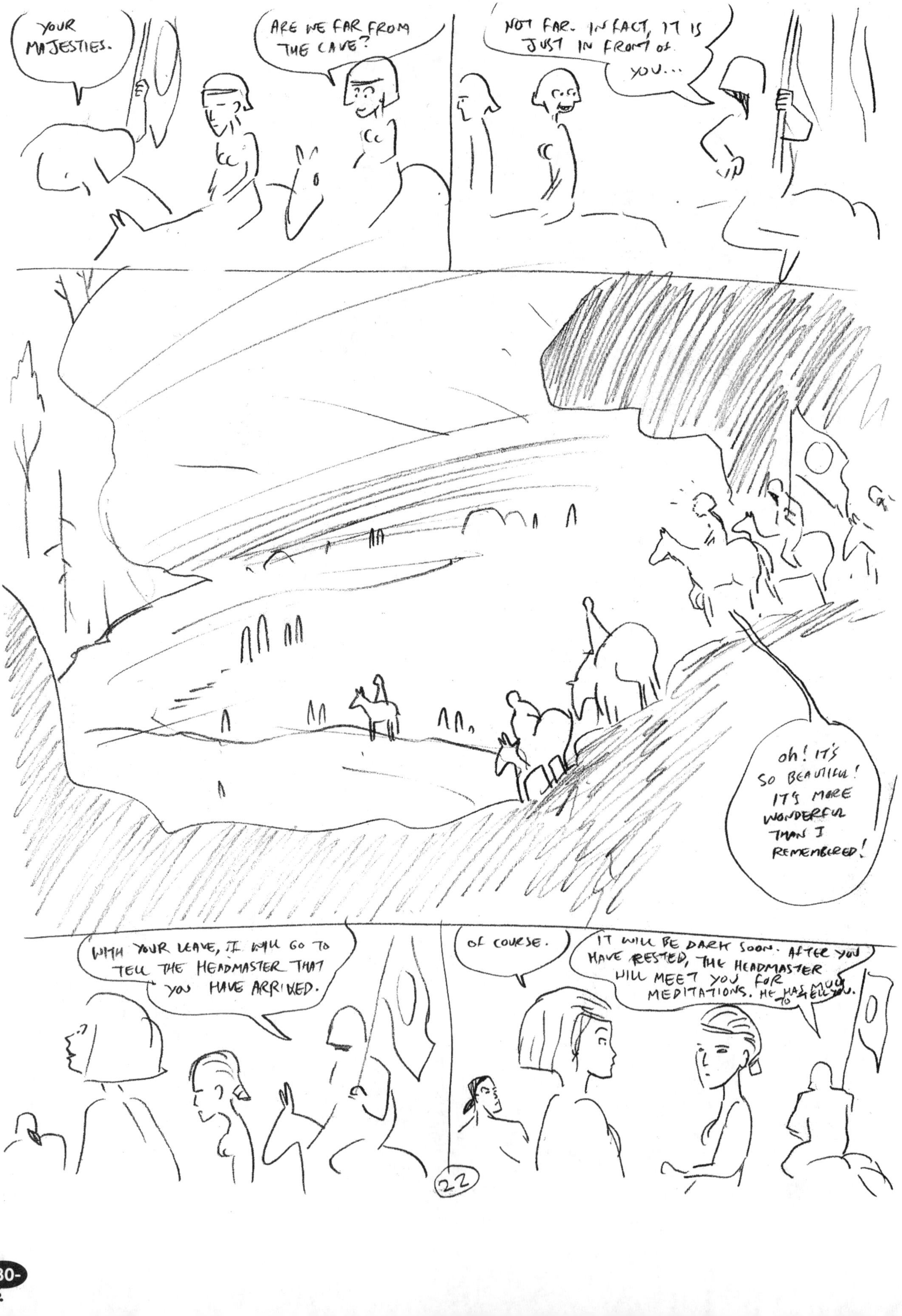
YOUR MAJESTIES.
ARE WE FAR FROM THE CAVE?
NOT FAR. IN FACT, IT IS JUST IN FRONT OF YOU...
OH! IT'S SO BEAUTIFUL! IT'S MORE WONDERFUL THAN I REMEMBERED!
WITH YOUR LEAVE, I WILL GO TO TELL THE HEADMASTER THAT YOU HAVE ARRIVED.
OF COURSE.
IT WILL BE DARK SOON. AFTER YOU HAVE RESTED, THE HEADMASTER WILL MEET YOU FOR MEDITATIONS. HE HAS MUCH TO TELL YOU.
22

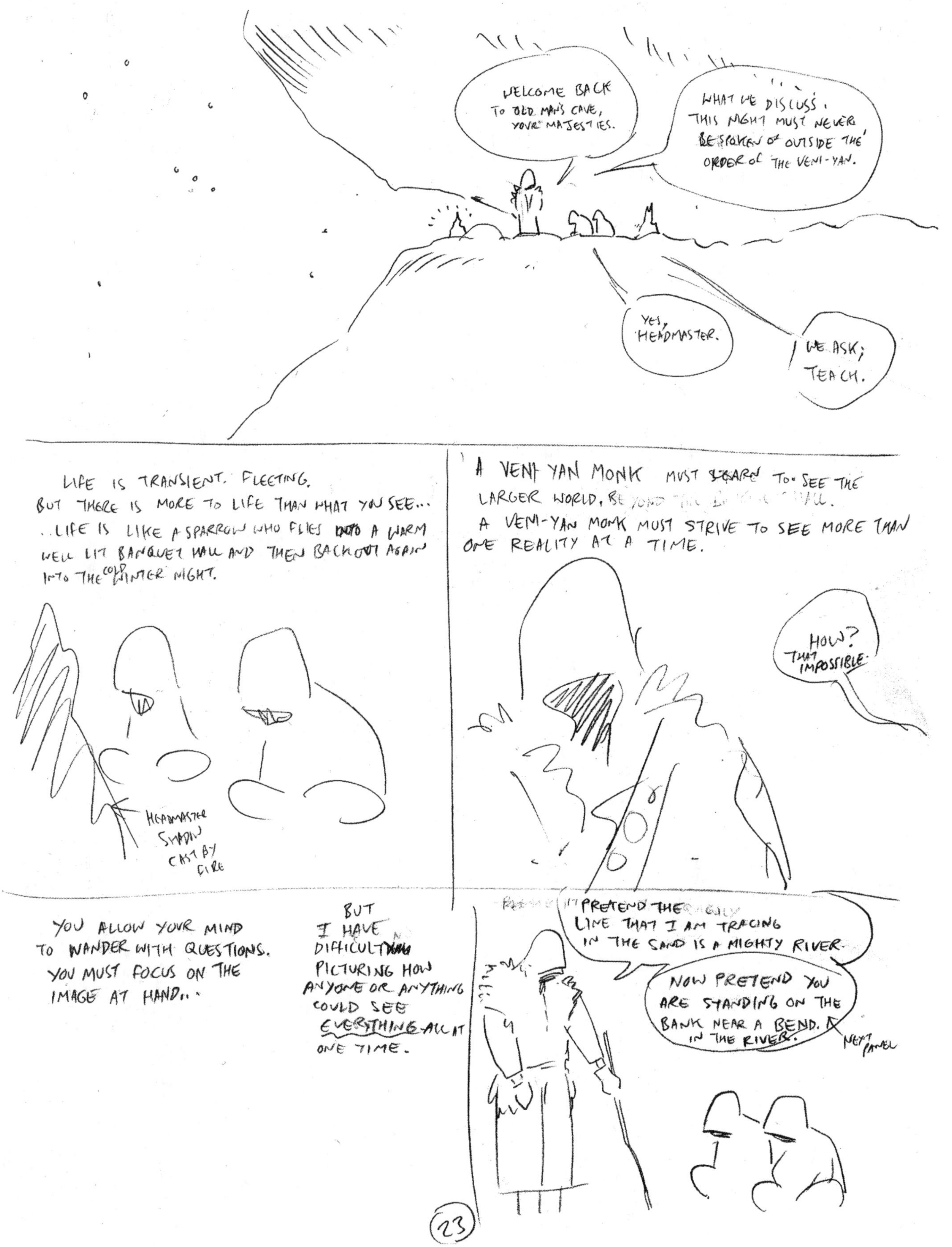

WELCOME BACK TO OLD MAN'S CAVE, YOUR MAJESTIES.
WHAT WE DISCUSS THIS NIGHT MUST NEVER BE SPOKEN OF OUTSIDE THE ORDER OF THE VENI-YAN.
YES, HEADMASTER.
WE ASK; TEACH.
LIFE IS TRANSIENT. FLEETING.
BUT THERE IS MORE TO LIFE THAN WHAT YOU SEE...
...LIFE IS LIKE A SPARROW WHO FLIES INTO A WARM WELL LIT BANQUET HALL AND THEN BACK OUT AGAIN INTO THE COLD WINTER NIGHT.
HEADMASTER SHADOW CAST BY FIRE
A VENI YAN MONK MUST LEARN TO SEE THE LARGER WORLD,
A VENI-YAN MONK MUST STRIVE TO SEE MORE THAN ONE REALITY AT A TIME.
HOW? THAT IMPOSSIBLE.
YOU ALLOW YOUR MIND TO WANDER WITH QUESTIONS. YOU MUST FOCUS ON THE IMAGE AT HAND...
BUT I HAVE DIFFICULTY PICTURING HOW ANYONE OR ANYTHING COULD SEE EVERYTHING ALL AT ONE TIME.
PRETEND THE LINE THAT I AM TRACING IN THE SAND IS A MIGHTY RIVER.
NOW PRETEND YOU ARE STANDING ON THE BANK NEAR A BEND. IN THE RIVER.
NEXT PANEL
23

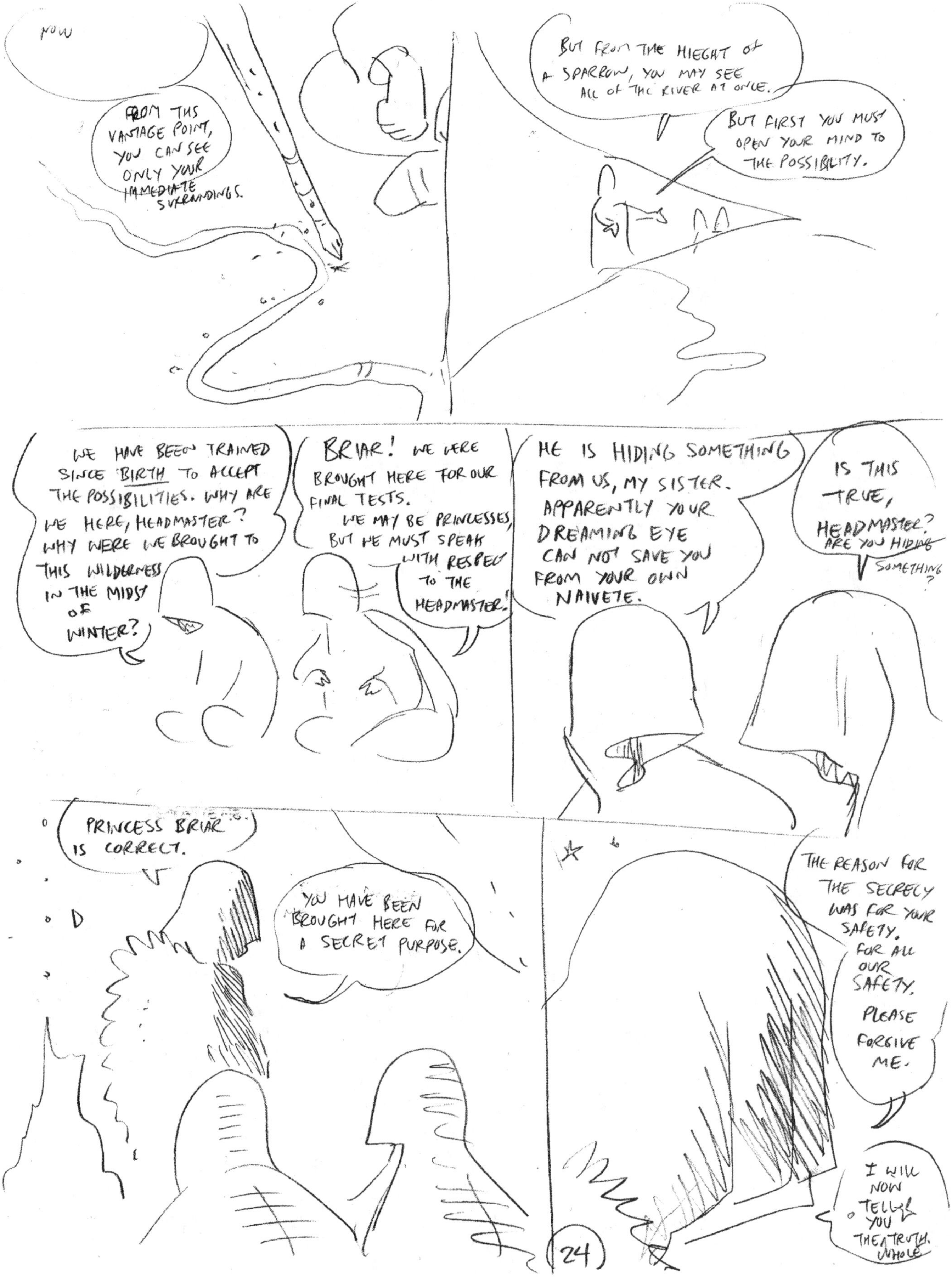
NOW
FROM THIS VANTAGE POINT, YOU CAN SEE ONLY YOUR IMMEDIATE SURROUNDINGS.
BUT FROM THE HIEGHT OF A SPARROW, YOU MAY SEE ALL OF THE RIVER AT ONCE.
BUT FIRST YOU MUST OPEN YOUR MIND TO THE POSSIBILITY.
WE HAVE BEEN TRAINED SINCE BIRTH TO ACCEPT THE POSSIBILITIES. WHY ARE WE HERE, HEADMASTER? WHY WERE WE BROUGHT TO THIS WILDERNESS IN THE MIDST OF WINTER?
BRIAR! WE WERE BROUGHT HERE FOR OUR FINAL TESTS.
WE MAY BE PRINCESSES, BUT WE MUST SPEAK WITH RESPECT TO THE HEADMASTER!
HE IS HIDING SOMETHING FROM US, MY SISTER. APPARENTLY YOUR DREAMING EYE CAN NOT SAVE YOU FROM YOUR OWN NAIVETE.
IS THIS TRUE, HEADMASTER? ARE YOU HIDING SOMETHING?
PRINCESS BRIAR IS CORRECT.
YOU HAVE BEEN BROUGHT HERE FOR A SECRET PURPOSE.
THE REASON FOR THE SECRECY WAS FOR YOUR SAFETY. FOR ALL OUR SAFETY.
PLEASE FORGIVE ME.
I WILL NOW TELL YOU THE WHOLE TRUTH.
24

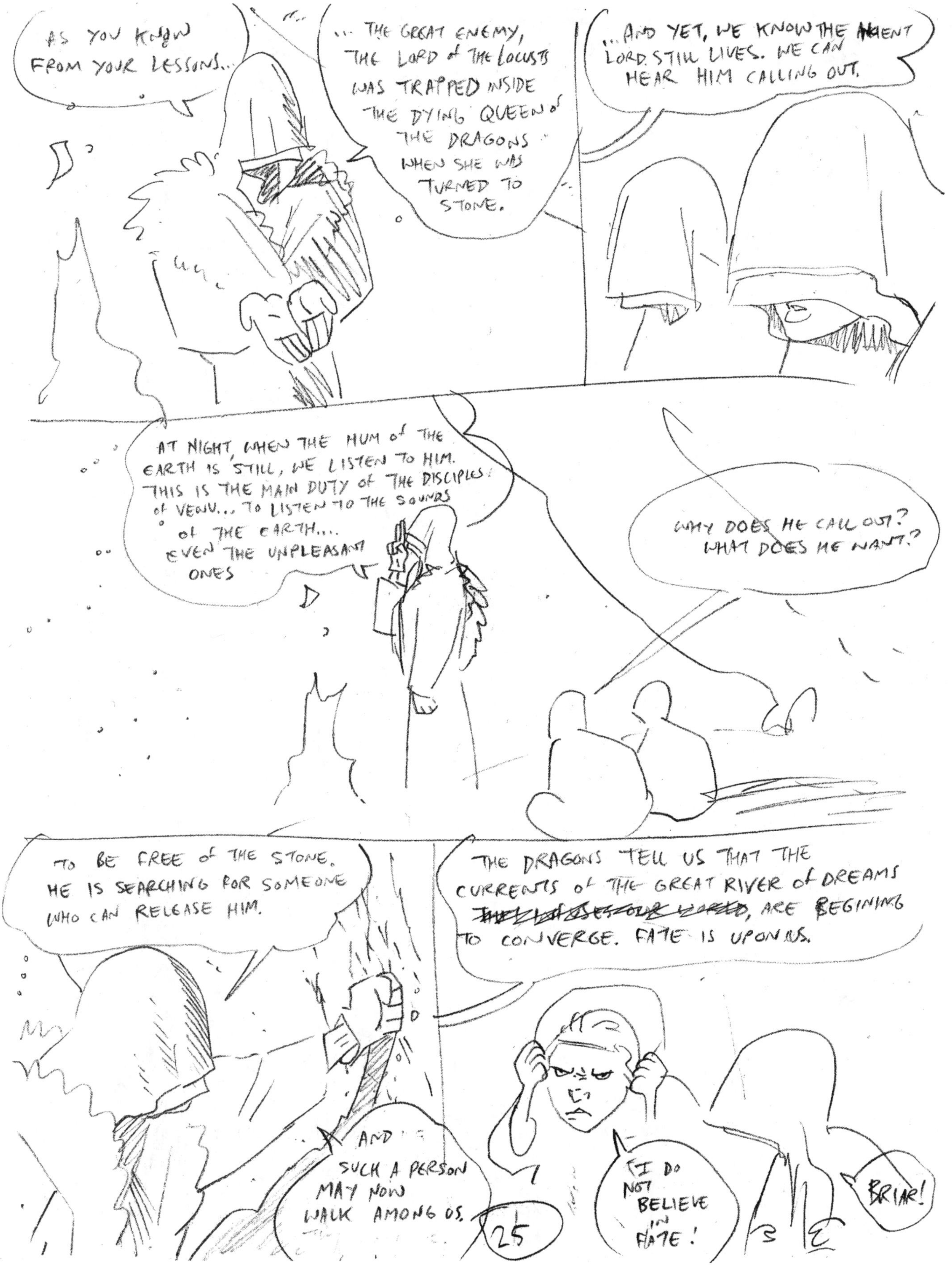
AS YOU KNOW FROM YOUR LESSONS...
... THE GREAT ENEMY, THE LORD of THE LOCUSTS WAS TRAPPED INSIDE THE DYING QUEEN of THE DRAGONS WHEN SHE WAS TURNED TO STONE.
...AND YET, WE KNOW THE ANCIENT LORD STILL LIVES. WE CAN HEAR HIM CALLING OUT.
AT NIGHT, WHEN THE HUM of THE EARTH IS STILL, WE LISTEN TO HIM. THIS IS THE MAIN DUTY of THE DISCIPLES of VENU... TO LISTEN TO THE SOUNDS of THE EARTH.... EVEN THE UNPLEASANT ONES
WHY DOES HE CALL OUT? WHAT DOES HE WANT?
TO BE FREE of THE STONE. HE IS SEARCHING FOR SOMEONE WHO CAN RELEASE HIM.
AND SUCH A PERSON MAY NOW WALK AMONG US.
THE DRAGONS TELL US THAT THE CURRENTS of THE GREAT RIVER of DREAMS
, ARE BEGINING TO CONVERGE. FATE IS UPON US.
I DO NOT BELIEVE IN FATE!
BRIAR!
25

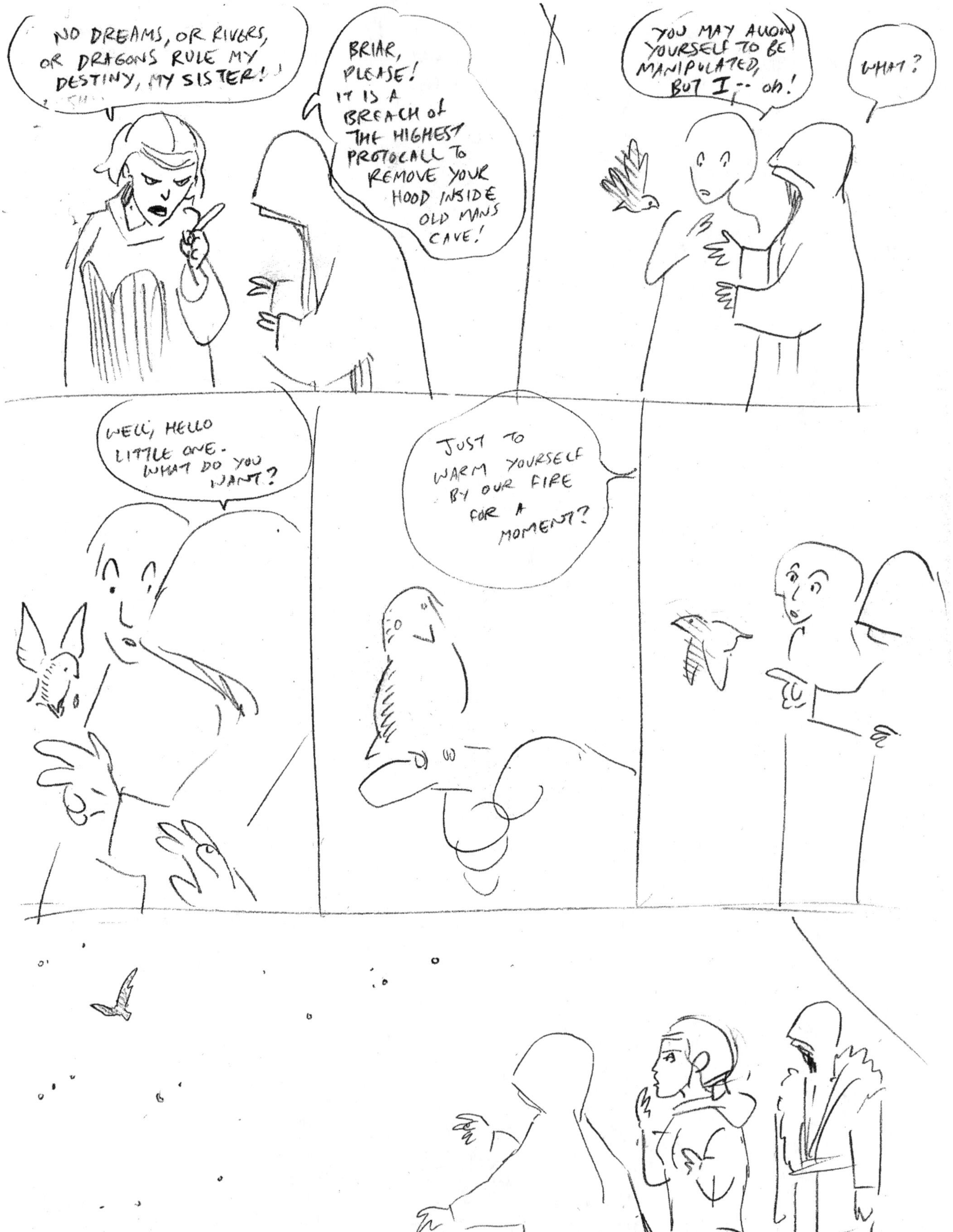
NO DREAMS, OR RIVERS, OR DRAGONS RULE MY DESTINY, MY SISTER!
BRIAR, PLEASE! IT IS A BREACH OF THE HIGHEST PROTOCALL TO REMOVE YOUR HOOD INSIDE OLD MANS CAVE!
YOU MAY ALLOW YOURSELF TO BE MANIPULATED, BUT I-- oh!
WHAT?
WELL, HELLO LITTLE ONE. WHAT DO YOU WANT?
JUST TO WARM YOURSELF BY OUR FIRE FOR A MOMENT?
26

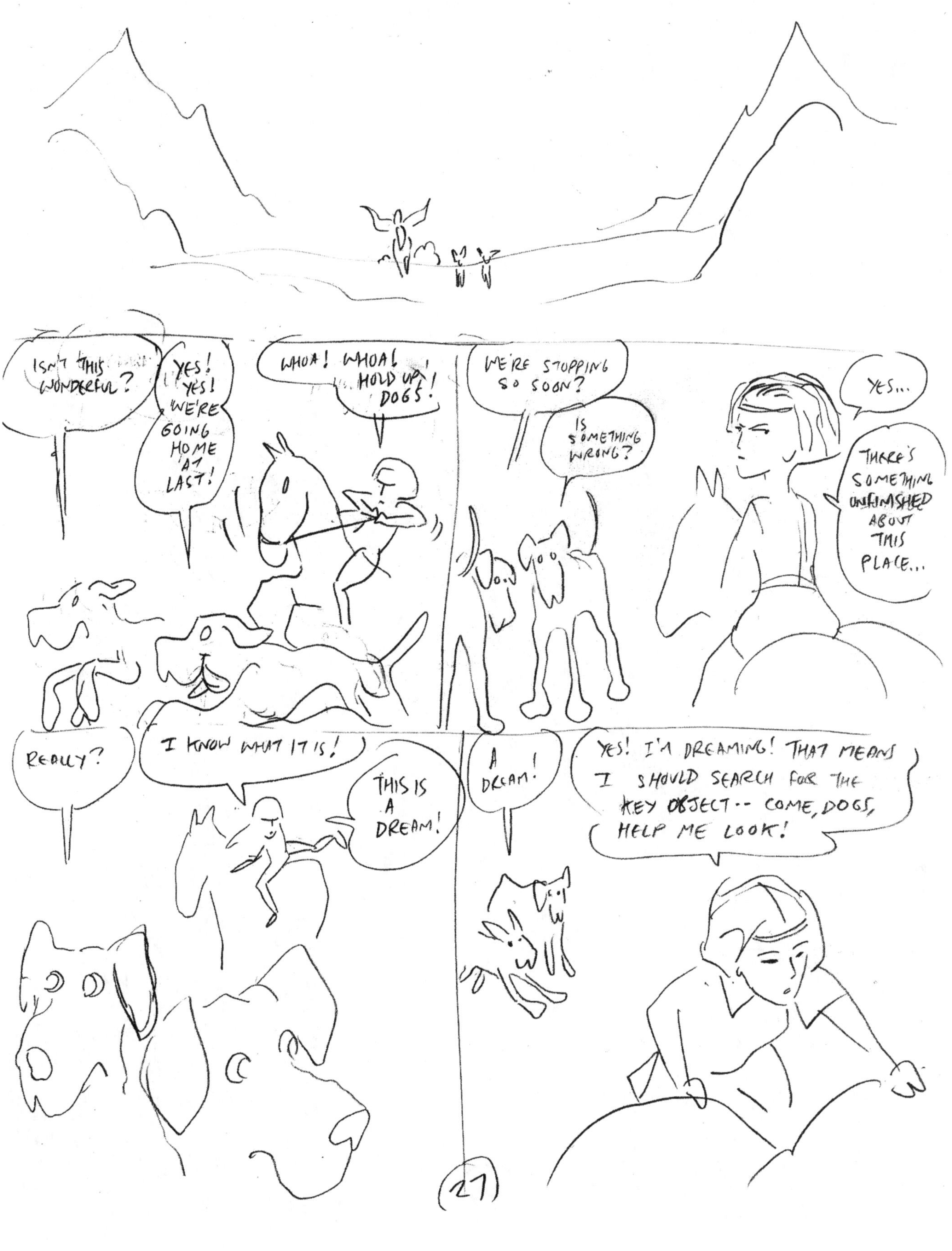
ISN'T THIS WONDERFUL?
YES! YES! WE'RE GOING HOME AT LAST!
WHOA! WHOA! HOLD UP, DOGS!
WE'RE STOPPING SO SOON?
IS SOMETHING WRONG?
YES...
THERE'S SOMETHING UNFINISHED ABOUT THIS PLACE...
REALLY?
I KNOW WHAT IT IS!
THIS IS A DREAM!
A DREAM!
YES! I'M DREAMING! THAT MEANS I SHOULD SEARCH FOR THE KEY OBJECT -- COME, DOGS, HELP ME LOOK!
27

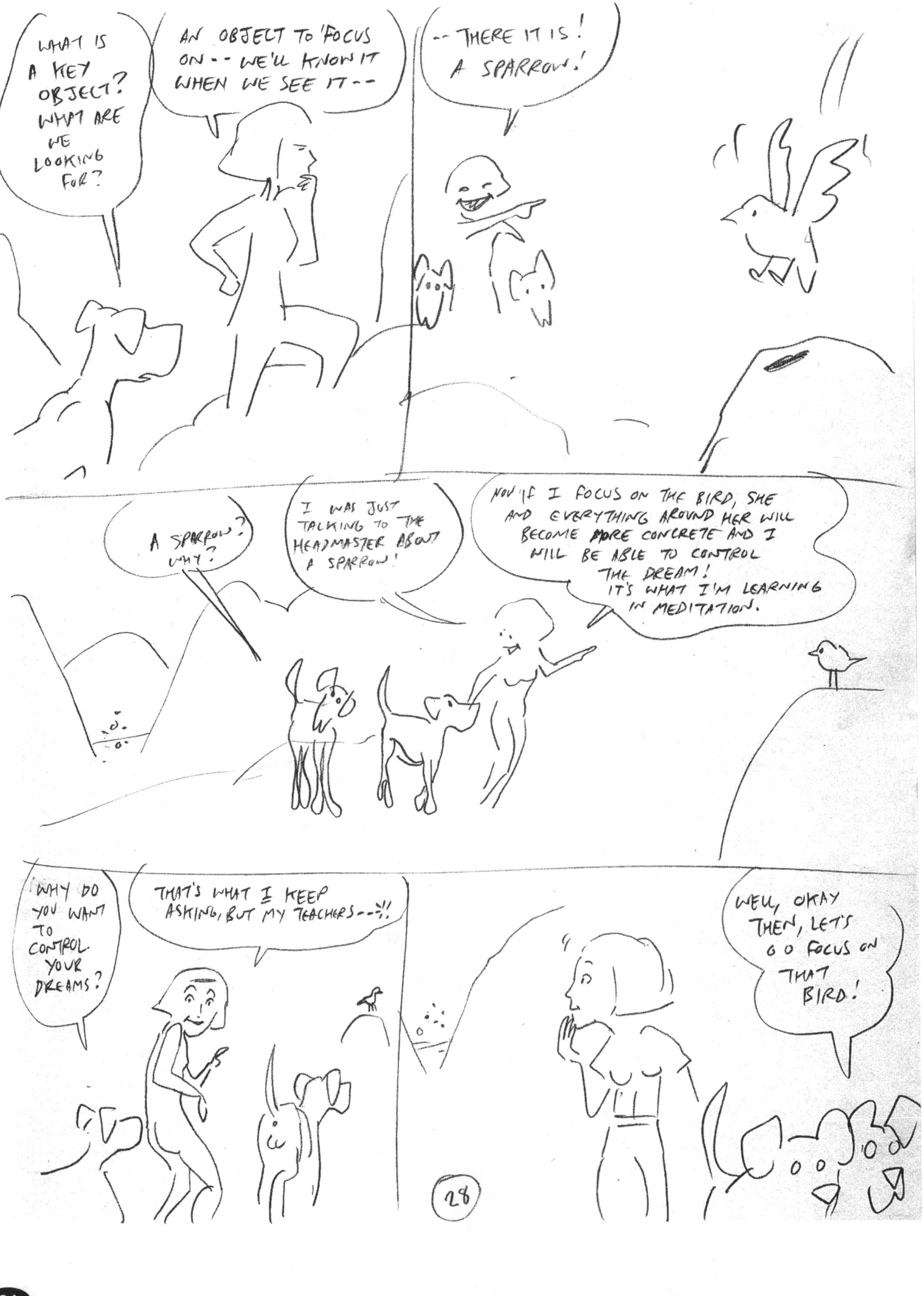
WHAT IS A KEY OBJECT? WHAT ARE WE LOOKING FOR?
AN OBJECT TO 'FOCUS ON -- WE'LL KNOW IT WHEN WE SEE IT --
-- THERE IT IS! A SPARROW!
A SPARROW? WHY?
I WAS JUST TALKING TO THE HEADMASTER ABOUT A SPARROW!
NOW IF I FOCUS ON THE BIRD, SHE AND EVERYTHING AROUND HER WILL BECOME MORE CONCRETE AND I WILL BE ABLE TO CONTROL THE DREAM! IT'S WHAT I'M LEARNING IN MEDITATION.
WHY DO YOU WANT TO CONTROL YOUR DREAMS?
THAT'S WHAT I KEEP ASKING, BUT MY TEACHERS --!
WELL, OKAY THEN, LET'S GO FOCUS ON THAT BIRD!
28

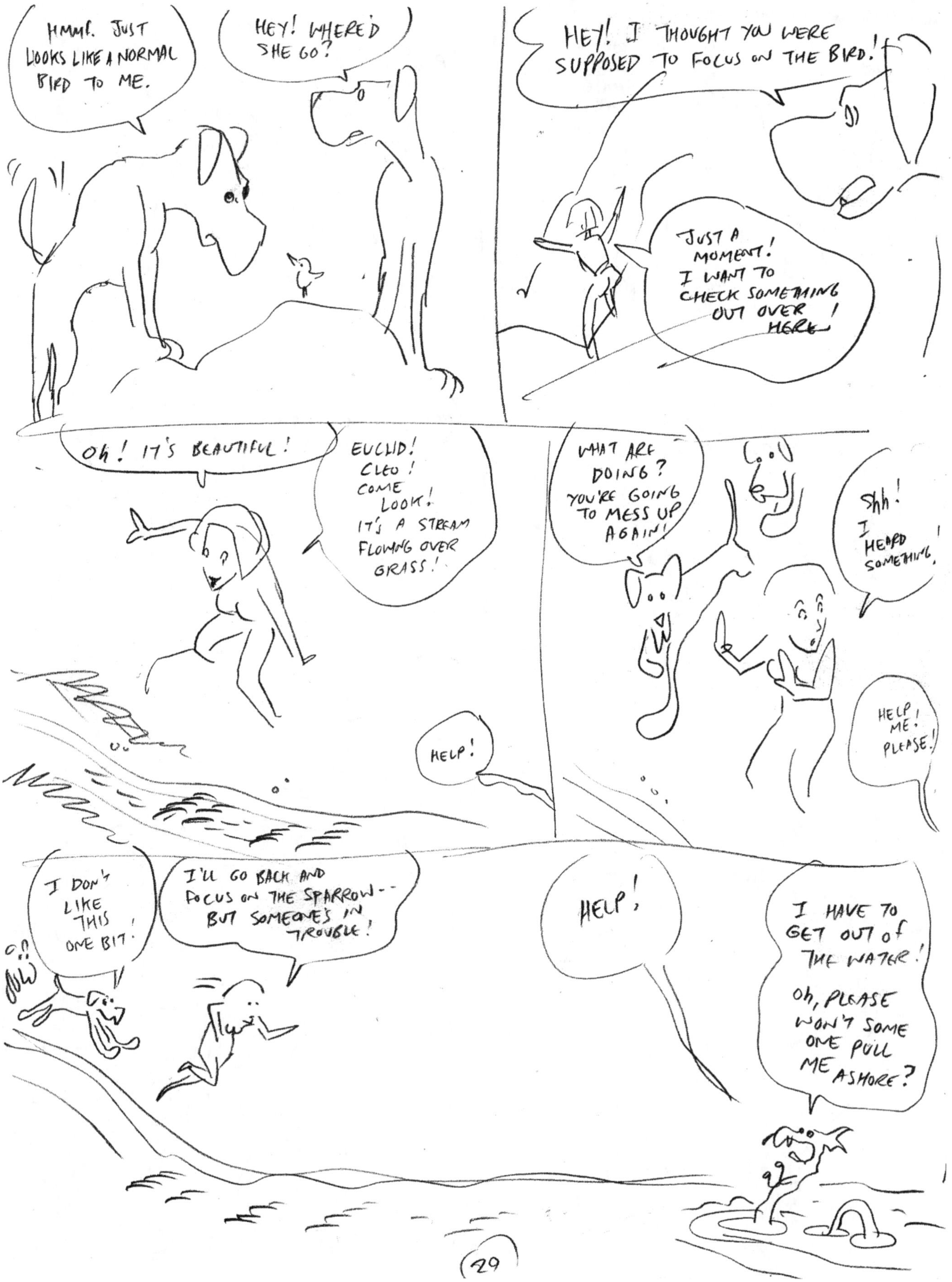
HMMM. JUST LOOKS LIKE A NORMAL BIRD TO ME.
HEY! WHERE'D SHE GO?
HEY! I THOUGHT YOU WERE SUPPOSED TO FOCUS ON THE BIRD!
JUST A MOMENT! I WANT TO CHECK SOMETHING OUT OVER HERE!
Oh! IT'S BEAUTIFUL!
EUCLID! CLEO! COME LOOK! IT'S A STREAM FLOWING OVER GRASS!
HELP!
WHAT ARE DOING? YOU'RE GOING TO MESS UP AGAIN!
Shh! I HEARD SOMETHING!
HELP! ME! PLEASE!
I DON'T LIKE THIS ONE BIT!
I'LL GO BACK AND FOCUS ON THE SPARROW-- BUT SOMEONE'S IN TROUBLE!
HELP!
I HAVE TO GET OUT OF THE WATER!
Oh, PLEASE WON'T SOME ONE PULL ME ASHORE?
(29

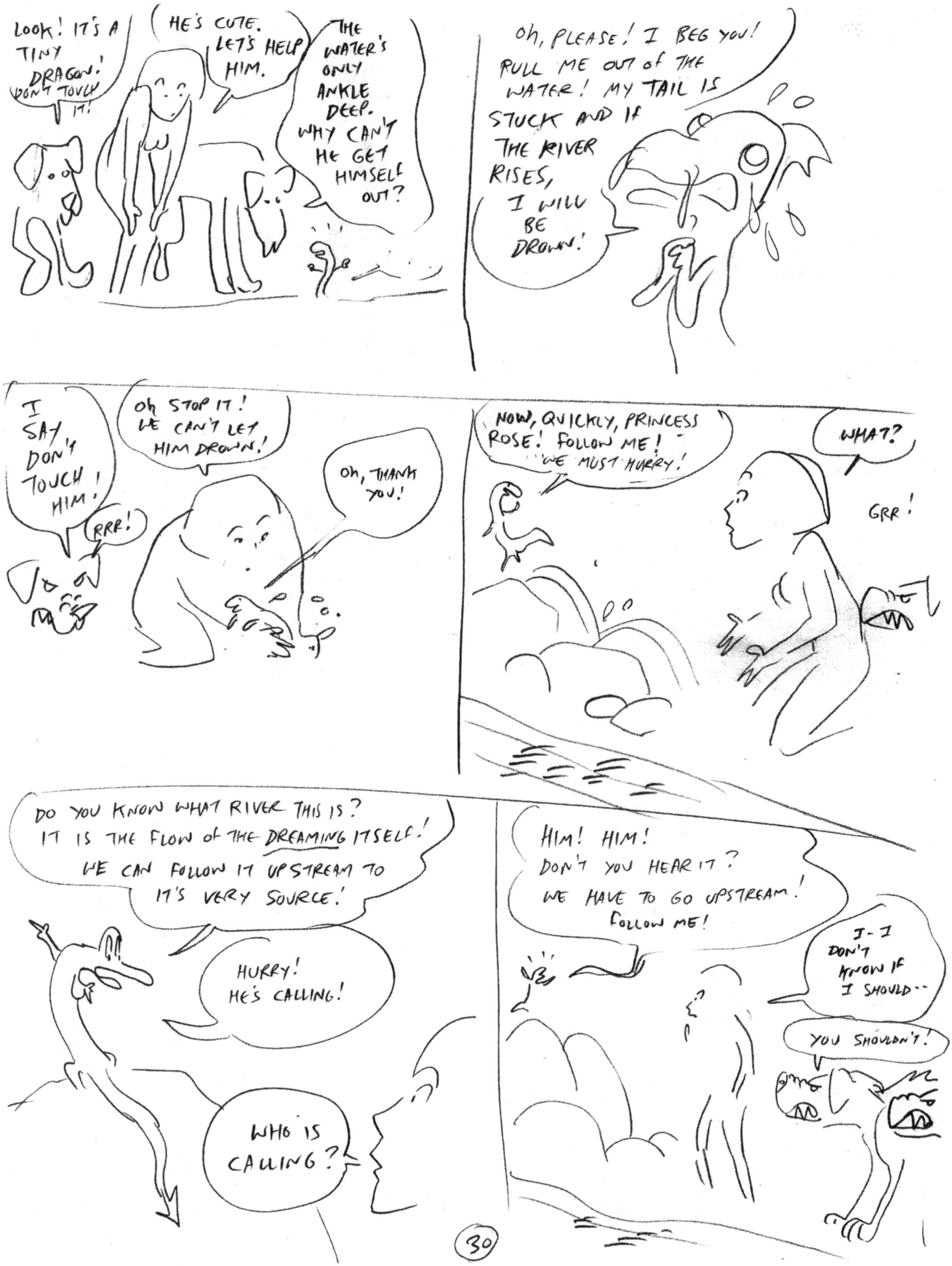

LOOK! IT'S A TINY DRAGON! DON'T TOUCH IT!
HE'S CUTE. LET'S HELP HIM.
THE WATER'S ONLY ANKLE DEEP. WHY CAN'T HE GET HIMSELF OUT?
Oh, PLEASE! I BEG YOU! PULL ME OUT OF THE WATER! MY TAIL IS STUCK AND IF THE RIVER RISES, I WILL BE DROWN!
I SAY DON'T TOUCH HIM!
RRR!
Oh STOP IT! WE CAN'T LET HIM DROWN!
Oh, THANK YOU!
NOW, QUICKLY, PRINCESS ROSE! FOLLOW ME! WE MUST HURRY!
WHAT?
GRR!
DO YOU KNOW WHAT RIVER THIS IS? IT IS THE FLOW OF THE DREAMING ITSELF! WE CAN FOLLOW IT UPSTREAM TO IT'S VERY SOURCE!
HURRY! HE'S CALLING!
WHO IS CALLING?
HIM! HIM! DON'T YOU HEAR IT? WE HAVE TO GO UPSTREAM! FOLLOW ME!
I-I DON'T KNOW IF I SHOULD...
YOU SHOULDN'T!
30

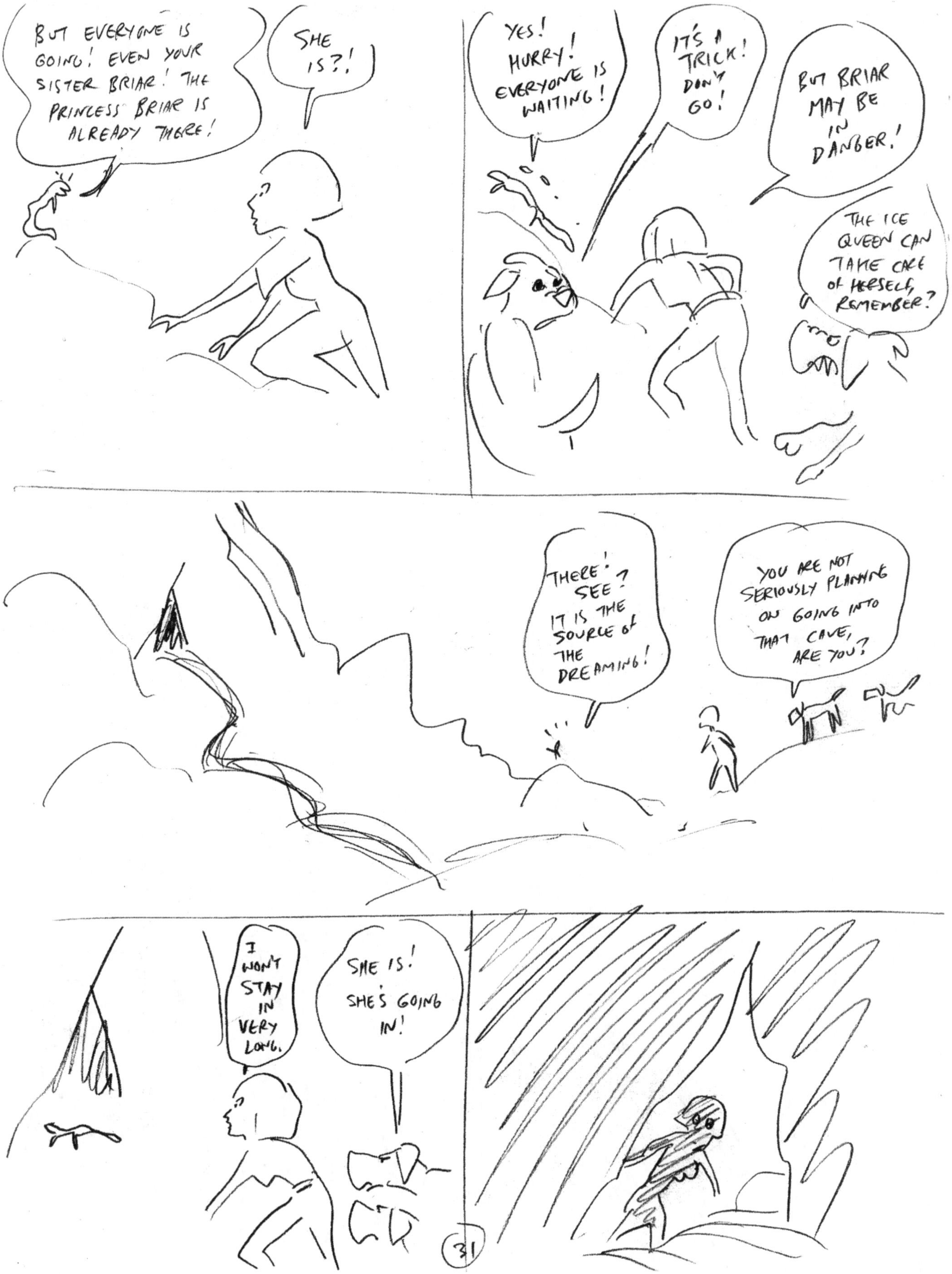
BUT EVERYONE IS GOING! EVEN YOUR SISTER BRIAR! THE PRINCESS BRIAR IS ALREADY THERE!
SHE IS?!
YES! HURRY! EVERYONE IS WAITING!
IT'S A TRICK! DON'T GO!
BUT BRIAR MAY BE IN DANGER!
THE ICE QUEEN CAN TAKE CARE OF HERSELF, REMEMBER?
THERE! SEE? IT IS THE SOURCE OF THE DREAMING!
YOU ARE NOT SERIOUSLY PLANNING ON GOING INTO THAT CAVE, ARE YOU?
I WON'T STAY IN VERY LONG.
SHE IS! SHE'S GOING IN!
31

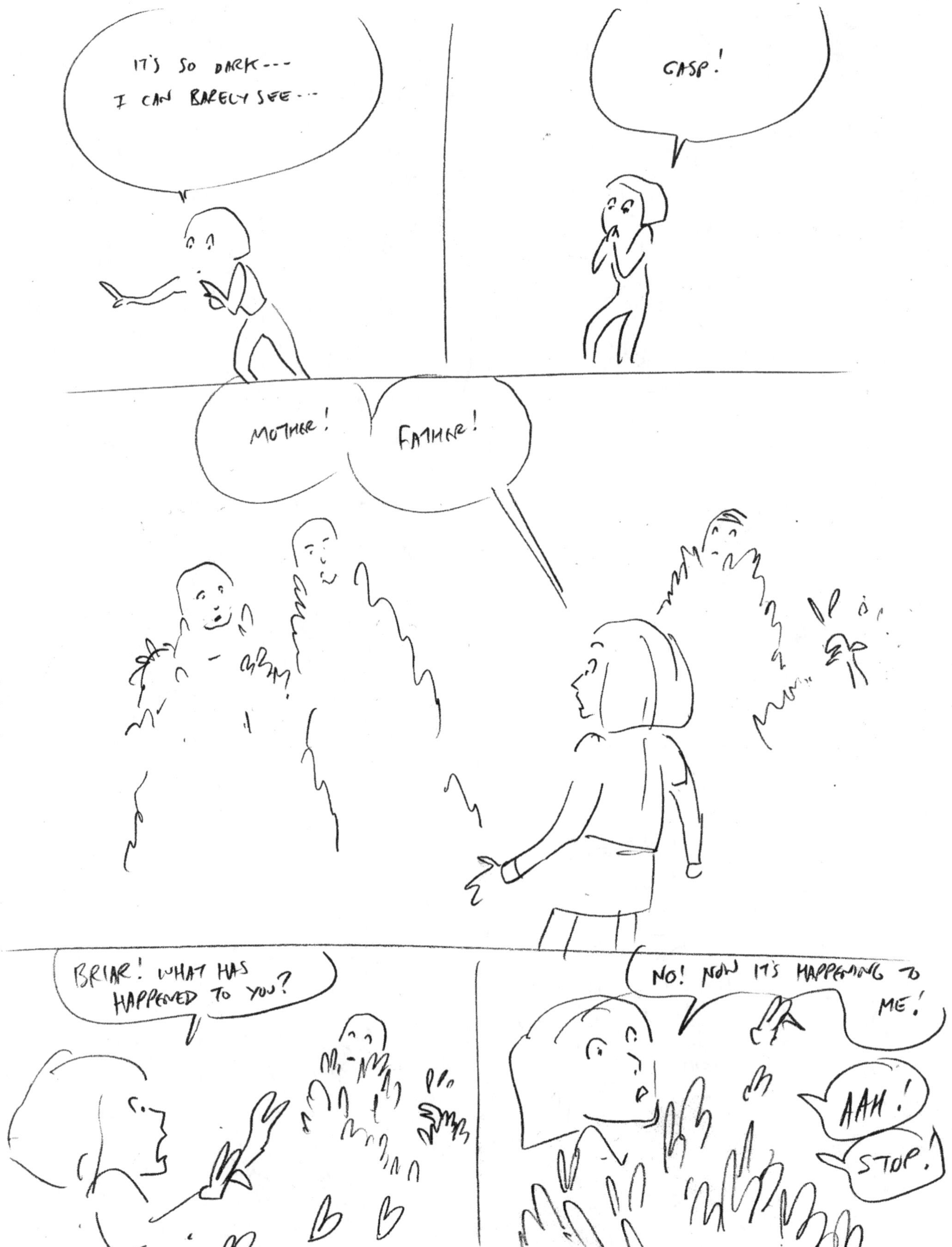
IT'S SO DARK---
I CAN BARELY SEE...
GASP!
MOTHER!
FATHER!
BRIAR! WHAT HAS HAPPENED TO YOU?
NO! NOW IT'S HAPPENING TO ME!
AAH!
STOP!
32

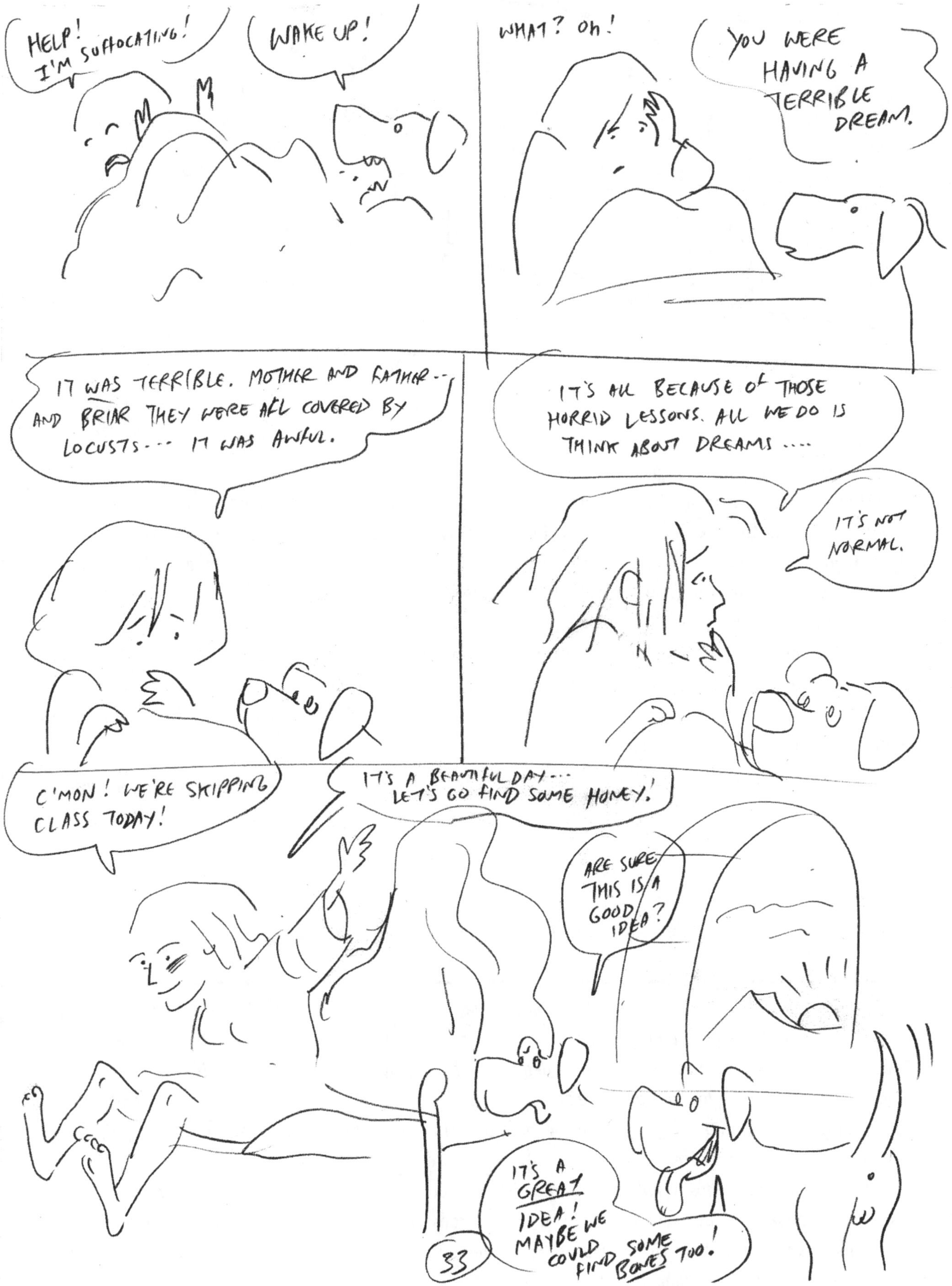
HELP! I'M SUFFOCATING!
WAKE UP!
WHAT? OH!
YOU WERE HAVING A TERRIBLE DREAM.
IT WAS TERRIBLE. MOTHER AND FATHER... AND BRIAR THEY WERE ALL COVERED BY LOCUSTS... IT WAS AWFUL.
IT'S ALL BECAUSE OF THOSE HORRID LESSONS. ALL WE DO IS THINK ABOUT DREAMS....
IT'S NOT NORMAL.
C'MON! WE'RE SKIPPING CLASS TODAY!
IT'S A BEAUTIFUL DAY... LET'S GO FIND SOME HONEY!
ARE SURE THIS IS A GOOD IDEA?
IT'S A GREAT IDEA! MAYBE WE COULD FIND SOME BONES TOO!
33

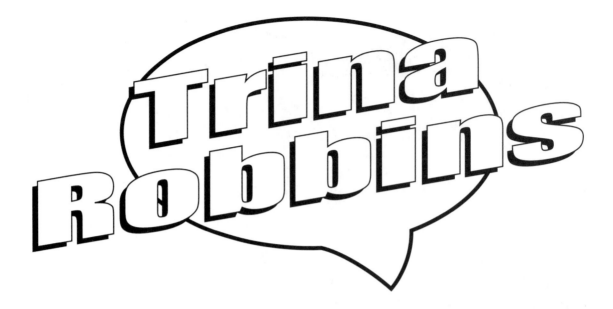

Why *GoGirl!* ? Why this script?

I'd given up selling a girl's comic to any publisher, when Anne Timmons suggested I write something for her to draw, and the temptation was irresistible. Amazingly, Image comics went for the idea! After a rocky start, when we realized that not enough retailers would order a girl's comic to allow us to publish in color, the black and white *GoGirl!* was born, and has held her own in a tough, male-dominated market.

Issue #1 introduced our plucky teen heroine and supporting characters. Each issue after that became a parody/homage of well-known popculture. Issue #2 parodied *It's a Wonderful Life*, and for issue #3, my inspiration was *Buffy, the Vampire Slayer*. I think this was our best issue yet; the one where all the characters and plot finally jelled.

– Trina Robbins, December 2001

Trina Robbins has flowed through the comics scene for over 30 years, presenting a strong and clearly female voice. In 1970, she produced the first comic ever created solely by female contributors, It Ain't Me, Babe. *This led to* Wimmin's Comix, *an underground anthology series that lasted 20 years. A strong proponent of comics by, for, and about females, she has exercised her beliefs in such ways as creating the series* California Girls *and being a founder of the group Friends Of Lulu, which exists to encourage female involvement in the comics scene.*

These days, Trina is most visible as a comics historian focusing on the often-overlooked women in comics history. Her books include The Great Women Superheroes, From Girls to Grrlz, *and* The Great Women Cartoonists, *which landed on Time.com's list of the best of comics for 2001. He current work is a volume on the interesting topic of murderesses.*

Her script was originally delivered as e-mail text; the font it is reprinted with is an arbitrary choice.

Subject: Script
    Date: Thu, 15 Feb 2001 14:49:11 -0800
    From: Trina Robbins <██████@██████.com>
      To: Annie Timmons <██████ @ ██████.com>

GOGIRL! #3
THE TEACHER FROM HELL
PAGE ONE (This page has already been drawn)
PANEL ONE
This is a big panel. No background. We see Lindsay from the chest up in
her GoGirl! outfit, looking out of the panel at the reader, punching
forward with her fist in Jack Kirby-style forced perspective. We don't
see who she's punching. She looks really mad, she's gritting her teeth.
Lindsay (2): I said *NO*!!!! (Tom; this needs to be a powerful, maybe
jagged-edged? - balloon, that looks like she's shouting)
Sound effect (3): POW! (Tom: maybe you can make this sound effect look
pop-art)

PANEL TWO
Camera draws back and now we see that we're in a gym and if you can show
it, there's a big round clock on the wall with hands that say 15 to 9. If
you can see even more, Lindsay's bookbag and backpack are on the floor,
against a wall. Lindsay has been working out with a trainer in a padded
outfit, the kind they wear for model mugging classes. (Anne, are you
familiar with model mugging? If not, I'll try to get you some reference.
 Basically, it's self defense classes where the students don't pull their
punches on the trainer, who is heavily padded.) The trainer, who wears a
helmet so you can't see the face, has just been hurled into a corner by
Lindsay's punch and has slumped to the floor. Lindsay bends over,
looking concerned.
Lindsay (4): Omigod, I'm sorry! Did I punch you too hard?

PANEL THREE
Tighter shot now, just Lindsay and the trainer. Trainer takes helmet off
and we now see that it's Lindsay's mom, Janet, under the helmet. She
looks dazed.   Little stars over her head would help give the impression
we want. Lindsay is still concerned.
Lindsay(5): Are you okay, mom?
Janet (6): Whew!
Janet (7): No, I'm fine, Lindsay.

PANEL FOUR
Janet gets up, dusts herself off. Lindsay looks up at the clock and
reacts with alarm.
Janet (8): But you pack a whallop. I'm gonna need extra padding —
Lindsay (9): Onooo! Look at the time! I'm late for class!

PANEL FIVE
Lindsay, still in her GoGirl! costume, flies out the window, holding her
bookbag by the strap, the bag sails through the air behind her. She
looks back as she flies away and calls back to Janet, who shouts up to
her.
Lindsay (10): Bye, mom! I'll change clothes when I get to school!
Janet (11): Lindsay, *wait*!

PANEL SIX
Janet standing alone in the gym, looking perplexed, talking to the air,
because Lindsay has flown away. She holds up a backpack.
Janet (12): You forgot your clothes!
PAGE TWO
PANEL ONE
This is a full-page splash panel with title and credits.

Lindsay, in her GoGirl! costume, making a graceful landing on the front steps of a typical high school, still holding her bookbag which flies behind her. Speed lines show how she's flown down from the sky. Let's have her feet not yet having touched the ground.
Caption, at top of panel (1): Lindsay Goldman's mom was Go-Go Girl, a superheroine in the 1970s. Lindsay's inherited her mom's ability to fly, and wearing her mom's old costume she becomes the teenage superheroine: GOGIRL! (this is the logo)
in THE TEACHER FROM HELL (this is the title)
Credits
Lindsay (2): (thought balloon) These early morning workout sessions with mom make me late for school!
PAGE THREE
PANEL ONE
Interior of school, Lindsay running through the hall, approaching a door that says "Girls".
Lindsay (1): (thought balloon) I'm lucky that my science teacher, Ms.Gomez, is so nice about me being late.
Lindsay (2): I'll just ch —

PANEL TWO
Lindsay stands in front of the girls' room door, looking mortified. She has just realized that she didn't bring her clothes.
Lindsay (3): Omigod, I left my clothes at the gym!

PANEL THREE
Medium shot. Lindsay walking through the door into her science classroom.
 She looks apprehensive because she's not only late, but she's wearing her superheroine costume. We don't see most of the classroom, maybe just one or two students on either side of the door, who turn to stare at her.
Lindsay (4): (thought balloon) This is *sooo* embarrassing!
Lindsay (5): Sorry I'm late, Ms. Gomez, I —-

PANEL FOUR
Now we see the teacher, she's a very stern and angry looking woman, frowning at Lindsay, arms folded across her chest.
Let's make her about 40, thinnish but not skinny, hair pulled back in a bun or a French twist, wearing a slightly severe suit with a knee-length skirt and flat heeled shoes. Lindsay's mouth opens in surprise and her body language also registers surprise, maybe her knees are bent and her head is forward: this is not Ms. Gomez! We can also see some more students: very pretty girls with big hair, and if you can see it, mini-skirts, giggling to each other about Lindsay. They are the Heathers, and they're always snotty to Lindsay. There's an empty seat in front of them where Lindsay will sit. We can also see more of the classroom, and there are Bunsen burners on each desk for their science project (whatever it is). If we can see the seat next to the empty seat, there's a very cute teenage guy sitting there. This will be Dylan, the star of the football team. If there's room, Haseena sits behind Dylan, looking sympathetic.
Lindsay (6): (Thought balloon) Not ...Ms...Gomez...
Teacher (7): And this must be our little superheroine.
Teacher (8): Ms Gomez took ill quite suddenly and I'm her replacement, Ms. Steele.
PAGE FOUR
PANEL ONE
A mortified Lindsay takes a seat in front of the Heathers, looking like she'd like to sink into the ground. The Heathers look at each other and giggle. If we didn't see Dylan in the past panel, we should see something of him now. He is NOT laughing at Lindsay, he might even smile at her in a friendly way. And if we didn't see Haseena in the past panel, we see her now, looking sympathetic.

Ms Steele still frowns and looks stern and angry.
Ms. Steele(1): Unlike Ms Gomez, I don't excuse lateness, no matter how special you *think* you are.
Ms. Steele (2): You may sit.
Heather #1 (3): (this speech balloon is a whisper balloon, so it's outlined in dashes: —) Can you believe her outfit?
Heather #2 (4): (another whisper balloon) It's *sooo* 20th century!

PANEL TWO
Big panel. Interior, the science classroom, the desks with Bunsen burners, as in last page. Dylan leans toward Lindsay to talk to her. Lindsay looks delighted. The two Heathers, seated behind Lindsay, frown; they don't like Dylan paying attention to Lindsay. The Bunsen burner on Dylan's desk is lit, and his books are piled up on his desk. (Note: Haseena's not gonna be doing any talking for the next few pages, but when you can fit her in, please do, always looking sympathetic)
Dylan (5): Lindsay, I'll fill you in on what you missed. We're testing the temperature of —-
Lindsay (6): (thought balloon) Dylan! The star of the football team and he knows I'm *alive*!
Lindsay (7): (thought balloon) Don't faint, girlfriend!
Off-panel speech balloon belonging to Ms Steele (8): Dylan, Lindsay does *not* require your help.

PANEL THREE
Ms Steele looms over Dylan looking, as usual, stern and angry. Lindsay hangs her head, embarrassed. Behind her, the Heathers giggle.
Ms Steele (8): Lindsay was *tardy*, and it's up to her to catch up with the class.
Ms Steele (9): She may discover that *science* takes more brains than *flying*.
Lindsay (10): (thought balloon) Sigh!

PANEL FOUR
Now Ms Steele is holding out big carton towards Dylan, who has risen from his seat to take it. We can tell from her body language (Top part of her body bent back with the weight) that the carton is heavy.
Ms Steele (11): Anyway, I need you to carry this heavy equipment to my car for me, Dylan.
Dylan (12): Okay, Ms Steele.

PANEL FIVE
Still the classroom. Lindsay sits at her desk, she's been working with her Bunsen burner. Next to her, Dylan's seat is empty but his Bunsen burner is still lit and his books are still piled on top of his desk. Behind her, the Heathers look towards the sound of the bell, and are already rising from their seats. Lindsay looks up at Ms Steele, who stands in front of the desks.
Caption at top of panel (13): Thirty long minutes later...
Sound Effect from outside of panel (14): BBBRRRINGGG!!
Ms Steele (15): Class dismissed! Remember to review pages 12 to 14 in your textbooks.
Lindsay (16): Ms Steele, where's Dylan? He never *returned*.

PANEL SIX
Lindsay and Ms Steele. Ms Steele faces towards the reader and away from Lindsay, who sits behind her. Thus, only the reader sees Ms Steel suddenly look demonic, the way in Buffy, the vampires' faces change when they become vampires. Her eyes can get little and beady, certainly her teeth get pointy, her nose flattens and maybe even her ears get pointy. Let's make this really obvious!
Ms Steele (17): Dylan left *early* for football practice.

Lindsay (18): (thought balloon) But his Bunsen burner's still on, and he's left all his books.   That's weird!

PAGE FIVE

PANEL ONE

Big panel. The science classroom. Dylan's seat, next to Lindsay's, is empty. This is the next day, so Lindsay is wearing ordinary clothes now, not her costume. We could put her in a simple T shirt and jeans, to contrast with the Heathers, sitting behind her, who have big hair and wear low-cut dresses. Lindsay is hunched over her desk, looking unhappy as Ms Steele stands over her and berates her. The Heathers point at Lindsay and giggle. Basically, whenever Ms Steele chastises Lindsay, the Heathers point and giggle. When they're not doing that, they're either whispering together or re-applying their lipstick, with the aid of big mirrors.

Caption (1): The next day...

Ms Steele (2): Late again, missy!

Ms Steele (3): *Playing superheroine* during school hours is *unacceptable*!

PANEL TWO

Still the classroom, different angle. Dylan walks in through the door. His body language should be stiff, but we don't see much of his expression yet. Lindsay perks up, she's relieved to see him

Lindsay (4): Dylan!

PANEL THREE

Dylan sits down next to Lindsay and now we see that his expression is a total blank. He doesn't look at Lindsay, just looks straight ahead and his eyes are round and starey, as if he's hypnotized. Lindsay starts to speak, then stops.

Lindsay (5: I was worr—-

PANEL FOUR

Ms Steele hovers over Lindsay, who stares at Dylan in confusion. Dylan still stares blankly straight ahead.

Ms Steele (6): Perhaps you should worry about *science* rather than *boys*, Lindsay!

Ms Steele (7): Tomorrow's test is *important*, and if you're not on time, you automatically get a zero!

PANEL FIVE

Ms Steele gestures towards a big carton sitting on her desk and addresses a boy behind Lindsay, who starts to stand up. Let's make him Hispanic, give him black hair. Lindsay still stares at Dylan, who stares blankly straight ahead.

Ms Steele (8): I need someone *young* and *strong* to carry this equipment to my car for me.

Ms Steele (9): Juan, you're captain of the football team, you'll do.

Lindsay (10): (thought balloon) There's something *funny* going on here...

PAGE SIX

PANEL ONE

Back at the gym.   Janet, in the trainer outfit again, Lindsay in her GoGirl! costume. Janet has been rushing Lindsay from behind, Lindsay has sidestepped, and Janet is in the act of falling forward onto a mat.

Janet (1): Whuff!

PANEL TWO

Janet has taken off her helmet. She sits on mat, looks up at Lindsay approvingly. Lindsay laughs.

Janet (2): Attagirl, Lindsay! By sidestepping, you use your attacker's force *against* him.

Lindsay (3): or *her*!

PANEL THREE
Lindsay looks at clock and runs over to pick up her bookbag and backpack.
Lindsay (4): Omigod, gotta run — or *fly*!
Janet (5): Slow down, you have half an hour. You can fly to school in 15 minutes.

PANEL FOUR
Clutching both her bags, Lindsay's about to take off through the window.
She looks back and talk to Janet. Janet runs over to her, holding up a small package.
Lindsay (6): It's that new teacher, Ms Steele! She's coming down hard on me for being late, and there's a test today—-
Janet (7): Wait! I have something for you!

PANEL FIVE
Closeup, Lindsay and Janet. Lindsay has opened the package, holds up a cell phone. She's delighted. Janet smiles.
Lindsay (8): Oh, mom, a cell phone! Thank you!
Janet (9): Next time you forget your clothes, I can phone you.
PAGE SEVEN
Big panel. Lindsay, in her GoGirl! costume, is flying through the air, not too high up, we have to be able to see the ground. She's flying over a suburban scene with one and two story houses and tees. There are some treetops close below her. She carries her book bag and wears her backpack. She looks stressed.
Lindsay (1): (thought balloon) Wish my new science teacher wasn't so *mean*! If I'm late for today's test, she'll fail me!
Lindsay (2): (thought balloon) And why is Dylan acting so weird?

PANEL TWO
Lindsay, still in the air, looks down at a cat caught up in the tree directly below her, while at the foot of the tree stands a little girl, looking up.
Lindsay (3): Could I be taking this too personally? Maybe he just doesn't *like* me—-
Lindsay (4): Whoa! Houston, we have a problem!

PANEL THREE
Lindsay flies down from the treetop with the cat in her arms. Speed lines show her descent. The happily smiling little girl is waiting below with her arms out to receive her cat.
Little Girl (5): GoGirl! Thank you!
Lindsay (6): No problem. This is what us superheroes *do*!

PANEL FOUR
Lindsay flies off, looking alarmed. Below, the little girls holds her cat with one arm and waves to Lindsay with the other.
Lindsay (7): *Onooo*! Saving that cat made me late!

PANEL FIVE
Lindsay, still in costume, bursts into the classroom, looking breathless.
Little sweat drops in the air around her should help give that impression, also her book bag and backpack could be all tangled up together. Ms Steele, sourfaced as ever, stands right at the door, conspicuously holding up her wrist with the watch on it and pointing to it with her other hand.
Ms Steele (8): Might as well turn around and fly home, miss *superheroine*.
Ms Steele (9): I *warned* you! You get a zero on this test!
Lindsay (10): But...

-97-

PAGE EIGHT
PANEL ONE
The school cafeteria. Lindsay mopes alone at a table, elbows on table,
chin resting on her hands. Haseena stands over her with a full tray,
looking, yes, sympathetic.
Haseena (1): Lindsay, aren't you eating anything?
Lindsay (2): I'm not hungry, Haseena.

PANEL TWO
Haseena has sat down opposite Lindsay, and tosses her an apple, which she
catches.
Haseena (3): C'mon, you gotta keep up your strength!
Lindsay (4): As if! I feel totally helpless.
Haseena (5):Don't let Ms Steele get you down. She has a thing against
superheroes or something.
Lindsay (6): There's something else—

PANEL THREE
Closer shot of the two girls. Haseena holds a sandwich, which she has
taken a bite of. Lindsay holds the apple and talks earnestly. Haseena
looks at her strangely; she thinks Lindsay's imagination is running away
with her.
Lindsay (7): Dylan and Juan are acting like zombies! And they each helped
Ms Steele carry stuff to her car. Could there be a connection??
Haseena (8): Lindsay—-

PANEL FOUR
Haseena tries to explain. Lindsay looks doubtful.
Haseena (9): Maybe they're both in a bad mood or something.
Haseena (10): Or they're worried about the big football game.
Haseena (10): I think you're getting kinda carried away. PAGE NINE
(Let's make this page a free-form collage. In two different panels, Ms
Steele is asking two different boys to help her carry stuff. To vary the
poses, in one panel, the boy is standing up at his desk, and in the
other, he precedes Ms Steele out of the classroom, carrying a cardboard
carton which we can tell is heavy by the way he bends backwards from the
waist to hold it. In another panel, Lindsay has just spilled the
contents of her test tube, and a sour-faced Ms Steele towers over her at
her desk. In the last panel, we have a closeup of Lindsay, with her
hands clapped onto either side of her face, looking upset.)
Caption above all the panels (1): And the next day...
PANEL ONE
Lindsay has managed to catch the sleeve of her sweater in fire by the
Bunsen burner. She's whacking at it with her other hand, looking
alarmed, as behind her the Heathers giggle and Dylan stares straight
ahead. Ms Steele stands over Lindsay, frowning.
Ms Steele (2): I didn't know superheroes were so *clumsy*, Lindsay!

PANEL TWO
Ms Steele, looming intimidatingly over Lindsay at her desk, as Lindsay
looks with horror at the liquid contents of her test tube, now spilling
all over her desk and onto her lap.
Ms Steele (3): You'll have to stay after class and mop that up.

PANEL THREE
Boy, carrying out carton with Ms Steele behind him.
Ms Steele (4): If you'll just carry that carton to my car, Julian —

PANEL FOUR
Closeup, Lindsay, upset, holding her head.
Lindsay (5): Something — is *very* — wrong!
PAGE TEN

PANEL ONE
2/3 page panel. The gym again. This time Lindsay, in her GoGirl! costume,
wears boxing gloves and is punching a punching bag with a look of intense
determination on her face. And this time, it's an off-panel voice that
says:
Off-panel voice (1): *NO!!!*

PANEL TWO
(The next two panels should run side by side on the bottom third of the
page)
Janet, who the off-panel voice belonged to, is now in the panel. Instead
of the model mugging outfit, she's in sweats, like a boxing trainer. She
addresses Lindsay, who wipes her forehead with a wrist (has to use wrist
'cause she's still wearing the boxing gloves.)
Janet (2): Don't hesitate like that. You've got to punch *through* your
target! You know that, Lindsay.

PANEL THREE
Now Lindsay has one glove off and is removing the other. She looks
discouraged. Janet is concerned. She puts her hand on Lindsay's arm.
Janet (3): Your performance is way down. Last week you nearly knocked me
out, and now you can't even kayo a punching bag. Is something wrong,
honey?

PAGE ELEVEN
PANEL ONE
Lindsay sits on the floor with her arms wrapped around her knees. Janet
kneels down on one knee and watches her.
Lindsay (1): Aw, mom, I don't know, it's like — I just don't *believe*
in myself anymore!

PANEL TWO
Closeup of Lindsay and Janet. Lindsay looks distressed. Janet gets more
and more concerned.
Lindsay (2): I don't feel *s-strong* anymore!

PANEL THREE
Same shot. Lindsay's face is starting to crumple.
Lindsay (3): I — I —

PANEL FOUR
Suddenly Lindsay is weeping on her mother's shoulder. Let's have her
face turned to the side facing us so we can see her cry, and let's see
tears. But keep it cute, not depressing. Janet is so shocked that she
hasn't even had the time to hug her daughter yet; her arms are still
stretched out on either side.
Lindsay (4): *BAW!!!!*

PAGE TWELVE
PANEL ONE
Still the gym. Now they're sitting on the floor side by side. Janet has
an arm around Lindsay's shoulder. With the other hand she offers Lindsay
a tissue from a box of tissues that sits on the floor next to her.
Lindsay blows her nose into a tissue.
Lindsay (1): S-so this new teacher really *picks* on me! I swear, mom,
she makes me feel like *two cents!*
Lindsay (2): And then there's all the boys who are acting like *zombies*
or something—
Lindsay (3): And they all get like that after they've helped Ms Steele
move stuff to her car!
Lindsay (4): *HONK!!*
Janet (5): Another tissue, honey?

PANEL TWO
Closeup of Lindsay and Janet in serious conversation. Lindsay looks a
little more hopeful.
Janet (6): Somebody's playing fast and loose with your *self-esteem,
Lindsay*, and it sounds like Ms Steele. Somehow, she's taken away your
faith in yourself.

PANEL THREE
Now they're standing up. Janet faces Lindsay and holds her by the upper
arms, giving her a pep talk.
Janet (7): Are you gonna let her *get away* with that? I believe in you,
but a superheroine has to believe in *herself*!

PANEL FOUR
Same pose, but closeup. Lindsay has started to get a determined
expression on her face.
Janet (8): If you let that — that *woman* get you down, then you're
letting her *win!*
Janet (9): And you have to believe in your *intuition*! If you think
there's more to this than just some boys feeling moody — *investigate!*
 Superheroes are *detectives*, too!

PAGE THIRTEEN
PANEL ONE
Full page splash panel. This should be a very upbeat page. Lindsay has
just taken off and is flying away from the gym's open window in a very
heroic pose — she's herself again. (and she has both her backpack and
her book bag, flying in the air behind her.) Janet stands in the window
with her fist raised, looking excited.
Janet (1): And show that witch what us superheroines are made of!

PAGE FOURTEEN
PANEL ONE
Lindsay in the air, swooping down above her school. (Remember, she still
has backpack and book bag in these panels — we'll need backpack later!)
Besides the school, you can see the parking lot below, with cars parked
in it.
Lindsay (1): There's the school — *wait* a minute!

PANEL TWO
Lindsay perched, almost Spiderman-style (But not!) on the roof,
overlooking the parking lot.
Lindsay (2): (thought balloon) Instead of going *in*, I'll just *wait*
here and see if Ms Steele has *another* boy carrying cartons to her car
for her.

PANEL THREE
Lindsay peers out over the edge of the roof. Down below are the small
figures of Ms Steele and a boy carrying a heavy carton. When we can see
the boy clearer, he'll be Black.
Lindsay (3): *Aha*! Didn't have long to wait. *This* time, she's got
Scott Miller, the *best fullback* on the football team!

PANEL FOUR
Now we're at ground level and Ms Steele and Scott are in the panel.
Lindsay isn't in the panel. Ms Steele and Scott stand in front of a car.
 Ms Steel has opened the trunk door all the way, still has her hand on
the handle. Scott is about to put the carton in the trunk.
Ms Steele (4): Just put it in the *trunk*, Scott—
Scott (5): Sure, Ms Steele.

PANEL FIVE
Suddenly Ms Steele brings the trunk door down upon Scott with all her
strength. We can see by what there is of Scott's body language that
she's knocking him cold: we don't see his head and shoulders, which are
in the trunk, but his arms and legs go flying upwards. Some "knockout"
stars emanating from within the trunk will also help. At the same time
that she does this, Ms Steele's face reverts to the demon likeness we saw
before.
Sound Effect of trunk closing (6): *WHAMMM!!*
Scott's speech balloon, from within the trunk (7): Hey wh — ulp!

PANEL SIX
The now demon-Ms Steele has the trunk door up again and is stuffing the
limp body of the unconscious Scott into the trunk. We see this at a
different angle, so that we can also see the roof of the school, where
Lindsay crouches, watching.
Lindsay (8): (thought balloon) Omigod!

PAGE FIFTEEN
PANEL ONE
Lindsay flying above the car, following it as it proceeds down a street.
She's in the act of removing the cell phone from her backpack (Told you
she'd need that backpack!)
Lindsay (1): (thought balloon) Oh mom, thank you for your good advice!
You totally rock!

PANEL TWO
Still flying above the car, she's pushing buttons on the cell phone.
Sound effect from cell phone (2): DIT-DIT-DIT-DIT-
Lindsay (2): (thought balloon) And thank you for this *cell phone*!

PANEL THREE
Closeup of Lindsay still in the air, cell phone held to her ear, look of
disbelief on her face. With the other hand she's hitting herself on the
side of her forehead.
Electronic-looking speech balloon (maybe with jagged edges?) emanating
from cell phone (3): You've reached Lindsay Goldman real estate. I can't
come to the phone right now, but if you'll leave a message —-
Lindsay (3): Oh mom, *duh!*

PAGE SIXTEEN
PANEL ONE
Seen from ground level. It's a scuzzy looking block, with garbage cans
and litter on the street, maybe a wino leaning against a building. The
buildings are several stories and have store fronts. The car is parked
in front of a boarded-up building. The trunk door is open and Ms Steele,
still with her demon face, has the limp, unconscious Scott draped around
her shoulders as she carries him towards the building's door. Up above
(but below roof level) hovers Lindsay, talking into her cell phone.
Lindsay (4): —-and she's some kind of *demon,* mom. Plus she's hecka
strong!
Lindsay (5): So when you get this *message*, you probably should head on
over. It's the boarded-up building — not the kind of place you'd expect
a *teacher* to live in.

PANEL TWO
Now Lindsay flies up towards the roof. She's put away the cell phone.
Lindsay (6): (thought balloon) — but then again, she's not *really* a
teacher!

PAGE SEVENTEEN
PANEL ONE

The hallway entrance to the apartment where Lindsay and Janet live. Janet, wearing a business suit and carrying a briefcase, looking happy, walks through the door.
Janet (1): (thought balloon) Closed the deal on the Hanover house! Yippee! I'll take Lindsay out for dinner tonight!

PANEL TWO
Janet has put her briefcase down, she stands in front of her answering machine, pushing the button.
Janet (2): (thought balloon) Turned off the cell phone -- didn't want interruptions. Let's see if there are any messages.

PANEL THREE
Janet stares at the answering machine with dismay as she listens to the message.
Electronic speech balloon coming from answering machine (3): --So you should probably head on over. It's the boarded-up building--
Janet (3): *Onoooo*! My baby!

PANEL FOUR
Janet, with a look of fear and panic on her face, impatiently rifles through her closet, looking for her costume.
Janet (4): Where's that *costume*? *Demons*, yet! Thinks she can handle it *alone*! Thinks she's *Buffy*, the *vampire* slayer!

PANEL FIVE
Janet holds up her costume on a hanger. She still looks anxious, and there's one tear (just one!) trickling down her cheek.
Janet (5): My baby *needs* me!

PAGE EIGHTEEN
PANEL ONE
Back to the roof of the building. Lindsay crouches on all fours, peering through a skylight.
Lindsay (1): A skylight! That's handy!

PANEL TWO
We see the interior — it's a loft. All four boys are chained by their wrists, above their heads, to the wall side by side. They don't look like zombies now, except for the unconscious Scott, who droops in his chains. The others look angry.
The demon Ms Steele is in the act of drawing a big circle on the floor, but she does not stand inside the circle. Next to the circle smoke arises from a fancy chalice, which stands on an ornate stand. A big fancy pitcher should also stand on the floor next to the circle, along with various assorted candles, and lying on the floor, a little wax figure, which we don't have to see clearly yet, but we'll need it later. Above, we can see Lindsay peering through the skylight, but none of them look up to see her.
Dylan (2): Hey, ugly! You won't get away with this! Our parents must have the whole police force out searching for us by now!
Lindsay (3): (thought balloon) Dylan and Juan and Julian! But that's *impossible!* They're at *school* — I *saw* them!

PANEL THREE
Demon/Ms Steele laughs maniacally. The boys continue to be chained and angry. We don't need to see Lindsay, now that we know where she is.
Demon/Steele (4): Hahaha! Nobody suspects you're even *missing*, because I've replaced you with *simulacra* — doubles of you that I *conjured* up! They can't really talk or do anything, but they *look* like you, and that's enough.
Juan (5): B-but *why*?

PANEL FOUR
As she speaks, demon/Steele pours liquid from the pitcher into the
circle, and smoke rises from where the liquid lands. (remember, she never
steps within the circle!)
Demon/Steele (6): Because you're *young* and *strong*! Football players
have the life force that I need to regain my *youth*! At 2,000 years,
I'm starting to look my age.
Demon/Steele (7): I'm summoning my little hungry friends from the *lower
reaches*. They find teenage boys *delicious*!

PANEL FIVE
Only Demon/Steele is in this panel. She passes her hands over the
circle, which is now filled with swirling mist. We can just see one or
two clawed hands with long pointy nails and maybe one forked tail
emerging from the mist.
Demon/Steele (8): When they consume your *bodies*, I will get your
souls! I will become *young* and *beautiful* again!

PAGE NINETEEN
PANEL ONE
Same scene, but we only need to see Dylan and Demon/Steele for this.
Dylan strains at his chains angrily. Demon/Steele laughs.
Dylan (1): Oh yeah? Well we have a *superhero* in our class. *GoGirl!*
will rescue us, you'll see.
Demon/Steele (2): How *touching!*

PANEL TWO
Now Demon/Steele holds up that wax figure, and we can see that it's a
crude representation of GoGirl!
Demon/Steele (3): GoGirl! is yesterday's news. I've put a spell on her
to weaken her. By now she's lost her self-esteem *and* her powers!
Speech balloon from outside of panel top (4): I don't *think* so!

PANEL THREE
GoGirl! leaps through the skylight, knocking the wax figure out of
Demon/Steele's hand with her foot. The figure goes flying off somewhere.
 This can be a big panel, and if we can see the chained guys, they're
watching and smiling. GoGirl! looks mad. Demon/Steele is surprised.
Demon Steele (5): Wh--?
Lindsay (6): I am *so* over that!

PAGE TWENTY
PANEL ONE
Looking grim, Lindsay delivers a kayo punch to Demon/Steele's chin,
sending her stumbling AWAY from the circle (remember the circle?), which
is still filled with swirling mist. Speed lines can show the punch.
Lindsay (1): Plus I am over *you*!
Lindsay (2): (Thought balloon) Don't ... hesitate. Punch ...*through*...
target.
Sound effect (3): *POW!*
Demon/Steele (4): Unnnhhh!

PANEL TWO
Lindsay has turned towards the chained boys. The circle on the floor
lies between them, still full of swirling mists. Behind her,
Demon/Steele, who had fallen to the floor, is not knocked out, and she
starts to rise, leaning on her elbows. Elated with her success, Lindsay
talks to the chained boys.
Lindsay (5): Wow, that was so cool! All I had to do was believe in
myself and her magic didn't work on me!

PANEL THREE
Lindsay still smiling and talking, oblivious to the fact that behind her,
Demon/Steele is now running at her full-force, with her arms outstretched
to push her into the circle. Dylan sees and calls out.
Lindsay (6): Why, I could —-
Dylan (7): GoGirl! Behind you!

PAGE TWENTY ONE
PANEL ONE
Grinning, Lindsay does the sidestep, and Demon/Steele runs right past her
into the circle fulla swirling mist.
Lindsay (1): (thought balloon) Use...attacker's force...*against* her.
Demon/Steele (2): *NOOOOO!!!!*

PANEL TWO
Lindsay and the chained boys watch as the clawed hands (remember them?)
drag demon/Steele down into the mists and whatever is under them. The
kids are not horrified, because she deserved it, but they're a bit
awestruck.
Demon/Steele (3): *AAARGH!!*
Lindsay (4): Ew, gross!

PAGE TWENTY TWO
PANEL ONE
Cut to Janet, in her costume, flying up a flight of stairs in the
building, still looking worried. You can see the landing that she just
left, and on that landing is a doorway with a door off it's hinges (she
just broke the door down). In the doorway stands a slatternly looking
and angry fat woman in a robe and bunny slippers, holding a screaming
baby on one arm, while with the other she shakes a fist at Janet. She
shouts at Janet.
Fat woman (1): —-and you break my door *again*, I call the *cops!*
Janet (2): Whew! *Wrong door*! Lindsay must be on the top floor!

PANEL TWO
Janet in front of top door, flying towards it with her fist out, in the
act of breaking it down. Maybe we can see the wood splinter.
Janet (3): Don't *worry*, baby! Mommy's coming! Mommy's —-
Sound effect of breaking door (4): *Keerash!!*

PANEL THREE
Janet, in doorway, with broken door hanging off one hinge, skids to a
stop as she takes in the scene openmouthed: The circle has disappeared,
Lindsay is in the act of unchaining Dylan, while Julian, who's awake now,
has already been freed and is in the act of unwinding the last chains off
himself. Juan and Scott are still chained, waiting their turn to be
freed. Lindsay looks back to Janet and smiles.
Janet (5): —-here?
Lindsay (6): Oh, hi mom. You're in time to help me get these chains off.

PAGE TWENTY THREE
PANEL ONE
Next day, in the halls of the high school. Lindsay, in normal clothes
now, walks with Haseena. They carry books and talk. There's a big
poster on the wall that reads: SPRING DANCE!
Haseena (1): So the simulacra *vanished* right in front of the whole
class, probably at the moment that the demon was dragged under. And Ms
Gomez—-?
Lindsay (2): The demon was holding her prisoner, too. She'll be okay.

PANEL TWO
Suddenly Dylan, Julian and Juan appear at the end of the hall, in the

direction that Lindsay and Haseena are headed. Haseena nudges Lindsay.
Julian and Juan and pushing a reluctant Dylan forward.
Haseena (3): (whisper balloon, drawn with dotted lines) Omigod, it's
Dylan!
Julian (4): (whisper balloon, dotted lines) Go on, dude, ask her to the
dance!

PANEL THREE
Closeup of Dylan and Lindsay speaking to each other. Dylan's nervous,
Lindsay's hopeful.
Dylan (5): Uh, hi Lindsay! I wanted to thank you for *saving* us, and
--
Lindsay (6): Yes, Dylan?
Lindsay (7): (Thought balloon) Ask me to the *dance*! Ask me to the
dance!
Dylan (8): — and I wanted to, um—-
Lindsay (9): *Yes*, Dylan?

PANEL FOUR
Still Lindsay and Dylan. He hands her two tickets. She looks
disappointed.
Dylan (10): And here are two tickets to the big game.
Lindsay (11): Oh. Thanks.

PANEL FIVE
Haseena and Lindsay walk off down the hall in one direction, while Dylan,
Julian and Juan walk off in the opposite direction. Lindsay's bummed,
Haseena consoles her.
Dylan (12): Dudes, I *couldn't* ask her! I mean, she's a *superhero*!
Why would she go to a dance with *me*?
Haseena (13): Never mind, Lindsay. *Boys*! Who can figure them out?
Caption (14): Join us in three months for more GoGirl! adventures!

This story has often been cited as the best to appear in *Astro City* to date, and I'm inclined to go a little further than that – it may be the best piece I've ever written.

A historical note: The germ of the story came from fellow writer Len Kaminski. We were talking one night, and he said, "You know what you should do in *Astro City* someday? You should do a story about some big universe-changing crossover epic, from the point of view of some poor hapless schmuck whose live is just blown to hell by all the temporal revisions." And as soon as he said it, the story all fell into place in my mind.

The only trouble was, I knew it was a short story – not a full 24 pages. So I saved the idea until I had a place to do a shorter story – and when the chance came around to do a 16-page story for a *Wizard* #1/2 issue, I jumped at it, and got to do the story as I'd first imagined it when Len made that suggestion.

A craft note: You'll note that a lot of the panel descriptions start with "On," or "Close on," or some other immediate description of the action or story moment we're looking at. This is something I picked up from Frank Miller, and it was a breakthrough for me – I had an unpublished script of his, and I'd noted how his panel descriptions almost always focused first and foremost on the one story moment that was most important to the panel, and filled in any extra details – setting, background, mood, whatever – afterward. Instead of describing the picture he envisioned, he was describing what the reader should see first, describing the moment, and it made the script cleaner, tighter and easier to follow. So I've tried to do that ever since, and it made my scripts that much better, that much more about *story* than about *description*.

– **Kurt Busiek, November 2001**

Kurt Busiek had toiled in comics for a long time without getting much fan attention before his miniseries Marvels *made him an "overnight" success. He remains a fan favorite and regular award winner, particularly for* Astro City, *which depicts a traditional superhero universe from a non-traditional perspective.*

ASTRO CITY #1/2
THE NEARNESS OF YOU

SCRIPT FOR 16 PAGES

KURT BUSIEK / WRITER
BRENT ANDERSON / PENCILLER
WILL BLYBERG / INKER
COMICRAFT / LETTERING
ALEX SINCLAIR / COLORS
JONATHAN PETERSON / EDITOR

LETTERING KEY:

UNDERLINED	BOLD LETTERING
ITALIC	ITALIC LETTERING
CAPITALIZED	DISPLAY LETTERING
(BL)	OVERSIZED LETTERING
(SL)	UNDERSIZED LETTERING
FX	SOUND EFFECT
(TH)	THOUGHT BALLOON
(WH)	WHISPERED BALLOON
(SB)	SPLASH/BURST BALLOON
(ELEC)	ELECTRONIC TRANSMISSION BALLOON

ANYTHING ELSE WILL BE SPECIFICALLY REQUESTED IN THE SCRIPT ITSELF. THANKS.

PAGE ONE - 2 PANELS

[1]   CLOSE ON A **YOUNG WOMAN'S FACE**, HER HAIR SWIRLING AWAY AS
        SHE'S SWUNG AROUND IN THE MIDST OF A DANCE. HER HEAD IS
        THROWN BACK AND TO OUR RIGHT, HER MOUTH OPEN IN A LAUGH.
        SHE HAS DARK SHORT HAIR AND A LIGHT DUSTING OF FRECKLES
        ACROSS HER NOSE -- SHE'S PRETTY, BUT NOT A HOLLYWOOD BEAUTY,
        MORE OF A HOMETOWN, GIRL-NEXT DOOR LOOK. SHE'S **MIRANDA**.
        1 Caption: Her name is Miranda.
        2 Caption: She has a low, throaty laugh, and a capped tooth from a
                       bicycle accident when she was eight years old.
        3 Caption: Her shampoo makes her hair smell like apples and like
                       wildflowers.

[2]   PULL BACK TO REVEAL **MIKE**, A YOUNG MAN IN HIS LATE TWENTIES,
        AND **MIRANDA**, DANCING. SHE'S IN HIS ARMS, HER SKIRT SWIRLING
        OUT NOT UNLIKE HER HAIR WAS IN THE LAST PANEL. THEY ONLY
        HAVE EYES FOR EACH OTHER. THE BACKGROUND IS MISTY,
        INDISTINCT.
        4 Caption: And he has never met her.
        5 Caption: But almost every night -- when he falls asleep --

[1]

PAGE TWO - 4 PANELS

[1]   CLOSE ON THE **TWO** OF THEM, IN A POSITION NOT UNLIKE
        LEYENDECKER'S THE DANCERS, HER BACK AGAINST HIS CHEST, HER
        HEAD TIPPED BACK TO REST BETWEEN HIS SHOULDER AND NECK.
        THEY'RE HAPPY.
        1 Caption: -- she's <u>there</u>.
        2 Caption: And she's so close, and so <u>tender</u> -- and her head rests in
                       the hollow of his neck in that old <u>familiar</u> way --

[2]   SUDDENLY, SHE'S GONE, AND **HE'S** PANICKY, GRASPING AT NOTHING --
        3 Caption: -- and then she's <u>gone</u> --

[3]   -- AND **HE** WAKES UP IN HIS BEDROOM, IN THE DARK, SPRAWLED ON A
        QUEEN-SIZED BED, THE SHEETS SNARLED AROUND HIM. HE'S IN
        BOXERS AND A T-SHIRT.
        4 Caption: -- and Michael Tenicek can forget about <u>sleep</u> for the rest of
                       the night.

[4]   **MIKE** WATCHES TV, UNSHAVEN, GLUM, STILL DRESSED FOR BED. STILL
        DARK OUTSIDE. PAST THE **NEWSCASTER** ON THE TV SCREEN IS THE
        HONOR GUARD SYMBOL.
        5 Caption: He's never <u>met</u> her. He <u>knows</u> he's never met her.
        6 TV (elec):   -- members of <u>Honor Guard</u> captured the self-styled
                       <u>Conquerlord</u> today at the U.N. Building in New York --

[2]

PAGE THREE - 1 PANEL

[1]   SPLASH PAGE. **MIKE** SITS ON A BENCH IN FRONT OF A BEEFY BOB'S, AT
        A CURBSIDE BUS STOP, WEARING A SUIT, A BRIEFCASE AT HIS SIDE.
        OTHER MORNING **COMMUTERS** WAIT AROUND HIM, SEATED OR
        STANDING. HOWEVER, ALL THE COMMUTERS BUT MIKE ARE TURNING,
        GASPING, DROPPING OPENED NEWSPAPERS, WHATEVER, AS THEY
        TURN TO SEE **JACK-IN-THE-BOX** FIGHTING THE **RAZORHAWKS** (THREE
        GUYS IN MECHANICAL WINGED SUITS) ATOP THE BEEFY BOB'S, THE
        RAZORHAWKS SWOOPING AT THE BOUNDING JACK, WHO POPS A FIST
        TO SLUG ONE OF THEM. THE FIGHT SHOULD LOOK AS IT'S TRAVELING
        FROM LEFT TO RIGHT PRETTY FAST, AND IN ANOTHER FEW SECONDS
        THESE GUYS'LL BE GONE. MIKE IS THE ONLY ONE NOT WATCHING; HE'S
        LOST IN THOUGHT.
             IN THE SKY ABOVE THIS ALL, WE SEE A GHOSTLY IMAGE OF
        MIRANDA'S FACE, VERY LARGE, MAYBE FORMED OUT OF CLOUDS,
        MAYBE JUST A GHOST-IMAGE.

        1 Caption: So how does he know she bites her <u>fingernails</u>? How does
                            he know she likes <u>roasted garlic</u> on her pizza?
        2 Caption: How does he know the little <u>sounds</u> she makes in her sleep?
        3 Caption: Michael Tenicek has never <u>met</u> her. He <u>knows</u> it.
        4 Caption: So why can't he get her out of his <u>mind</u>?
        5 Title: THE NEARNESS OF YOU

PAGE FOUR - 5 PANELS

[1]   FROM MIKE'S P.O.V., AT A BAR, LOOKING AT A **FRIEND** OF HIS, A
       CONCERNED-LOOKING BLACK GUY IN A SWEATER AND JEANS.
              1 Guy: Mike! Earth to Mike!
              2 Guy: Have you heard a word I've said, Mike? You look awful!
              3 Guy: You've got to get some sleep, man...

[2]   FROM MIKE'S P.O.V., AT HIS DESK AT WORK, AS HIS ANGRY **BOSS** SLAMS
       A PILE OF PAPERS DOWN ON THE DESK, HOLDING UP HIS OTHER
       HAND, THE THUMB AND FOREFINGER SHOWING "THIS CLOSE."
              4 Boss: These need to be totally redone, Tenicek. Did you even
                          bring your head in to work that day?
              5 Boss: I don't know if you're looking for a new job, but let me tell you
                          -- you're this close to needing one. You get me?

[3]   FROM MIKE'S P.O.V., AT A NICE RESTAURANT. HIS **DATE**, A YOUNG
       WOMAN WHO LOOKS NOTHING LIKE MIRANDA, IS GETTING UP AND
       TURNING AWAY, ANNOYED, ABOUT TO LEAVE.
              6 Woman: I don't know why I bothered. Everyone says you're a flake,
                          but you seemed like a nice guy.
              7 Woman: A word of advice, the next time you ask someone to dinner?
                          Show up.

[4]   LOOKING PAST **MIKE**; HE'S IN THE DOORWAY OF HIS BEDROOM,
       LOOKING AT THE BED, THE COVERS MESSED UP, EVENING. HE'S STILL
       DRESSED, IN A DRESS SHIRT AND SLACKS; HE DOESN'T WANT TO GO TO
       SLEEP.
              8 Caption: It used to be kind of nice, when it only happened once every
                           couple of months or so.
              9 Caption: A mystery girl. His "dream girl," he called her to himself. But
                           that was before it was once a week. Then twice. Then --

[5]   **MIKE** WALKING DOWN THE SIDEWALK AWAY FROM US, TURNING
       BACK TO EYE A GORGEOUS **BLONDE** AS SHE WALKS TOWARD US, A
       CONFIDENT, UMA THURMAN TYPE. OTHER **PASSERSBY** AROUND. DAY.
       MIKE'S IN A SUIT.
              10 Caption: And it's not even like she's his type -- or what he always
                           thought was his type.
              11 Caption: She's not the kind of woman who turns his head on the
                           street. Not what he'd pick, if you asked him.

[4]

-111-

PAGE FIVE - 4 PANELS

[1]   A DREAM PANEL, FROM MIKE'S P.O.V. **MIRANDA** IS STANDING AT THE
        SINK, HER HANDS PLUNGED INTO SOAPY WATER AS SHE WASHES
        DISHES, HER HEAD AND SHOULDERS TURNING TOWARD HIM TO GREET
        HIM, SMILING BROADLY, WELCOMINGLY. THIS IS HOME.

1 Caption:	But still -- he goes to <u>sleep</u> --
2 Caption:	-- and he's seen that smile a <u>million</u> times. He knows just how she likes to have her <u>neck</u> rubbed.
3 Caption:	He knows so much <u>about</u> her --

[2]   **MIKE** SITS ON THE EDGE OF HIS BED IN THE DARKNESS, HOLDING HIS
        HEAD. HE'S IN BOXERS AND A T-SHIRT.

4 Caption:	-- and it's <u>terrifying</u>.
5 Caption:	Is he <u>cracking up</u>? Is he going <u>insane</u>? For God's sake, what comes <u>next</u>?

[3]   **MIKE** IN HIS KITCHEN, TALKING ON THE WALL-MOUNTED PHONE,
        WEARING A SWEATER.

6 Caption:	He knows he's never met her. He <u>knows</u>.
7 Mike:	<u>Mom</u>? Hi. No, I'm good, I'm <u>fine</u>.
8 Mike:	Listen, Mom --

[4]   CLOSE-UP -- **MIKE** RESTS HIS FOREHEAD ON THE WALL ABOVE THE
        PHONE AS HE TALKS, HIS FACE SHADOWED. HE'S GRASPING FOR
        STRAWS.

9 Mike:	-- do you remember a girl named <u>Miranda</u>?
10 Mike:	Maybe a couple of years <u>younger</u> than me? Short dark hair? Really light freckles across the bridge of her <u>nose</u>?

PAGE SIX - 6 PANELS

[1]   **MIKE** AT HIS DESK IN THE OFFICE, IN A SUIT, TALKING ON THE PHONE, WORRIED.

    1 Mike: Maybe in the <u>dorm</u>, Bob? On one of the other floors?

[2]   **MIKE** AT A PAY PHONE, A PARK SCENE BEHIND HIM, HE'S IN A "FOX-BROOME" SWEATSHIRT AND GYM SHORTS, HOLDING A BASKETBALL AS HE TALKS ON THE PHONE.

    2 Phone (elec):   -- doesn't sound like the kind of chick you <u>ever</u> chased back in <u>high school</u>, hoss.

    3 Phone (elec):   Not like it makes a difference. With me it was <u>blondes, blondes, blondes</u>, 'til Shelly showed up, and then <u>pow</u>!

[3]   **MIKE** SITTING IN HIS LIVING ROOM, A CORDLESS PHONE TO HIS EAR, SITTING IN A MOSTLY DARK ROOM, IN T-SHIRT, BOXERS AND BATHROBE.

    4 Mike: -- <u>know</u> it's late, Chet. Sorry -- I didn't mean to <u>wake</u> you.

    5 Mike: But -- look, back in <u>sixth grade</u>, I've been trying to remember all the --

    6 Mike: <u>Chet</u>?

[4]   **MIKE** SITS ON THE COUCH, HIS FOREARMS RESTING ON HIS THIGHS, THE PHONE DANGLING FROM HIS HAND. HE'S GLUM, WE'RE PULLED BACK, DISTANCED FROM HIM.

    No Copy

[5]   ON HIS **HAND**, HOLDING SOME PILLS, TAPPED FROM A PRESCRIPTION BOTTLE OUT INTO HIS PALM.

    7 Caption: The <u>pills</u> -- they stopped it, knocked him out. For a little while. Then she started to show up <u>anyway</u>.

    8 Caption: Maybe -- maybe if he took <u>more</u> of them --

[6]   **MIKE** HEARS A SOUND BEHIND HIM AND STARTS TO TURN --

    9 FX: SHK

    10 Mike: <u>Huh</u>?

    11 Mike: What's that --

PAGE SEVEN - 2 PANELS

[1]   -- AND WE GET A CLOSE-UP ON HIS **FACE** AS HIS EYES GO WIDE --
        1 Mike (sl):   -- noise?

[2]   -- AND THERE, IN HIS APARTMENT, STANDS (OR HANGS) THE **HANGED
        MAN**, MIST CURLING AROUND HIM AS ALWAYS. BIG PANEL.
        No Copy

[7]

PAGE EIGHT - 6 PANELS

[1]   MIKE GAPES, AMAZED AND SCARED. THE HANGED MAN HOVERS
DISPASSIONATELY IN FRONT OF HIM, HIS HEAD LOLLING.
        1 Mike: Th-the Hanged Man?!
        2 Mike: But y-you never leave Shadow Hill -- !
    3 Caption (hm):   I go where I am needed. And tonight, one of the places I am
                  needed is here.
          [John: The Hanged Man doesn't speak. Instead, he communicates
              through magic, a sort of telepathy; his words, marked (hm),
            should be in gothic-looking (but readable) captions. Thanks.]

[2]   ON MIKE, CONFUSED.
    4 Caption: He does not hear the words. Rather, they simply appear in
                  his mind --
        5 Mike: Here -- ?
    6 Caption: -- not so much spoken as inscribed.

[3]   ON THE HANGED MAN.
    7 Caption (hm):   Your dreams trouble you. And in turn they trouble reality. You
                  fear you are going mad.
    8 Caption (hm):   But you are not.

[4]   THE HANGED MAN REACHES A BONY ARM OUT --
    9 Caption (hm):   Here ...

[5]   -- AN ALARMED MIKE STARTS TO BACK AWAY ---
    10 Mike: Hey -- what --

[6]   -- AND THE HANGED MAN'S FOREFINGER TOUCHES MIKE'S FOREHEAD.
MISTS SWIRL UP AROUND MIKE AS HE GOES INTO A TRANCE.
    11 Caption (hm):   ... I shall show you.
     12 Caption: And suddenly --

PAGE NINE - 4 PANELS

[1]   CLOSE ON **A MOUTH** BLOWING A REFEREE'S WHISTLE (THIS YOU CAN SHOW FROM THE SIDE, BRENT).
        1 Caption: -- it's <u>1943</u>, in the <u>First National Bank</u> on Novick Avenue --
        2 FX: WHEEEEEEEET

[2]   PULL BACK TO REVEAL: WE'RE IN A BANK LOBBY, CIRCA 1943. THE **TIME-KEEPER**, A SUPER-VILLAIN WHO CAN STOP TIME, STANDS ON ONE OF THOSE TABLES THAT YOU FILL OUT DEPOSIT SLIPS AT, HIS **MEN** OUT ON THE FLOOR AMONG THE **CUSTOMERS**, WHO ARE FROZEN IN TIME BY THE WHISTLE-BLAST. THE TIME-KEEPER IS A SHORT, BEAKY-LOOKING GUY WITH A RECEDING HAIRLINE AND LONGISH HAIR, GIVING HIM A BIRDISH LOOK; HE WEARS A VERTICALLY-STRIPED SHORT-SLEEVED REFEREE'S SHIRT, A BOW TIE, BLACK PANTS AND HIGH-TOP SNEAKERS. ONE HAND HOLDS A WHISTLE, WHICH IS ON A LANYARD AROUND HIS NECK; THE OTHER HOLDS A LARGE POCKET-WATCH CONNECTED BY A CHAIN TO HIS BELT. HIS MEN WEAR DOMINO MASKS AND JACKETS WITH A CLOCK-FACE ON THE BACK.
        3 Time-Keeper: Very <u>good</u> --- they're frozen <u>stock-still</u> in time!
        4 Time-Keeper: To <u>work</u>, my Tempus Fugitives -- time waits for <u>no man</u>!

[3]   SUDDENLY (BIG PANEL), IN THROUGH THE PLATE-GLASS WINDOW CRASH THE **ALL-AMERICAN** (A PATRIOTIC HERO WHOSE COSTUME IS DESIGNED AROUND A FOOTBALL UNIFORM) AND **SLUGGER**, HIS KID SIDEKICK, WHOSE COSTUME IS DESIGNED AROUND A BASEBALL UNIFORM. SLUGGER CARRIES A BASEBALL BAT. THE **TIME-KEEPER** REACTS IN SHOCK.
        5 FX: KRASSSSH
        6 All-American: <u>Hold</u> it, Time-Keeper! I'll have to see your O.P.A. Bank-Robbery <u>Coupon Book</u>!
        7 All-American: <u>Rationing</u>, you know!
        8 Time-Keeper (SB):   The <u>All-American</u>!
        9 Slugger: And don't forget <u>Slugger</u>, the Junior Dynamo!
        10 Slugger: We captured one of your men's <u>chrono-packs</u>, buster -- and duplicated your <u>time-field</u>! And <u>that</u> means --

[4]   CLOSE ON THE ACTION AS SLUGGER'S **BAT** SHATTERS THE TIME-KEEPER'S **POCKET-WATCH**.
        11 FX: KSSH
        12 Slugger: -- your time's <u>up</u>!

[9]

PAGE TEN - 5 PANELS

[1]   ON **MIKE**, IN THE DARKENED APARTMENT, CONFUSED. THE MISTS ARE
        RETREATING SOMEWHAT.
        1 Mike: But -- all this was so long ago --
        2 Mike: -- what does it have to do with me --- ?

[2]   THE **HANGED MAN** LOOKS AT HIM, IMPASSIVE.
        No Copy

[3]   ON **MIKE**, THE MISTS RISING, LOOKING SORTA SHEEPISH.
        3 Mike: Okay, okay, I get the message.
        4 Mike: I'll wait and see...
        5 Caption: And the mists rise up around him once more ---

[4]   IN THE **TIME-KEEPER'S** LAIR (CLOCKS AND A GEAR MOTIF
        EVERYWHERE). HE'S GESTICULATING WITH A NEWSPAPER AND A LIFE
        MAGAZINE, OTHERS PILED HELTER-SKELTER ON A TABLE NEARBY. THE
        TABLE ALSO HOLDS A FORTIES RADIO. WE DON'T NEED TO SEE BOTH
        THE MAGAZINE AND THE NEWSPAPER CLEARLY THIS PANEL, BUT
        BETWEEN THIS AND THE NEXT WE SHOULD SEE THEM BOTH. THE
        LAMPLIGHTER, SEEN ON THE LIFE COVER, IS DRESSED IN COLONIAL
        GARB (TRICORN HAT, CLOAK, KNEE-BREECHES, BUCKLE SHOES) A
        MASK, AND CARRIES A GLOWING LANTERN.
        6 Caption: -- and the Time-Keeper has escaped from jail, but finds his
                         plans blocked on all sides --
        7 Time-Keeper: The All-American! The Astro-Naut! The Lamplighter!
        8 Time-Keeper: Is there no end to these costumed crusaders?!
        9 Headline: **ASTRO-NAUT CAPTURES ERSATZ ED**
        10 LIFE Cover: **WHO IS THE LAMPLIGHTER?**
        11 Radio (elec; sl): -- Blackout Bandits foiled today by the All-American and Slugger --

[5]   CLOSER ON THE **TIME-KEEPER**, GESTICULATING, ANGRY, DETERMINED.
        12 Time-Keeper: Very well! I've spent my life mastering time -- working, while
                         others mocked me as an idiotic dreamer!
        13 Time-Keeper: If these "superheroes" stand in my way, I'll simply go back in
                         time --
        14 Time-Keeper (SB): -- and prevent them from ever being born!!

[10]

PAGE ELEVEN - 5 PANELS

[1]　　THE **TIME-KEEPER**, WEARING HI-TECH (WELL, FORTIES HI-TECH) GLOVES, RIPS A HOLE IN REALITY, THE GLOWING EFFECT OF IT VERY DRAMATIC. THIS PANEL SHOULD HAVE STRONG DIAGONAL ACTION (NOT UNLIKE THAT PANEL WE BOTH LIKED IN NIGHT FORCE, BRENT), SO WE GET A SENSE OF THE MOTION OF IT.

　　　　1 Caption:　　-- and Michael Tenicek <u>knows</u>, without understanding why, that the patterns of time can be <u>rewoven</u> and <u>altered</u> --

[2]　　THE **TIME-KEEPER** HAS STEPPED THROUGH THE RIFT INTO THE TIME DOMAIN, AND IS LOOKING UP AT THE MASSIVE FIGURE OF **ETERNEON**, A COSMIC SIXTIES/SEVENTIES VILLAIN IN COOL ARMOR.

　　　　2 Time-Keeper:　<u>Eh</u>? Who are <u>you</u>?
　　　　3 Eterneon (e):　I am <u>Eterneon</u>, Lord of Time.
　　　　4 Eterneon (e):　Go <u>back</u>, little human. You are <u>disturbing</u> my domain -- wielding forces you cannot <u>hope</u> to comprehend.
　　　　[John: Eterneon (e) gets some kind of funky cosmic lettering. Thanks.]

[3]　　ON THE **TIME-KEEPER**, SHOUTING HIS DEFIANCE, CHRONAL ENERGY CRACKLING AROUND HIM LIKE LIGHTNING --

　　　　5 Time-Keeper (SB):　I don't <u>care</u>!
　　　　6 Time-Keeper:　I'm not going to be a <u>nothing</u> anymore! I'm not going to be a <u>loser</u>!
　　　　7 Time-Keeper:　I've <u>broken</u> time! I've bent it to my <u>will</u>!

[4]　　THE **TIME-KEEPER** LEAPS FORWARD, GROWING, SUFFUSED WITH THE ENERGY. AGAIN, STRONG DIAGONAL ACTION; THE ANGER OF THIS AND THE POWER OF IT ARE AS IMPORTANT AS WHAT'S ACTUALLY HAPPENING, MAYBE MORE SO.

　　　　8 Time-Keeper:　And if <u>you</u> won't bow to me <u>too</u> --

[5]　　ON THE **ENERGY** AND THE **SPEED LINES**, CRACKLING WITH POWER AND RAGE.

　　　　9 Time Keeper (SB):　-- I'll <u>kill you</u> -- !
　　　　10 Caption:　-- or, if handled roughly, they can be <u>torn asunder</u> -- !

[11]

PAGES TWELVE & THIRTEEN - 7 PANELS TOTAL

THIS IS A DOUBLE-PAGE SPREAD, WITH PANEL ONE BLEEDING BEHIND EVERYTHING, AND PANELS 2-7 SUPERIMPOSED ALONG THE BOTTOM.

[1]   THE **TIME-KEEPER**, NOW GIANT AND GLOWING, IS GRAPPLING WITH **ETERNEON** AS A TIME-STORM, SOMETHING LIKE A CROSS BETWEEN THE INSIDE OF A TORNADO, A HURRICANE AND A WHIRLPOOL, SWIRLS AROUND THEM. VERY VIOLENT, VERY BIG.
         1 Caption: He feels the power of the time-storm their battle triggers --
         2 Caption: -- and sees the changes it wreaks --

[2]   WE SEE THE **SILVER AGENT** LEAPING OFF A ROOFTOP TOWARD A **TYRANNOSAURUS REX**. EARLY SIXTIES.
         3 Caption: He sees time thrown into chaos --
         4 Silver Agent: Hey, Rover! Up here!

[3]   WE SEE **M.P.H.** STRUGGLING TO HIS FEET AS **VIKINGS** CHARGE TOWARD HIM, THEIR **LEADER**, WIELDING A BIG-ASS DOUBLE-BLADED AXE, CHARGING OVER THE TOP OF A PARKED CAR, HIS FOOT PLANTED ON ITS ROOF.
         5 Caption: -- all eras collapsing, entangling with each other --
         6 M.P.H. (sl):   Not Vikings. Tell me it's not Vikings...

[4]   WE SEE **SAMARITAN** EVAPORATING AS **WINGED VICTORY** REACHES THROUGH HIM, TRYING TO CATCH HIM.
         7 Caption: He sees heroes unmade --
 8 Winged Victory (SB):   Samaritan!

[5]   WE SEE THE **FIRST FAMILY** FACING TOWARD US, TURNING TO LOOK OVER THEIR SHOULDERS AS IN THE BACKGROUND, ASTRO CITY FADES AWAY. THIS IS THE MID-SEVENTIES, SO **NICK** AND **NATALIE** ARE TEENAGERS, AND THERE'S NO REX OR ASTRA YET.
         9 Caption: -- and worse --
         10 Dr. Furst: Astro City --
         11 Natalie: -- it's disappearing!

[6]   WE SEE THE **SILVER AGENT**, THE **OLD SOLDIER**, THE **N-FORCER**, **BEAUTIE**, THE **LAMPLIGHTER** AND **STARWOMAN** CHARGING FORWARD, WRESTLING WITH DARK BLACK **TENTACLES** FROM NOWHERE THAT IMPEDE THEIR PROGRESS.
         12 Caption: And he sees the last, desperate battle --

         [more]

PAGES TWELVE & THIRTEEN - 7 PANELS TOTAL (continued)

[7]   AND WE SEE THE **HANGED MAN**, THE **HALCYON HIPPIE** (THE BEATNIK IN A NEW INCARNATION, WITH STYLIZED LONG HAIR AND BEARD, A VEST AND LOVE BEADS), **NICK FURST** (AS AN ADULT) AND **WINGED VICTORY** FLOATING IN A MYSTIC CONFIGURATION AS AN "INFINITY" FIGURE MADE OF ENERGY ARCS AROUND AND BEHIND THEM. THE HALCYON HIPPIE IS IN A LOTUS POSITION, THE OTHERS IN CRUCIFORM.

        13 Caption: -- to <u>reweave</u> time -- to <u>undo</u> the damage --

        14 Caption: -- and to set all, once more, to <u>rights</u>.

PAGE FOURTEEN - 6 PANELS

[1]   WE'RE BACK IN MIKE'S LIVING ROOM, PULLED BACK FROM THE
      CHARACTERS. **MIKE** IS TAKING THIS ALL IN, AND THE MIST THAT WAS
      AROUND HIM IS FLOWING BACK TO THE **HANGED MAN**, IN THE
      SHADOWS BEYOND HIM.
              1 Mike: When ... when did this all <u>happen</u>?
              2 Caption: <u>Yesterday</u>. Five <u>decades</u> ago. Does it <u>matter</u>?

[2]   ON **MIKE**, SLOWLY ARTICULATING WHAT HE'S LEARNED.
              3 Mike: I ... <u>understand</u>, I think.
              4 Mike: She <u>died</u>, didn't she? I knew her, and she died in that ... that
                            <u>maelstrom</u> ...
              5 Caption (hm):   She was your <u>wife</u>. And she never <u>existed</u>.

[3]   ON THE **HANGED MAN**.
              6 Caption (hm):   The chronal reconstruction was not exact. Air Ace first battled the
                                Barnstormers on a Sunday, not a Monday...
              7 Mike: My ... <u>wife</u>?
              8 Caption (hm):   ...and as a result, her <u>grandparents</u> never <u>met</u>.

[4]   ON THE **HANGED MAN**.
              9 Caption (hm):   For the most part, the new reality is <u>whole</u>. But close bonds such
                                as yours ... they create a <u>weakness</u> in the fabric of time...
              10 Caption (hm): ... one that could let through ... <u>dangerous things</u>. But the
                                weakness is <u>healed</u> by your understanding.

[5]   ON THE **HANGED MAN** AND **MIKE**; MIKE'S HEAD IS COMING AROUND
      AT THE HANGED MAN'S OFFER.
              11 Caption (hm): I cannot <u>return</u> her to you ... that is beyond even my power. But if
                                the pain is <u>too much</u> ...
              12 Caption (hm): ...I <u>can</u> allow you to forget...

[6]   ON **MIKE**, UNSURE.
              13 Mike: <u>Forget</u> her?
              14 Mike: I ... uh ...

PAGE FIFTEEN - 6 PANELS

[1]   ON **MIKE**; HE'S MADE HIS DECISION. THE **HANGED MAN** ACCEPTS IT --
          1 Mike: <u>No</u>. I don't want to forget.
         2 Caption (hm):   As you <u>wish</u>.

[2]   -- AND TURNS STARTING TO GLIDE TOWARD THE WALL --
         3 Caption (hm):   You will not <u>remember</u> this visit, though your sense of
                              understanding will <u>remain</u>.
         4 Caption (hm):   And now, I have <u>others</u> to visit tonight, so...

[3]   -- AND **MIKE** HOLDS OUT A HAND, CALLING TO HIM TO STOP,
SUDDENLY UNSURE. LOOKING PAST MIKE AT THE **HANGED MAN**,
MAYBE AN ARM IS ALREADY PASSING THROUGH THE WALL?
         5 Mike: <u>Wait</u>!
         6 Mike: <u>Others</u>? What -- uh -- what do <u>most</u> people choose?
         7 Mike: Do they <u>forget</u>, or --

[4]   3/4 REAR PROFILE ON THE **HANGED MAN** AS HE TURNS HALFWAY
BACK.
         8 Caption: For a moment, he thinks he sees the twitch of a <u>smile</u> under
                           that burlap hood --

[5]   CLOSE ON THE **HANGED MAN**.
         9 Caption (hm):   <u>No one</u> forgets. No one.
        10 Caption (hm):   Good <u>night</u>, Michael Tenicek. Sleep <u>well</u>.

[6]   THE HANGED MAN IS GONE, AND ONLY A FEW TENDRILS OF MIST
REMAIN. **MIKE** IS LOOKING AT WHERE HE ONCE WAS...
        11 Caption: And then he's <u>gone</u> --
        12 Caption: -- and the memory of him <u>fades</u> like smoke on the summer
                         breeze --

PAGE SIXTEEN - 3 PANELS

[1]   ON **MIKE**, IN BED, ASLEEP, SPRAWLED ON HIS BACK.
          1 Caption: And Michael Tenicek <u>sleeps</u>, without drugs or fear --

[2]   AND **MIRANDA'S** THERE, TURNING TOWARD US AND SMILING AS SHE
          BRUSHES HER HAIR (MAYBE SHE'S IN A ROBE OR NIGHTGOWN?) --
          2 Caption: -- and the <u>dreams</u> come. The dreams of <u>Miranda</u>.
          3 Caption: He <u>knew</u> her. He <u>knows</u> that. In another time, another world
                              -- he <u>knew</u> her.
          4 Caption: And he <u>loved</u> her

[3]   AND WE END WITH AN EXTERIOR SHOT OF MIKE'S NEIGHBORHOOD, AS
          THE **HANGED MAN**, TRAILING MIST, GLIDES UPWARD AND FORWARD,
          HEADED FOR HIS NEXT "HOUSE CALL"...
          5 Caption: And that makes all the <u>difference</u>.
          6 Blurb: You Are Now Leaving Astro City
                              Please Drive Carefully

Greg Rucka had already established himself as a novelist before he broke onto the comics scene with the award-winning *Whiteout*. This script is from the first issue of *Whiteout: Melt,* the second miniseries.

I'll let Greg's staccato script speak for itself. But I do have to say that I've never seen another comics writer use endnotes.

– Nat Gertler, December 2001

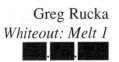
<u>Page 1</u>

<u>ONE:</u>
This is a landscape, a huge wide longshot of the polar plateau, running in along the Queen Maude Mountains (just for perspective, you understand). Tiny specks of SCOTT's party working their way south.

STETKO (caption):   It was **war**.

STETKO (caption):   Calling it anything else is bullshit, pure and simple.

<u>TWO:</u>
This is actually a POV shot from SCOTT's view—looking ahead at the vast blurry flatness, the hints of a tent visible as well as a flag pole, a piece of fabric snapping in the wind.

STETKO (caption):   It wasn't until Amundsen reached Madeira that he told the stunned crew of the *Fram* where they were headed.

STETKO (caption):   Then he sent a telegram to Scott, who was wintering in Melbourne…

<u>THREE:</u>
Reverse, with side of a tent in the FG, as well as a portion of the Norwegian flag flying on its pole, as SCOTT trudges his way closer. Face hidden under hood and wrap, but the eyes should hint at what we'll see in Panel 6.

Behind SCOTT are WILSON, OATES, EVANS, and BOWERS [GR: not that the names matter, but I know you dig that historical accuracy stuff, Steve.] All the men look whipped, and are pulling their own sledges.

Snow whips around them in the wind.

STETKO (caption):   'Beg leave to inform you *Fram* proceeding to Antarctic. Amundsen.'

STETKO (caption):   Talk about passive/aggressive.

<u>FOUR:</u>
OTS SCOTT, as he leans into the tent, reaching for the note that waits on the floor. In the tent are some supplies of food, maybe a blanket or two. Token courtesy from Amundsen. The note is addressed to ROBERT F. SCOTT.

STETKO (caption):   Scott and his party reached the Pole on January 17, 1912…

1

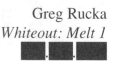

STETKO (caption):   …33 days **after** Amundsen.

STETKO (caption):   Amundsen had **another** message for Scott waiting there…

FIVE:
CU of the paper in SCOTT's hand, opened. Handwritten in English is the following:

Scott—
    I WIN.
        Amundsen

STETKO (caption):   Didn't really say that.

SIX:
CU of ROBERT FALCON SCOTT, his expression as he suffers the most crushing defeat imaginable. Remember, he had tried twice already to reach the pole—he was doing this for his country as well as himself—and he knows that, not only has he failed, but he and his crew are all liable to die.

Incredibly tragic in this moment, I think.

[GR: I've got a reference photograph of Scott if you need it.]

STETKO (caption):   It didn't **need** to.

2

Page 2

ONE:
View of SCOTT's party, trudging towards us from the far BG. Obscured by snow. The full party.

STETKO (caption):   Evans, Scott's second-in-command, died one month later.

TWO:
View of SCOTT's party, now minus Evans.

STETKO (caption):   Oates killed himself a month after that, walked out of the tent in the middle of a blizzard…

STETKO (caption):   'I am just going outside and may be some time,' he said.

THREE:
View of SCOTT's party, SCOTT, leading, now looking back. Now minus Evans and Oates.

STETKO (caption):   Very British of Oates. Very proper.

STETKO (caption):   They never found his body.

FOUR:
SCOTT, BOWERS, and WILSON. Frost on their faces. Frost-bitten, emaciated—they starved as much as froze to death—hunted and haunted.

STETKO (caption):   The blizzard started on March 21, 1912.

STETKO (caption):   Scott's last entry was dated March 29.

FIVE:
Interior of Scott's tent. SCOTT, BOWERS, and WILSON all dead, frozen solid.

STETKO (caption):   Their bodies were found eight months later.

STETKO (caption):   Casualties of war.

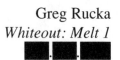

Page 3

ONE:
View of an airplane flying in the Antarctic sky. Not sure what the model would be, but it's a German airplane, and it's about 1939, now.

STETKO (caption):   The race to the pole over, the new war was waged for the continent itself.

STETKO (caption):   No tanks, no bombers, no offensives.

STETKO (caption):   Rather a bloodless land grab, and when the snow-dust settled—

TWO:
New angle on the airplane, banking, and we see it's side door is open and a FIGURE is dumping out bags of tiny metal objects.

STETKO (caption):   —Argentina, Australia, Chile, France, New Zealand, Norway, and the UK all made claims to Antarctica.

STETKO (caption):   The US and the Russians **didn't**, but both have reserved the right to do so if the mood should strike them.

THREE:
CU of one of the METAL SWASTIKAS stuck into the ice. Beyond it [depending on how you want to draw this] are scattered dozens more.

STETKO (caption):   During WW2 the Nazis made their play for the Ice …

STETKO (caption):   …scattering thousands of metal swastikas all over the polar plateau, sort of the way a dog **pisses** on its territory.

STETKO (caption):   It didn't work. Nobody cared.

FOUR:
GLOVED hand of GI JOE is reaching for one of the swastikas in previous. On his arm is an AMERICAN FLAG. Beyond JOE are countless other SOLDIERS, moving heavy equipment, Caterpillar tractors. It's 1946 now.

STETKO (caption):   Operation Highjump was a different story.

STETKO (caption):   Officially a training mission, Highjump brought 4700 men to the Ice, building bases and airfields…

4

FIVE:

All of those SOLDIERS are now busily erecting a base. Now they're SOVIET
SOLDIERS, though, if you can manage the distinction.

STETKO (caption):   …and the Soviets responded in kind.

STETKO (caption):   The Cold War and the Ice, a match made in heaven.

Page 4

ONE:

A group of ARGENTINE SOLDIERS are firing machine guns at us. The guns are canted a little high, as if firing over the heads of their targets (which, in fact, they are).

STETKO (caption):   Overt acts of war, though, **those** have been rare…

STETKO (caption):   …Argentina opened fire on the UK in 1952…

TWO:

Angle showing the SOLDIERS with their backs to us. They've stopped firing. In the BG a group of BRITISH SCIENTISTS are running for a nearby plane. The Union Jack has fallen by the side of a burnt out station.

STETKO (caption):   …**warning** shots as the Argentines and the Chileans tried to flex some territorial muscle.

THREE:

A landing strip cut into the Ice. Two huts have been built, one with Argentina's flag, one with Chile's, stand nearly side-to-side. Maybe twenty soldiers are united around them.

Converging on their point are easily one hundred ROYAL MARINES, armed and ready.

STETKO (caption):   Britain responded with a couple **boatloads** of Royal Marines.

FOUR:

Same location, but the huts are gone and so are all of the soldiers. Barren, icy, not worth dying for at all.

STETKO (caption):   One of the many factors, incidentally, that lead to the war in the Falklands.

FIVE:

Extreme long shot, the endless polar plateau. Sastrugi carved into the surface.

NO COPY.

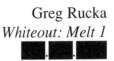

Page 5

ONE:
Political shot, like a photograph. This should be the biggest panel here.

Several men gathered around a table with four identically bound treaties all set on a table. All the men are smiling for the camera. The following nations are represented—maybe there are tiny flags on the table: Argentina, Australia, Belgium, Chile, France, Japan, New Zealand, Norway, the USSR, the UK, and the USA.

STETKO (caption):   June 23, 1961.

STETKO (caption):   The Antarctic Treaty—drafted two years **earlier**—comes into effect.

STETKO (caption):   Article I, Subsection 1, addresses the military issue.

STETKO (caption):   "Antarctica shall be used for **peaceful** purposes only. There shall be **prohibited**…

STETKO (caption):   …any measure of a military nature, such as… military bases…military maneuvers…testing of any type of weapon."

TWO:
A HANDSHAKE over the bound copies.

STETKO (caption):   Nearly 80% of the world's governments have added their signatures to the Treaty since its ratification.

THREE:
Another photograph. Two men, arms around each others' shoulders. RUSSIAN is holding a miniature Soviet flag in his hand, holding it out towards the camera. The other, AMERICAN, is holding a miniature American flag. Both are smiling.

STETKO (caption):   There has been no known breach of the treaty…

FOUR:
Another photograph, wide shot. The RUSSIAN has moved to one side, and is talking with KGB DUDE, looking over his shoulder at the AMERICAN.

AMERICAN has moved to the opposite side where he is talking to CIA DUDE. AMERICAN is looking over his shoulder at the RUSSIAN.

Both men are still smiling at one another.

7

-131-

STETKO (caption):   …no military action or **violation**…

STETKO (caption):   …to this very day.

-132-

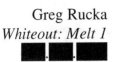

Page 6

ONE:
CU—and if this is difficult for the reader to make out at first, that's just fine. Should be small, and part of the following sequence of four panels, all in one row.

We're looking at a SCIENTIST's throat while a SPESNAZ pushed his combat knife up and into it, entering at the trachea, moving up to the chin, and then cutting out to the left.

Knife has just entered trachea. No blood.

NO COPY.

TWO:
CU, same, and now the blade has reached the chin. Remember, the knife blade has entered at an upwards angle—the tip is probably through the roof of this poor bastard's mouth right now.

Barest leaking of blood from the entrance wound.

NO COPY.

THREE:
CU, same, the knife now slicing out to the left. Still just a bare hint of the blood.

NO COPY.

FOUR:
CU, same, but the knife is out, and now the blood is gushing forth.

NO COPY.

FIVE:
This should be the rest of the page. We're inside Tayshetskaya, a Russian research base just inside Wilkes Land. We're in a lab.

In FG, the SCIENTIST we've just watched being murdered is pitching forward in the FG, eyes still open, wondering how he just died. Behind him, knife down, one hand still extended in the act of releasing him, is SPESNAZ 1[i]. He's a big motherfucker, and if we could see beyond his mask, we'd see the look of grim satisfaction on his face.

In BG we see that other SPESNAZ—Numbers 2 and 3—are doing much the same thing to other SCIENTISTS. There is already one body on the floor. <u>All are using their knives</u>.

NO COPY.

Page 7

ONE:
Angle through the doorway, looking into the lab. Another SCIENTIST is dead on the floor in the FG.

Inside the lab, in BG, we see the three SPESNAZ moving. ONE and TWO are pulling a cabinet back from the wall. THREE is opening a pouch on his belt.

NO COPY.

TWO:
CU of THREE's hands as he plants a small Semtex charge (it's gonna look like a small cube of play-dough) against the wall. Two wires run from the cube.

NO COPY.

THREE:
Angle from opposite corner, SPESNAZ 1 and 2 are facing towards us, covering their heads and ears. SPESNAZ 3 is opposite the cube, turning away. The wires run to the detonator in his hand.

SPESNAZ 3:   <Cover!>

FOUR:
Small explosion.

SFX: KRBAM

FIVE:
Reveal, same angle as previous, that the blast has opened a hole in the wall and floor. Smoke wisping around.

SPESNAZ 1 (off):   <Get down there.>

SIX:
From the doorway again. SPESNAZ 1 is coming towards us, stepping over bodies. SPESNAZ 2 and 3 are disappearing down the newly opened hole.

NO COPY.

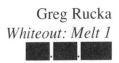

Page 8

ONE:
Close angle on the entrance to Tayshetskaya, as SPESNAZ 1 stands outside, gesturing back the way he came. SPESNAZ 4 is by the doorway, looking at him.

SPESNAZ 1:   <Help them.>

TWO:
Angle view of Tayshetskaya, the compound. It's a small facility—fourteen men—and SPESNAZ 1 stands outside of the Main Building. Two other buildings are standing nearby, as well as a third, elongated sausage like structure. In the open space of the compound are a couple of the camp vehicles—SnoCats—and six parked snowmobiles, three with trailers. The snowmobiles are all facing away from the entrance.

By the side of the "sausage" is SPESNAZ 5 (SASHA)[ii], kneeling.

SPESNAZ 1:   <How is it going?>

SASHA: <Almost done.>

THREE:
Low angle along the side of the "sausage." Since all printing on the structure is in Cyrillic, we're going to emphasize this with the universal symbols for No Smoking and Flammable, both of which are painted on the structure.

SASHA is planting the last of a sequence of shaped charges against the base. If you can manage it, another charge might be visible further down the length of the "sausage."

SASHA: <Ready when you say.>

FOUR:
View of entrance as SPESNAZ 1 moves out of the way as SASHA comes to join him. From the hallway is emerging SPESNAZ 2, carrying a crate—about the size of a Stinger missile. We cannot see what's written on the crate.

SPESNAZ 1:   <Load them.>

SPESNAZ 1:   <Sasha? Inside and give me a count.>

SASHA: <Right away.>

FIVE:

11

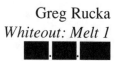
High angle looking down on the compound as SPESNAZ 1 remains standing by the entrance. SPESNAZ 2 has loaded his crate onto the back of his snowmobile and is climbing aboard. SPESNAZ 3 and 4 are now emerging with identical crates.

NO COPY.

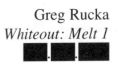

Page 9

ONE:
Wide shot showing Tayshetskaya, view from a distance. The Main Building is in BG, with SPESNAZ 1 by the door. All of the other SPESNAZ are on their snowmobiles, except SASHA. They've finished loading.

In the FG, crouched, is BUNIN.

BUNIN (small):   <…God dear God please help me…>

TWO:
SPESNAZ 1 is turning to face the door as SASHA comes back, running.

SASHA: <Thirteen.>

SPESNAZ 1:   <There are supposed to be—>

SASHA: <I **know**.>

THREE:
OTS SPESNAZ 1 as he starts barking orders. The SPESNAZ on the snowmobiles are getting off them and scattering to comply.

SPESNAZ 1:   <One got out! Find him!>

FOUR:
OTS BUNIN, watching as the SPESNAZ below scatter and begin searching.

BUNIN: <…no no no oh shit, oh shit…>

Page 10

ONE:
Looking at where BUNIN has been laying on the ice. He's getting up and making a break for it—ever try running on ice?—panicked and justly terrified. He's wearing standard ECW, and is carrying a pouch of some sort—he was out getting samples.

BUNIN: <…run just run—>

TWO:
Angle as SASHA sees BUNIN running. SASHA is bringing his machine gun to bear.

SASHA: <Got him! Got him he's—>

THREE:
View of BUNIN falling, body catching all of a three-round burst from SASHA's silenced MP-5. <u>One of the rounds catches BUNIN in the head.</u>

SPESNAZ 1 (off):   <**DON'T** SHOOT—>

SFX: thwp thwp thnk

FOUR:
SPESNAZ 1 has grabbed SASHA and is rattling the other man.

SPESNAZ 1:   <I said **don't** shoot, you fucking cunt!>

SASHA: <But he—>

SPESNAZ 1:   <Get the body, put it by the tanks!>

FIVE:
Wide angle. All the SPESNAZ but SASHA are back on their snowmobiles. SASHA is setting BUNIN's body by the tanks.

SPESNAZ 1:   <Move that cow's ass of yours, Sasha! Come on!>

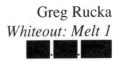
Page 11

ONE:
CU of BUNIN's corpse lying further from the tanks than is prudent. A charge on the sausage is visible in the BG.

NO COPY.

TWO:
Tayshetskaya in mid-explosion. The "sausage" has erupted in flame, already spreading to the other structure. BUNIN's body is beginning to burn. The SnoCats are on their sides, tumbling away, canopies shattering in the blast.

The six snowmobiles are all zipping away, already out of the range of the blast.

[This is, as they say in the porn industry, the money shot. Make it as big and nasty and impressive as you like.]

NO COPY.

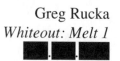

Page 12

ONE:
View of STETKO, leaning back on a bench, legs extended. She's in a tank-top and shorts and sneakers, taking in the sunlight, wearing her shades. Her mauled hand is cradling a bag of popcorn, and she's scattering a handful with the other. She looks relaxed and about as happy as she's liable to get. She is, for our reference, about 18 months older than when last we saw her, which puts her at around 34 years old, now. Maybe another line or two on her face. Her hair is longer than before, maybe just below the shoulders, although it's currently tied back in a high pony-tail.

She's in the Christchurch Botanic Gardens, and surrounded by lush greenery heavily in bloom. If we were working in color, this would be a visual assault after the monochromatic world on the last seven pages.

She's having a generally nice vacation, feeding the birds.

STETKO (caption):   I'd forgotten how much I like being **warm**.

STETKO (caption):   How much I like seeing **green**—

TWO:
CU STETKO's expression as her smile turns into a patented Carrie pokerface at the sound of the voice.

MILLER (off panel):   Deputy Marshal Stetko? Deputy Marshal Carrie Stetko?

THREE:
Angle looking past STETKO on the bench as she leans forward, scattering more popcorn for the birds. MILLER is approaching from the side. He's in his late 30s, white, wearing a suit and looking fairly agitated.

STETKO doesn't even look at him.

MILLER: I've been looking all over Christchurch for you—

STETKO: And who the hell are you?

MILLER: Miller, I'm from the consulate. I **tried** paging you—

STETKO: Left it in my room.

FOUR:
Different angle, STETKO continues to feed the birds. MILLER still stands off to a side, looking slightly unsure of how to proceed.

16

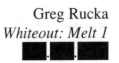

FIVE:
STETKO is now leaning back again. MILLER is still in the same position.

MILLER: There's been an **incident**…at Tayshetskaya…

SIX:
BIRDS nibbling at a pile of spilled popcorn.

MILLER (off panel):   …you're wanted at the consulate.

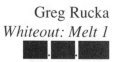

Page 13

ONE:
Briefing Room at the US Consulate in Christchurch. Large conference table, high-backed leather chairs. At the far end of the room hangs the Great Seal of the United States of America. An American flag hangs from a pole in the corner.

Coming through the door to the right are MILLER and STETKO.

At the head of the table is ROSS.

At the end of the table by Ross is GERETY.

ROSS: Marshal Stetko, I'm David Ross. Pleasure to meet you.

STETKO: Why are you ruining my vacation, Mr. Ross?

ROSS: Miller, make sure an LC-130 is standing by.

MILLER: Sir.

TWO:
Angle OTS on ROSS, where STETKO is looking at MILLER, who is now leaving the room.

STETKO: If that plane's for **me**, don't bother. I've **still** got eight days before I'm back on the Ice.

ROSS: Why don't you have a seat?

THREE:
STETKO has taken the near chair, looking both peeved and curious. ROSS is opening a file folder on the table in front of him.

ROSS: You know **Tayshetskaya**, Marshal?

STETKO: One of the Russian research **stations** in Wilkes Land. About a thousand klicks from McMurdo.

ROSS: Not anymore.

FOUR:
ROSS has slid the open folder to STETKO. She's reaching for it with her good hand.

STETKO: Meaning?

18

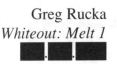
ROSS: Meaning between 0420 and 0520 local this morning, Tayshetskaya **exploded**. Boom. Gone.

FIVE:
CU STETKO's reaction, mild surprise, as she looks down at the document before her.

ROSS (off panel): Radio traffic between Vostok and Leningradskaya has been hot since then.

ROSS (off panel): There were 14 men at Tayshetskaya, Marshal. Support and science. All are presumed dead.

Page 14

ONE:
New angle, STETKO looking at ROSS. GERETY is waiting patiently in his seat.

STETKO: It's a tragedy, Mr. Ross. But it's a **Russian** tragedy.

STETKO: Why are you telling this to **me**?

ROSS: James?

TWO:
OTS STETKO, looking at GERETY, who is just as mellow and calm as can be.

GERETY: It might **not** have been an accident.

STETKO: And you are?

GERETY: James.

THREE:
STETKO's reaction. She's getting close to losing her patience with this.

STETKO: Of course. **Another** fucking spook. CIA? NSA?

FOUR:
New angle, looking across the table. STETKO still facing GERETY, ROSS at the end, following the conversation.

GERETY: Tayshetskaya wasn't **only** a research station, Marshal.

GERETY: We have intelligence indicating the site was also used as an **arms** depot. Conventional as well as biological agents.

STETKO: Bullshit.

Page 15

ONE:
OTS GERETY, STETKO across the table, leaning forward and getting more fed-up.

GERETY: Marshal, you're not **naïve**. You've been on the Ice for five **years**…

GERETY: You **know** Article I is followed in **spirit**, not in letter.

GERETY: Tayshetskaya doubled as a former-Soviet staging ground in case a **hot** conflict ever broke out on the Ice.

GERETY: Much like McMurdo.

STETKO: Even **if** I grant what you say, you don't **want** me...

TWO:
Angle along the table, from the side and maybe just below the lip, as STETKO turns her head to look at ROSS. GERETY is still looking at STETKO. Both men are perfectly calm and reasonable.

STETKO: …send a member of your **cloak** and **dagger** brigade—

ROSS: We **can't**. It'd take us a minimum of 72 hours to get an agent in place, and that's **if** the weather is with us.

GERETY: But **you**, Marshal, you're good to run right now…

THREE:
STETKO, ROSS, and GERETY. STETKO practically growling.

GERETY: …you're **known** on the Ice. You have official status as US law enforcement—

STETKO: Not my **jurisdiction**—

GERETY: —there **is** no jurisdiction. They can't officially refuse you. You go, they've got to accept the help in the spirit of the Treaty.

FOUR:
OTS ROSS, STETKO looking up at him, mild surprise and some legit concern.

STETKO: That's total bullshit.

21

-145-

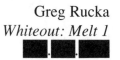

ROSS: Yes. But it'll get you to the site. And you know a lot of the
                               Russians already, don't you?

FIVE:
CU reaction STETKO. Attitude change, not as hostile, but now more legitimately upset.

STETKO: Some. Mostly out of Vostok and Leningradskaya.

STETKO: Shit.

22

Page 16

ONE:
POV STETKO, now looking back at GERETY. GERETY is entirely reasonable, almost friendly. And clearly not telling her all the facts.

GERETY: We want you to get on site as soon as possible and evaluate the situation. Determine the cause of the incident.

TWO:
View of STETKO on one side, GERETY on the other. ROSS watching.

STETKO: That's all?

GERETY: It's **enough**. You'll report to me. We've already spoken with Marshal McEwan in Hawaii. He knows you're working with us.

STETKO: I **haven't** said I'll do it.

THREE:
Angle from GERETY's shoulder, as ROSS appeals gently to STETKO.

ROSS: This is an issue of the national interest, Marshal. Your country **needs** you.

FOUR:
New angle, showing STETKO's contempt for this particular appeal.

STETKO: This would be the **same** country that **exiled** me to the Ice four years ago?

STETKO: Read you **files**, Consul Ross. I'm **thin** on patriotism right now.

FIVE:
CU GERETY. Almost smug.

GERETY: We'll bring you back to the world.

SIX:
CU STETKO's reaction. A cross between amusement and contempt.

NO COPY.

23

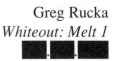

Page 17

ONE:
STETKO has brought her glare back to GERETY, and it's severe, one of her laser-burn looks. GERETY is just as almost-smug as before.

GERETY: It's what you **want**, isn't it? To get transferred back **home**?

GERETY: The Field Office in Phoenix, maybe? Somewhere **warm**?

TWO:
STETKO continues to glare at GERETY. ROSS watching. GERETY's expression is the same.

STETKO: Don't yank my chain, **James**.

GERETY: No yanking, I promise you.

GERETY: You do what we ask, **when** we ask, and I'll make certain you find your way home.

THREE:
POV GERETY, looking at STETKO. Her expression has softened, thinking.

NO COPY.

FOUR:
STETKO's POV, she's looking at her mauled hand.

GERETY (off panel):   What do you say, Marshal?

FIVE:
POV GERETY again, looking at STETKO. She is raising her right hand, setting her elbow on the table in front of her. We can see the missing fingers, and there's no question that Gerety sees them, too.

NO COPY.

SIX:
Same frame as previous, but STETKO has made a fist and is now looking at GERETY/ us.

STETKO: You've got a deal.

24

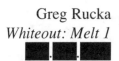

Page 18

ONE:
Exterior establishing of the ruins of Tayshetskaya, from the air. Blackened buildings, some fires still smoldering, but smaller. Smoke is rising into the air. We can make out people moving amongst the wreckage, and one or two airplanes already on the ground.

STETKO (caption):	Miller has the LC-130 ready and the weather—for **once**—is on my side…

TWO:
CU STETKO, looking out the window in the co-pilot seat of the Twin Otter. She's got her shades on, and the blissed out look she gets when staring at the Ice.

DELFY is flying, craning his neck to spot a place to land.

STETKO (caption):	…even so, it's still 30 hours since leaving Christchurch that Delfy flies us in.
STETKO (caption):	I'm **not** surprised to see the fires still burning.

THREE:
POV STETKO, looking at where the smoke is rising, the fires still burning.

STETKO (caption):	The only thing on the Ice **more** dangerous than the weather…
STETKO (caption):	…is **fire**.

FOUR:
View as the Twin Otter sets down in the BG. In FG we can see the Emergency Crews—mostly Russians, some Americans, some Aussies—working the site. TWO MEN in ECW are carrying burnt bodies and laying them out in a line. All the bodies are covered with black plastic tarp. There are 14 of them (though you don't have to show them all).

View of PYOTR DANILOVICH SEROV, in his mid-forties, regular ECW but hood down. He's got a radio hooked to his jacket epaulet, the small handset clipped to his collar, and a clipboard in his hand. He's not a happy camper—lots of dead bodies. He is the doctor out of Leningradskaya, and thus has become the de facto ruler of this particular scene of carnage.

SEROV:	<Jesus Christ this mess I don't need.>
STETKO (caption):	Must have been a hell of a blast.

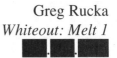
FIVE:
CU SEROV's expression. Sour, traditionally Russian bad mood.

NO COPY.

SIX:
CU SEROV's expression, but it's turned into a huge smile.

SEROV: Marshal Carrie!

-150-

Page 19

ONE:
SEROV, still holding the clipboard, is catching STETKO in a bear-hug. In BG, some of the rescue crew have stopped to watch. Most are smiling. Almost all know Stetko in passing, and she's certainly unique.

SEROV:	<**Every**one! It's our cowgirl!>
STETKO:	Pyotr Danilovich!
SEROV:	My favorite fucking American! You've come see our… how you say?…bar-be-cue?

TWO:
Angle showing the bodies laid out in the FG. EBG STETKO is pulling away from SEROV—both grinning. Carrie is heading towards the bodies. DELFY has emerged from the plane and is coming along, as well.

STETKO:	That's truly disgusting, Pete.
STETKO:	You know what happened yet?

THREE:
Reverse, showing STETKO in FG, side view, crouching down on her haunches to begin examining the line of corpses.

SEROV is in BG, full on, looking at her, now serious. DELFY is further back, joking with one of the other crew.

SEROV:	What happens was Hell open on earth, Carrie. Diesel tanks caught with crew inside. Big **blast**, then big flames.
STETKO:	No survivors?
SEROV:	Nyet.
STETKO:	You prelim any of these guys yet?
SEROV:	Da. From blast trauma. Or they get smoke, then burn to death, never wake up.

FOUR:
CU SEROV, eyebrow raised, curious.

SEROV: You looking something special? America looking, too?

STETKO (off):   Nah. You know me, Pete…

FIVE:
CU STETKO pulling up the edge of one of the tarps.

STETKO: …I'm just **morbid**.

SEROV (off):   America sends you, though, Da?

STETKO: Da.

SIX:
Angle as STETKO lowers tarp, back on her haunches, looking up at SEROV.

STETKO: What were they researching here?

SEROV: Um…is atmosphere, I think. Not certain.

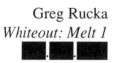

Page 20

ONE:
New angle, maybe looking down slightly. STETKO has moved to the next body in the line, still on her haunches, and lifted another tarp. SEROV still to a side on line with her, along the bodies.

STETKO: What bases are giving aid?

SEROV: All Russian bases in area. Also McMurdo and Mawson.

STETKO: …

STETKO: Pete, take a look at this.

TWO:
Reveal that Stetko has pulled up the tarp covering the badly burnt face of BUNIN. The entrance wound is hard to identify, but the back of the skull is missing a chunk of bone.

STETKO (caption):   Well, shit.

STETKO (off panel):   That a bullet wound?

THREE:
STETKO, still on her haunches, is looking at the corpse while SEROV examines the head wound under the tarp.

SEROV: Da. Da, or from heat fire. Bullet probably.

STETKO: Interesting, huh?

STETKO: Somebody has a gun.

STETKO: Question is, was this poor son of a bitch shot **before** he got roasted or after?

FOUR:
View as STETKO gets to her feet, looking at the rubble that is the Main Building. SEROV is still crouched by the body, examining it.

SEROV: …maybe only heat…

STETKO: Mind if I look around?

SEROV: …hmm? Nyet, nyet…go…

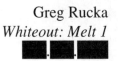

FIVE:

Shot from behind STETKO as she gingerly begins picking her way through the wreckage. It's hot, and some areas are still smoking.

STETKO (caption):   If that guy was shot…

STETKO (caption):   …if that guy was **shot** than this is **no** accident.

Page 21

ONE:
CU STETKO, thinking as she continues through the rubble.

NO COPY.

TWO:
POV STETKO, looking into what was the remnants of the lab. There is a blackened patch of ground—actually the hole the Spesnaz blew—partially covered with debris.

NO COPY.

THREE:
STETKO closer to the hole, not yet able to recognize it for what it is.

STETKO (caption):   …the hell? Looks like a **hole** in the—

FOUR:
The ground where STETKO has been standing just snapped out from under her, and she's falling.

STETKO: AH!

SFX: krrSNAP

-155-

Page 22

ONE:
STETKO landing hard on her side. No detail around her. It's hot and dark down here, and water is still dripping from the heat above.

STETKO: Ow fuck ow ow! Dammit!

TWO:
Angle looking up STETKO as she looks up at the hole. Out of reach. Patch of light falling on her.

STETKO: Lovely. Fucking lovely.

THREE:
STETKO, reaching into a parka pocket with her good hand.

NO COPY.

FOUR:
CU STETKO, turning the head of a Mini-Maglite with her teeth.

NO COPY.

FIVE:
View as STETKO shines the light around her.

Page 23

ONE:
POV STETKO, the beam of light. It's clearly a storage space, and fairly large. Shelves run along each side, and crates are packed into the center. A couple of snowmobiles—circa 1980s—are half-covered with tarps.

STETKO (caption):   Waddya know.

TWO:
POV STETKO as the beam falls across crates and crates of ammunition. Cyrillic markings on the containers, but the numbers 7.62 X 39MM are clear.

STETKO (caption):   Looks like they were right…

THREE:
Angle on STETKO holding the Mini-Mag in her mouth while she muscles one of the crates open.

STETKO (caption):   …naughty Russians…

FOUR:
POV STETKO, looking into a crate full of KALASHNIKOV AK-47 AUTOMATIC RIFLES.

STETKO (caption):   …storing weapons.

STETKO (caption):   AK-47s.

FIVE:
STETKO looking around, holding the Mini-Mag.

STETKO (caption):   Let's see what else they've got…

SIX:
ECU STETKO, her reaction. Stunned.

STETKO (caption):   …oh, fuck.

33

Page 24

ONE:
POV STETKO. The Mini-Mag beam is highlighting an open crate with a great big
RADIATION SYMBOL stenciled on its side. Beside it are two other crates, also open.

STETKO: Oh fuck.

STETKO: Oh fuck oh fuck a lot.

TWO:
ECU of the RADIATION SYMBOL.

STETKO (caption):   Nukes.

STETKO (caption):   They had **nukes**.

THREE:
OTS STETKO as she moves closer, confirming that all three crates are empty. The
RADIATION SYMBOL is perfectly clear, no mistaking it.

STETKO (caption):   And of course they're **gone**.

STETKO (caption):   Just perfect.

FOUR:
STETKO turning quickly, hearing something behind her.

STETKO (caption):   Just fucking per—

FIVE:
OTS STETKO.

KUCHIN is in front of her, lit by the Mini-Mag and the light from above.

He is dressed <u>identically</u> to the Spesnaz earlier. No weapons visible.

STETKO (caption):   —fect?

END OF PART 1

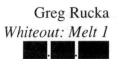
---

[i] The Spesnaz guys here need to be consistent. There are six of them, and until issue 3 we probably won't see any of them outside of their ECW, so don't worry about their faces. But try to keep the sizes consistent, of course.

Their ECW is important—Arctic camouflage, very sleek, very professional soldier. Not the bulky parkas, but rather fitted gear that doesn't hinder their movement. All of them are armed with a submachine gun across their backs and a pistol either at the hip or thigh—no shoulder holsters. The weapons are specific—I want the tech here to be accurate—so contact me for references. Their submachine guns all have brass-catchers. Additionally, all have a knife, either on their belt, boot, or thigh. You can vary their look by giving some of them additional pieces of kit—some would have grenades, some would have extra ammunition, one of them has a radio pack.

There are no markings whatsoever on their ECW—been removed—and their faces are entirely covered by mask and goggles.

Should be a group of scary looking guys, frankly.

[ii] Sasha is in no way important—I just needed one of them to have a name, so Spesnaz 5 is Sasha. We may use him more later, but there you go. If you want to identify him in some particular way, that's fine by me.

This assignment actually came to me from my then-neighbor, author Faruk Ulay. He was guest editor of an issue of the experimental literary and cultural magazine *Fol*, and had four more pages to fill. With his love for comics, he turned to me and asked me to put together a story that fit into the issue's theme, "imperfection".

There are two things about *Fol* of which you should be aware. One is that it's a large magazine, even larger than oversized U.S. comics such as the *Marvel Treasury Editions*, even twice the size of the Paul Dini/Alex Ross superhero books. As such, there was little need to worry about the amount of dialogue, as I would have plenty of room for both large legible lettering and art. The other is that it's a Turkish magazine. Faruk translated all of the dialogue, and poor Steve Lieber, who drew the tale, had to hand-letter it in a language he didn't know.

The fully illustrated work appears after the script. It has been relettered (via computer) into English. This is the first time that this story appears in a language that either Steve or I can read.

Nat Gertler has written comics ranging from The Flintstones *to, well, artsy material for Turkish magazines. He is most identified with* The Factor, *a self-published alternative miniseries. His work on that book brought him a nomination for the coveted Eisner award.*

Steve Lieber served his years in the mainstream, drawing Hawkman *for DC Comics. His current acclaim, however, comes from his work on* Whiteout, *an arctic thriller miniseries written by Greg Rucka which garnered four Eisner award nominations. Its follow-up series,* Whiteout: Melt *won the Eisner for best limited series. Steve is working with Greg again, chronicling the adventures of Batman in* Detective Comics, *while he also illustrates a Warren Ellis graphic novel about Vikings visiting feudal Japan.*

Degeneration
Script by Nat Gertler
█████████ Ave., Apt █
Pasadena, CA 91101
(██) ██-█
Internet: █@███████
For Fol

Steve: Feel free to call me if you have any questions, problems, insults, etc. I am not one of those people who thinks that everything has to be absolutely to the original script right down to the last little scar. I am, however, one of those persons who needs to be involved in any changing of what I've written. This is not by accident. There are reasons for all the things that I've put in, and while I try to keep the script informed with my intent, there are always subtle things about the construction of the story that do not quite get put into words, or even that I am not fully aware of the reason for them until I am faced with the prospect of changing them. So talk to me; I am flexible, but I need to be involved.

The setting is going to be New York City, so you can breath a little sigh of relief. I assume that you have good reference on the history of men's dress (I wish I had better reference myself, but such is life.) I'm typing this before I type the rest of the script, but will note that I do not expect to be doing much in the way of exteriors, so you needn't worry too much about that.

The printed page size is 14 1/2" by 19 1/2". The paper that they tend to use is a thick, non-glossy stock. The printing is quite high quality. Everything should be hand-done; I remember mentioning to hand-letter it, but I should also note that no zip-a-tone is to be used.

I'll try to put my Alan Moore-style script-writing hat for some of this, since you like that level of details I've never quite hit full-Alan (and am not sure I'd want to), but came reasonably close in writing parts of Mister U.S. (not just the pseudo-Watchman part), the frankly lackluster *Death & Taxes*, and the one-page framing bit for a two-part *Intruder* backup I did with Joe Staton. (Added later: Well, I didn't get near full-Alan this time for the individual panels. I got in range for the scene setting, though…)

(COVER PAGE)

My current concept of this (which changes about every fifteen minutes) is to have a thick, black border bleeding to the edges. The image, centered, is a shot of a hand-drawn family tree. (If the tree itself is not included in what I send you, call me up and yell at me.) The tree should be enlarged (FARUK: I know you wanted to avoid mechanical elements, but is it okay for him to use photocopying to enlarge and degrade this image?), and look like it is a multiple-generation photocopy of something that has been written by hand and added to by others over the years. Horizontally centered over this image, and within the lower half vertically, is a title/credit box. The title should "degenerate" as it goes along; the first letter should be written very precisely in a serifed font, and the style should simplify and grow sloppy until the final letter is sloppy. I am *not* separating out the efforts in the credits, because I think doing so makes it sound less like a full collaboration (not that it is a full mutual both-doing-everything collaboration, but when trying to push to an artsy audience like this, it's probably better to make it not sound mechanical.)

FARUK: The title I have chosen is a good one in English, because it means to grow worse, but it contains the word "generation", which in its familial meaning is much to the heart of what we're discussing. However, a literal translation of the word into Turkish is not likely to have the same subtleties, I suspect. Still, a literal translation would not be a bad title, but if you have an idea for something interesting in Turkish, I'm interested.

TITLE BOX: DEGENERATION
              BY NAT GERTLER AND STEVE LIEBER

-161-

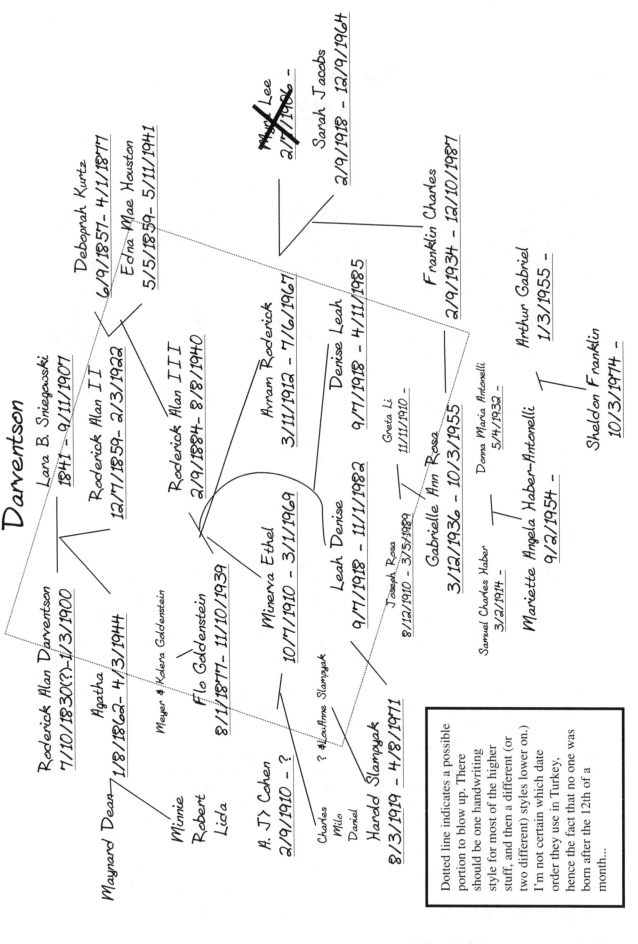

Darventson

Roderick Alan Darventson
7/10/1830(?)-1/3/1900

Lara B. Sniegowski
1841 - 9/11/1907

Deboprah Kurtz
6/9/1857- 4/1/1877

Roderick Alan II
12/7/1859- 2/3/1922

Edna Mae Houston
5/5/1859- 5/11/1941

Mark Lee
2/7/1906 -

Sarah Jacobs
2/9/1918 - 12/9/1964

Roderick Alan III
2/9/1884- 8/8/1940

Avram Roderick
3/11/1912 - 7/6/1967

Franklin Charles
2/9/1934 - 12/10/1987

Arthur Gabriel
1/3/1955 -

Maynard Dean

Agatha
1/8/1862- 4/3/1944

Meyer & Kolena Goldenstein

Minnie
Robert
Lida

Flo Goldenstein
8/1/1877- 11/10/1939

Minerva Ethel
10/7/1910 - 3/1/1969

Denise Leah
9/7/1918 - 4/11/1985

Greta Li
11/11/1910 -

Donna Maria Antonelli
5/4/1932 -

Sheldon Franklin
10/3/1974 -

A. J> Cohen
2/9/1910 - ?

Charles
Milo
Daniel

? LouAnne Slampyak

Harold Slampyak
8/3/1919 - 4/8/1971

Leah Denise
9/7/1918 - 11/1/1982

Joseph Rosa
8/12/1910 - 3/5/1989

Gabrielle Ann Rosa
3/12/1936 - 10/3/1955

Samuel Charles Haber
3/2/1914 -

Mariette Angela Haber-Antonelli
9/2/1954 -

Dotted line indicates a possible portion to blow up. There should be one handwriting style for most of the higher stuff, and then a different (or two different) styles lower on.) I'm not certain which date order they use in Turkey, hence the fact that no one was born after the 12th of a month...

PAGE ONE

(1)

SETTING: An office in New York City, modern day. It's late fall or early winter, around 7:30 PM, so it's dark outside. This is a large office, the CEO office for a brokerage that's probably worth something in the $25 million range (which isn't large as brokerages go). It's clearly a designer office, done in modern-pseudo-art-deco. The office is on the corner of a high floor of a skyscraper, so two of the walls are basically big windows. Of the two remaining walls, the right one (if you're facing them) has bookshelves, black and high, bearing a mixture of never-touched leatherbound financial volumes and heavily riffled computer printouts and bound sets of quartlerly reports. Thre's also a door to a private washroom. The left wall has a large recessed black double door and an entertainment center with a stereo, a large screen TV, and a VCR; these things are built into the wall. The carpet is plush, cream-colored like the walls. This is the office of a person who frantically tried to make it look like he didn't really do work, because his leadership was supposed to be effortless, although that was far from true.

There is a desk facing the entrance door. It has a heavy, polished black stone top, and space directly under that for about 4 inches of drawers. The desk is supported by black metal sides; instead they head from the edge of the top downward and inward, curving back at the bottom to provide feet. This has the effect of accentuating the information that the desk does not have file drawers on the side – this is not the desk of someone who is supposed to keep his own files, and heaven forbid that it looks as though he does. The chair is high-backed, padded, black leather; this is the chair of someone who spends his time leaning back in deep contemplation, not of someone who leans forward to work. There are visitor chairs of a similar design in front of the desk, but they have lower backs . There is a small table between the visitor chairs, with a carved wooden cigar box and a black cigar ashtray.

Toward the right of the desk is a computer set-up, just a large screen and a keyboard on a small desk; the processor is a tower model on the floor, the sort used by people who may be looking at stock status on the screen, but certainly aren't going to be sticking any floppies into the machine. It's a Windows box, with far more power in it than would ever be used; it was a top of the line machine 18 months ago.

There are those art-deco flared wall lights on the walls, in between bookshelves on the bookshelf wall and at spots on the other wall far enough from the TV that their light would not be distracting. These are not really meant to provide light but more to provide a designy glow. The real lighting for the room usually comes from recessed incandescent lights in the ceiling. There is also a torchierre light in the window corner, there to illuminate the bust of the firm's founder, which stands beside it on a simple glossy black rectangular pillar. The bust is of a man with a sharp 1860's haircut, clean-edge. The features are chiseled and strong, the chin prominent, the eyes wide and intelligent, the eyebrows have a hairy flair at the outside edges, as is often used with demonic characters, although he is not demonic. The expression on the face is not the usually sleepy look one often sees on busts; this is more of a fierce, I'm-in-the-middle-of-doing-something-so-don't-get-in-my-way look. The simple silver plate on the bust's pedestal reads *Roderick Darventson I, founder, Darventson Investments*. (FARUK: Remember to translate that!)

This is all setting. We don't have to see all this stuff, but that's what the office is like.

Currently sitting in the office chair is Sheldon Darventson, and he does not look like he quite belongs there. . Facially… well, you'll have to read through page 2 before you can really envision it (because his face is related strongly to his fathers, and we have to go through the whole history to really paint it), but basically he has thick, dark hair, dark, thoughtful eyes, a round, warm face, simply curved eyebrows; he looks like an intelligent-but-warm person rather than a hard-edged businessman. He's a little on the short side, a bit padded out but not really overweight. His matter of dress is not messy but not businesslike either; he has on a light one-color sweater over a casual collared shirt.

Sheldon is seated at the desk. He is seated in the big chair, but he is leaning forward from it, rather than leaning back into it. He's using a Macintosh laptop that is open on the desk; this is both a likely computer for someone just out of college and fits in with the break-in-the-pattern that we're going to find out Sheldon is. He and the computer are at a somewhat odd angle, to catch the light well, because the only light on in the room is the torchierre in the corner; the overhead lights and the art deco wall things are turned off. (Sheldon's been in this office all day. When he came in, the sunlight was good, so there was no need to turn a light on. When the light failed, he just turned for the nearest light to turn it on; the switches for the rest of the lights are over by the entrance, and that would have meant getting up and heading over to turn them on. This is a simple efficiency (and intensity of concentration) rather than a laziness at work.) The bust is casting a shadow that falls on the desk, keeping the lighting from being complete. The chair has to be angled so the high back isn't blocking the light.

Also on the desk is a photocopy-paper box marked FAMILY RECORDS (Faruk!) ; the lid is off – in fact, the lid has been put on the bottom of the box. A couple of papers are sticking out from the box. The desk also has a pen set, and a backpack – not new, but not ratty, and again seeming out of place.

At this moment, he has one hand still on the keyboard, and is holding up a slightly ragged paper – the family tree, but we can't see that from this angle.

"This angle" is that we're looking toward the desk from the inside. We need to be able to see the lamp, the bust (although it need not be clear), Sheldon, the box, and the desk. We need to be able to see Sheldon well enough to basically establish him visually here, but given that, we can be far enough back that we can get the sense of the room (or at least that we can see that the wall to his side is a window, as the one behind him is; "Corner office" is a good sensibility to have, and there should be at least the suggestion of the night Manhattan skyline through the window. Yeah, it's trite, but it works.

1 CAPTION: COMPUTERIZING MY FAMILY HISTORY IS DIFFICULT. I HAVE A PHOTOCOPY OF A PHOTOCOPY OF AN OLD CARBON-COPY OF A HANDWRITTEN FAMILY TREE. THE NAMES ARE BLURRED, AND THE ADDITIONS ARE OFTEN SLOPPY.

2 CAPTION: HER MOTHER'S NAME CAN'T BE "CHOLERA"...

3 CAPTION: WHAT I'M REALLY DOING IS AVOIDING THE WORK THAT FACES ME, TAKING THE REINS OF THIS BROKERAGE HOUSE.

(2)

Small panel. In the doorway, holding open the one door she entered through of the double doors, is Dee. Dee is Sheldon's secretary; she was Sheldon's father's secretary, and possibly even his grandfather's secretary at the end of his life. She's a sharp-looking black woman of 60, dressed quite professionally. This is the sort of secretary you need when you play in the big leagues; she's educated, capable, flexible, and quite dedicated. She's still here because her boss is still here. She gets paid quite well, because someone like this can make a big difference. She carries herself with well-earned confidence without inappropriate aggressiveness. I suspect she had more than a little to do with the company not falling apart during Sheldon's father's rein. (Okay, okay, that's probably more than you need to know about her.)

4 DEE: MISTER DARVENTSON? IT'S 7:30. IF YOU HAVEN'T ANYTHING MORE FOR ME, I WAS HOPING IT WOULD BE OKAY FOR ME TO LEAVE.

(3)

Vertical panel, two tiers. It's an overhead view of the room, oriented so that Sheldon is at the top, Dee at the bottom. There should be plenty of room for balloons in-between.

5 SHELDON: SEVEN-THIRTY? THEN WHY DIDN'T YOU LEAVE HOURS
AGO?

6 DEE: AS LONG AS YOU'RE WORKING, I CAN STAY, SIR.

7 SHELDON: I'M NOT REALLY WORKING. JUST TAKING CARE OF SOME
FAMILY BUSINESS.

8 DEE: IT'S *ALL* FAMILY BUSINESS.

(4)

Sheldon is leaning against the bust pillar–hands on its top edge, leaning forward against it, staring at the bust in profile.

9 CAPTION: SHE'S RIGHT. SINCE YOU STARTED THIS FIRM IN THE
1860'S, THIS FAMILY AND THIS BUSINESS
HAVE BEEN ONE AND THE SAME.

(FARUK: "One and the same" is an English term indicating two separately described things that are actually the same object; i.e. "Superman and Clark Kent are one and the same" is just another way of saying "Superman is Clark Kent", but it adds emphasis. Don't just literally translate the term.)

(5)

Close–up on the bust, a face-front shot. We can see the plaque.

10 CAPTION: We've all tried to be you, and we've all gotten worse and worse at it.

PAGE TWO

Steve, this page has been killing me. I was envisioning all sorts of tricky things. I had it locked in my mind that we had to show each of these guys "in action", in some sort of full shot… plus we need some non-standard layout, plus a lot of text. And no matter how I crunched it, it didn't work. And suddenly I came up with this, and at the moment it seems like a *really good* idea to me, but I can't say for sure if that's because it really works, or if it's just so bloody simple to write and to understand. So if you look at it and say "uggh, no, this won't do it all!", call me and let me know. I don't think you will. I think it really works. But then again, I like to suck ketchup right from the packets you get from fast-food places, so my judgment is not beyond question.

Anyway, what this is is 6 matching head-and-shoulder shots, running from upper left to lower right. (The shot should largely match with the shot of the bust at the end of the previous page.) They should be placed so that the lower-right corner of each shot overlaps the upper-left corner of the next; don't be afraid to make the overlap big enough so that a small part of the face is overlapped. And don't bother leaving much margin on the page; let's really use it.

There's a caption that goes with each head shot. For the first three, it goes to the right of the picture, not overlapping the picture at all. For the last three, it goes to the left (keep those from going too close to the left edge, so we don't lose text in the fold.) What this means is that there's going to be a little dead space to the left of pictures 2 and 3, and to the right of 4 and 5. What I'd like to put there as a page background is one of those stock price charts, you know the ones with the jaggy lines showing the stock's history. Even though it starts with a small up, it quickly trends down and continues to jaggedly go down. Do include widely-spaced horizontal and vertical graph paper lines.

The overall background should probably be black (that might be good for the whole project), so the graph will have to be white on black.

(1)

This is the same guy that the bust is of. He should be wearing proper business attire for 1870 or so. This is a successful and powerful man, and he looks it. This guy should look perfectish. He's smiling a perfect smile, teeth showing.

1 CAPTION: RODERICK DARVENTSON, *SELF-MADE MAN*. DIDN'T MAKE A MISSTEP WHEN HE FOUNDED HIS OWN FIRM AND GRABBED ONE OF THE VALUABLE SEATS ON THE NO-LONGER-OPEN-TO-ALL STOCK EXCHANGE. WITH AGGRESSIVENESS AND HONESTY, HE TURNED IT INTO ONE OF NEW YORK'S LEADING BROKERAGE HOUSES.

(2)

This could be the spitting image of the first shot, except the smile is a bit crooked, and the teeth are a bit askew. Suit circa 1910.

2 CAPTION: RODERICK JUNIOR, THE COMPACT VERSION OF HIS FATHER, HARVARD ECONOMICS *SUMMA CUM LAUD*, FILLED HIS FATHER'S ROLE

EASILY WHEN THE OLD MAN PASSED WITH
THE CENTURY. HE TOOK BOLD RISKS WITH
THE BUSINESS, SOME *BAD*, MOSTLY *GOOD*.

(FARUK: "PASSED WITH THE CENTURY" = DIED WHEN THE CENTURY ENDED.)

(3)

Softer face (the points on the eyebrows are gone), softer chin, no smile. Suit circa 1930.

3 CAPTION: RODERICK III, "RODDY" TO HIS HARVARD FRIENDS, WAS
SMART BUT *TIMID*. HIS AVERSION TO RISK
DROVE AWAY CUSTOMERS DURING THE
MONEY-FOR-ALL TWENTIES, BUT THOSE
WHO TOOK HIS *BEARISH* ADVICE IN '29
BECAME BOTH RICH AND DEVOTED.
DARVENTSON INVESTMENTS STAYED
AFLOAT WHILE OTHER STOCKBROKERS HIT
THE *SKIDS* OR THE *SIDEWALK*.

(FARUK: Not sure that will translate well. "Hit the skids" means basically to go broke. My goal is to say "went broke or committed suicide" in some interesting way. "Bearish" in stock terms means that one thinks that stocks are going to do badly; "pessimistic" might make a reasonable equivalent)

(4)

Smaller eyes, darker hair, less intelligent look. Post-war suit. (I figure that Roderick III went and married a Jewish woman of "traditional" Jewish looks, hence the darkening influence and the refusing to name the child after the then-living father.)

4 CAPTION: AVRAM R. DARVENTSON ("CHIP", OR TO HIS AMHERST
CHUMS, "SLOTH") KEPT GENERATING
SMALL BUT STEADY PROFITS FOR INVESTORS
DURING THE WAR YEARS, WHILE OTHER
BROKERS ENRICHED THEIR CLIENTS FROM
GOVERNMENT-BACKED INDUSTRY.

(5)

Balding, chubby, and it looks like the collar is too small for him. Suite circa 1970.

5 CAPTION: GRAMPA WORKED TO KEEP THE COMPANY THE SAME AS
HE HAD ALWAYS KNOWN. MEANWHILE,
OTHER BROKERAGE HOUSES WERE
MERGING, *GROWING* AND *MUTATING*
INTO MULTI-STRENGTHED POWERHOUSES.

THE STRESS OF TRYING TO STAY IN PLACE
SHOWED IN HIS DRINKING, AND THAT
CAUSED HIS DEATH BEHIND THE WHEEL.

(FARUK: "Behind the wheel" = driving; i.e., he died from a drunk driving accident.)

(6)

Balding, sweaty, tie loosened and collar opened, no suit, one eye slightly squinted. This man looks in bad condition… and he looks almost nothing like Roderick I.

6 CAPTION: DAD KNEW WHAT WAS EXPECTED FROM HIM, AND TRIED.
IT TOOK HIM SIX COLLEGES, BUT HE GOT
HIS MASTERS IN ECONOMICS. AND
THROUGH THE MONEY-HUNGRY '80'S, HE
KEPT THE BUSINESS SOLVENT, WITH THE AID
OF CONSULTANTS AND UPPERS. THE
FORMER GOT HIM IN AND OUT OF LEGAL
TROUBLE; THE LATTER PUT HIM IN THE
GRAVE LAST WEEK.

(FARUK: "Uppers" are drugs to give you energy, alertness, and raise mood.)

PAGE THREE

(1)

Sheldon is digging through the papers in the box.

1 CAPTION: That put me in the *president's chair*, a position my father had long groomed me for, a position I had never wanted.

2 CAPTION: I can never be my father, much less the man my father *tried* to be. And my archaeology degree does not lend itself to this work. So for the moment, I'm just digging through my family's past.

(2)

Sheldon's hand is pulling an old, brittle folded piece of paper out of the box. It's got handwriting on it, but we're not close enough to see what it is.

3 CAPTION: Each generation tried to be a copy of the generation before. But copies are *always* imperfect. And copies of copies just *multiply* the flaw.

4 CAPTION: I shouldn't be...

5 CAPTION: What's this old thing?

(3)

Sheldon stands, reading the letter out loud to the empty room. This should be side shot, with Sheldon at panel left, and the side window in the background. He's holding the letter up to his face, not bending his neck down to read it. He is holding it gingerly, with both hands, for this is an old and brittle piece..

6 CAPTION: It's a letter, handwritten by Roderick Senior himself.

7 SHELDON: "Mother, father, I'm sorry I left you without warning. Maybe it's some flaw in me, but I cannot take over that farm."

8 SHELDON: "I know that keeping it in the family means a lot to you, but I need to find my own path. I am in New York now. I think I've found my place."

(4)

Shocked, Sheldon whips his head around to look towards the bust.

NO COPY

(5)

Sheldon has picked up the bust, cradling it under the chin in his left hand, and is holding it up, staring it straight in the eye. This is a close in shot, seen from Sheldon's right, so that we basically get a symmetry of two faces facing each other (although the face shapes should still be clearly different). Sheldon's look is thoughtful, confident. (Roderick's look hasn't changed, of course.)

9 SHELDON: I AM JUST LIKE YOU, OLD MAN.

(6)

(Small panel; I suggest stacking this and panel 7 vertically within the tier.) Sheldon's hand rolling the trackball of the laptop computer. We should be able to see the keyboard and the bottom edge of the screen, just so the reader can better tell what this is.
NO COPY

(7)

(See above) The mouse pointer, clicking on a screen button marked SAVE. (FARUK: We'll need the proper Turkish file-saving command word. Alas, we'll probably lose the nice effect that we have in English, with Save meaning not only to store, but also to rescue.)
NO COPY

(8)

Seen from outside the office, Sheldon is coming through one of the double doors and pulling it shut behind him. He has the laptop in the other hand, and his backpack on his back. He is looking straight ahead, where he is going (and toward the reader), not looking back at all. He is determined, and he is relieved. (If we had more space here, I'd say let's make it the left-side door that's open, so that we can pick our angle to see through the opening and into the office, right across to where the light has been left on and is shining on the bust in the opposite corner. But this page is too crowded for that at this point, I figure.) Since this is the last panel, we should announce the end of the story in some form. However, since the story is told with captions, I don't want to captionize The End, which would make it read as part of the story rather than as a delimiter. Instead, what you should do is to cut a quarter circle shape out of the lower right corner of this panel. With a little space between the panel border and it, draw a nice big dot (maybe half an inch across) that uses that quarter circle for a quarter of it. This is a period, put to mark the end of the story. Sound okay?

10 CAPTION: (PLACE IT ON THE UPPER PORTION OF
                THE PANEL) I WON'T BE
                RETURNING.

-170-

arventson

30(?) - 1/3/1900

Larra 1841 - 9/11/1907

AGATHA
11/8/1862 - 4/3/1944

RODERICK ALAN II
12/7/1859 - 8/8/1940

Meyer & Kolera (?)
Goldstein

Roderick Al
2/9/1884 - 8/8/1

FLO GOLDSTEIN
8/1/1877 - 11/10/1939

DA

Minerva Ethel
10/7/1910

Leah Denise

Avram Roderick
3/11/1912 -

DENISE

?LOUANNE

DEGENERATION

NAT GERTLER
&
STEVE LIEBER

AMPYA

SARAH
JAC
18 - 12/

JOSEPH P
8/12/1910
3/5/1989

GRL
11/11/1910

FRANKLIN CHARLES
/1934 - 12/10/1

COMPUTERIZING MY FAMILY HISTORY IS DIFFICULT. I HAVE A PHOTOCOPY OF A PHOTOCOPY OF AN OLD CARBON-COPY OF A HANDWRITTEN FAMILY TREE. THE NAMES ARE *BLURRED*, AND THE ADDITIONS ARE OFTEN SLOPPY.

HER MOTHER'S NAME *CAN'T* BE "CHOLERA"...

WHAT I'M *REALLY* DOING IS AVOIDING THE WORK THAT FACES ME, TAKING THE REINS OF THIS *BROKERAGE HOUSE*.

MISTER *DARVENTSON?* IT'S 7:30. IF YOU HAVEN'T ANYTHING MORE FOR ME, I WAS HOPING IT WOULD BE OKAY FOR ME TO LEAVE.

SEVEN-THIRTY? THEN WHY DIDN'T YOU LEAVE HOURS AGO?

AS LONG AS YOU'RE WORKING, I CAN STAY, SIR.

I'M NOT REALLY WORKING. JUST TAKING CARE OF SOME *FAMILY BUSINESS*.

IT'S *ALL* FAMILY BUSINESS

SHE'S RIGHT. SINCE YOU STARTED THIS FIRM IN THE 1860'S, THIS FAMILY AND THIS BUSINESS HAVE BEEN ONE AND THE SAME.

WE'VE ALL TRIED TO BE YOU, AND WE'VE ALL GOTTEN WORSE AND WORSE AT IT.

RODERICK DARVENTSON 1

FOUNDER -

DARVENTSON INVESTMENTS

RODERICK DARVENTSON, *SELF-MADE MAN*. DIDN'T MAKE A MISSTEP WHEN HE FOUNDED HIS OWN FIRM AND GRABBED ONE OF THE VALUABLE SEATS ON THE NO-LONGER-OPEN-TO-ALL STOCK EXCHANGE. WITH AGGRESSIVENESS AND HONESTY, HE TURNED IT INTO ONE OF NEW YORK'S LEADING BROKERAGE HOUSES.

RODERICK JUNIOR, THE COMPACT VERSION OF HIS FATHER, HARVARD ECONOMICS *SUMMA CUM LAUD*, FILLED HIS FATHER'S ROL EASILY WHEN THE OLD MAN PASSED WITH THE CENTURY. HE TOOK BOLD RISKS WITH THE BUSINESS, SOME BAD, MOSTLY *GOOD*.

RODERICK III, "RODDY" TO HIS HARVARD FRIENDS, WAS SMART BUT *TIMID*. HIS AVERSION TO RISK DROVE AWAY CUSTOMERS DURING THE MONEY-FOR-ALL TWENTIES, BUT THOSE WHO TOOK HIS *BEARISH* ADVICE IN '29 BECAME BOTH RICH AND DEVOTED. DARVENTSON INVESTMENTS STAYED AFLOAT WHILE OTHER STOCKBROKERS HIT THE *SKIDS* OR THE *SIDEWALK*.

AVRAM R. DARVENTSON ("CHIP", OR TO HIS AMHERST CHUMS, "SLOTH") KEPT GENERATING SMALL BUT STEADY PROFITS FOR INVESTORS DURING THE WAR YEARS, WHILE OTHER BROKERS ENRICHED THEIR CLIENTS FROM GOVERNMENT-BACKED INDUSTRY.

GRAMPA WORKED TO KEEP THE COMPANY THE SAME AS HE HAD ALWAYS KNOWN. MEANWHILE, OTHER BROKERAGE HOUSES WERE *MERGING*, *GROWING* AND *MUTATING* INTO MULTI-STRANGTHED POWERHOUSES. THE STRESS OF TRYING TO STAY IN PLACE SHOWED IN HIS DRINKING, AND THAT CAUSED HIS DEATH BEHIND THE WHEEL.

DAD KNEW WHAT WAS EXPECTED FROM HIM, AND TRIED. IT TOOK HIM SIX COLLEGES, BUT HE GOT HIS MASTERS IN ECONOMICS. AND THROUGH THE MONEY-HUNGRY '80'S, HE KEPT THE BUSINESS SOLVENT, WITH THE AID OF *CONSULTANTS* AND *UPPERS*. THE FORMER GOT HIM IN AND OUT OF LEGAL TROUBLE; THE LATTER PUT HIM IN THE *GRAVE* LAST WEEK.

THAT PUT ME IN THE *PRESIDENT'S CHAIR*, A POSITION MY FATHER HAD LONG GROOMED ME FOR, A POSITION I HAD NEVER WANTED.

I CAN NEVER BE MY FATHER, MUCH LESS THE MAN MY FATHER TRIED TO BE. AND MY ARCHAEOLOGY DEGREE DOES NOT LEND ITSELF TO THIS WORK. SO FOR THE MOMENT, I'M JUST DIGGING THROUGH MY FAMILY'S PAST.

EACH GENERATION TRIED TO BE A *COPY* OF THE GENERATION BEFORE. BUT COPIES ARE *ALWAYS* IMPERFECT, AND COPIES OF COPIES JUST *MULTIPLY* THE FLAW.

I SHOULDN'T BE...

WHAT'S THIS OLD THING?

IT'S A LETTER, HANDWRITTEN BY RODERICK SENIOR HIMSELF.

"MOTHER, FATHER, I'M SORRY I LEFT YOU WITHOUT WARNING. MAYBE IT'S SOME FLAW IN ME, BUT I CANNOT TAKE OVER THAT FARM."

"I KNOW THAT KEEPING IT IN THE FAMILY MEANS A LOT TO YOU, BUT I NEED TO FIND MY OWN PATH. I AM IN NEW YORK NOW. I THINK I'VE FOUND MY PLACE."

I *AM* JUST LIKE YOU, OLD MAN.

I WON'T BE RETURNING.

Kevin Smith has long been a fan of comics, but it wasn't until he was already well established as an independent filmmaker that he broke into writing comics. This, the script for his first published story, features the Jay and Silent Bob characters who had already been popularized in *Clerks*, *Mallrats*, and *Chasing Amy*, and would prove even more vital in *Dogma* and *Jay and Silent Bob Strike Back*.

Kevin's script resembles film scripts in many ways. The most obvious is the use of establishing lines such as INT QUICK STOP – NIGHT to quickly establish the location (INT standing for "interior", the inside of the building, as opposed to EXT, "exterior"). The panel descriptions are terse (often shorter than the panel's dialog) but effective. In most cases, he's describing the scene simply and not calling for a specific camera angle. This could be because he trusts the artist (and well he should, since this story was illustrated by the eminently respectable Matt Wagner) or it could be simply that, as a director used to directing his own scripts, he seldom needs to specify in the script what he can specify at other times and in other ways in his films.

While this was Kevin's first appearance in comics, it was far from his last. He continues to write adventures of his film characters, and has also built a strong following writing mainstream superhero books such as *Daredevil* and *Green Arrow*.

– *Nat Gertler, December 2001*

Walt Flanagan's Dog

by

Kevin Smith

First (and only) Draft
July 27, '97
View Askew Productior

JAY AND SILENT BOB in WALT FLANAGAN'S DOG!

PAGE ONE

INT QUICK STOP - NIGHT

1) Tight on a can of Yoo-Hoo as a hand sets it on a counter.

2) The clerk (DANTE) hits buttons on the cash register, while balancing the pay phone receiver between his shoulder and ear. Only the back of the Yoo-Hoo purchasing CUSTOMER is visible - a trench-coated, baseball-cap-backwards wearing burly dude with long hair. Smoke rises from the unseen cigarette gripped (presumably) betwixt his unseen lips.

                         DANTE
                    (into phone)
              No, I have to work again tomorrow night...
              A sorority meeting, hunh? Come on; call them
              what they are - all-chick daisy-chains... Well
              that's what I heard...
                    (to customer)
              Seventy five.

3) We're in tight on the customers hands, as he pulls change from a full dime bag.

                         DANTE V.O.
              I don't work Saturday, though... Because
              I'm closing Friday night... You're going?!
              I can't believe you sometimes...

4) The customer (his back still to us) sets the change (and sundry lint, seedlings, and bud-shavings) on the counter, as Dante continues his phone call.

                         DANTE
              Veronica, it's a cable access game show... at a
              mall, no less - how interesting can it be?...
              Sociologically?... Don't give me that college talk...

5) The customer, exits, his face still unseen, the can now missing from the counter, a line of smoke left in his wake. Dante reaches for the change on the counter.

                         DANTE
                    (to leaving customer)
              Thanks.
                    (to phone)
              So then we can hang out all Saturday...
              After your class... What are we going to
              do?... Clothes on or off?...

6) Dante makes a face at the hand full of dirty change and detritus in his hand as he examines it closer.

                              DANTE
          What do you expect? I'm a guy?...
                    (off change and junk)
          Ugh...

7) A closeup of Dante's thumb and forefinger, between which is a weed
seedling; his eye peers at it.

                              DANTE
          I wasn't talking about that... Come on -
          would I ever be that...

EXT QUICK STOP - NIGHT

8) A tongue seals a Phatty Boombatty Blunt, bursting with sweet, sweet buds.

                              DANTE V.O.
          ...blunt?

                              JAY V.O.
          Ahhhh...

PAGE TWO AND THREE
SPLASH PAGE (leave space for credits box) -

Outside of Quick Stop, the wide-eyed and smiling ear-to-ear JAY holds aloft the newly formed Blunt. SILENT BOB (the customer from inside) joins him, shaking the can of Yoo-Hoo.

                    JAY
        BEHOLD!!! ONE GRADE 'A', CHOICE PRIME CUT
        PHATTY BOOM-BATTY BLUNT!!!

PAGE FOUR

EXT QUICK STOP - NIGHT

1) Jay holds the Blunt up to Silent Bob's face. Silent Bob pops open the can of Yoo-Hoo.

> JAY
> 'Tis a thing of beauty, Tons-of-fun. This is
> going to net our little empire a cool twenty
> bucks from some foolish high-schooler.
> Call me king of the mark-up... noonch!

2) Jay tucks the Blunt into Silent Bob's coat (presumably into an inside pocket), while Silent Bob sips from the Yoo-Hoo, one eye on his compatriot. Behind them, in the background, RANDAL exits the Video Store.

> JAY
> You hold onto it, though, tubby. If I get
> possession one more time, I'm gonna be
> tube-steakin' some big fuck up in county.
> And I eat it for only one fat fuck, right?

3) Jay pulls his fist back, enraged, as if to hit Silent Bob. Silent Bob wipes his mouth on his sleeve, paying little attention to his compatriot. In the background, Randal locks the Video Store door.

> JAY
> EWWWW!!! You fucking faggot! How many
> times do I gotta tell you: I hate guys! I hate
> guys so much, I can't even stand to see *myself*
> naked! I'm all about the clam!

4) Randal walks past the pair, and Jay goes shocked-wide-eyed at the casual insult Randal lets slip from the corner of his mouth. Silent Bob sips his Yoo-Hoo.

> RANDAL
> Fucking junkie...

5) All piss-and-vinegar, Jay screeches at the out of frame Randal. It's the classic comic-book pissed pose: one arm bolt straight with a fist clenched, the other raised high in the air with a finger pointing in an "I've-got-something-to-say" fashion, shoulders hunched, body bent a bit, feet raised just slightly off the ground, mouth inhumanly open, spittle flying. Silent Bob's eyebrows raise only slightly at Jay's vulgar diatribe.

> JAY
> YOU COCK-SMOKING CLERK!!! I'LL FUCKING
> TEAR YOUR SWEATY SACK OFF AND MAKE
> YOU WEAR IT LIKE A FUCKING CLOWN NOSE!!!
> I'LL PUT YOU IN A DRESS AND BITCH SLAP
> YOU AROUND, RIGHT IN FRONT OF WHICH-
> EVER CLAM-DIGGER IS CLAIMING TO BE YOUR
> FUCKING FATHER THIS WEEK!!! DO YOU HEAR
> ME?!?! LOOK INTO MY EYES, YOU FUCK?!?!
> DOES IT LOOK LIKE I'M JOKING?!?! NOTHING
> TO SAY NOW, RIGHT?!?!

EXT QUICK STOP - NIGHT

1) Randal leans out of the convenience store door.

> RANDAL
> I just called the cops on you, dude.

2) Jay goes wide-eyed and silent, the rage replaced by shock. Silent Bob arches an eyebrow.

3) Jay walks past Silent Bob in the opposite direction of the convenience store, muttering.

> JAY
> Come on, Silent Bob. We got shit to do
> anyway.

EXT NEIGHBORHOOD - NIGHT

4) The tiny figures of Jay and Silent Bob walk down a quiet suburban street in an overhead shot. Jay's hands are jammed firmly in his pockets, cowed and angry about it. Smoke trails behind Silent Bob.

> JAY
> ...that fuckin' guy think he is?! Calls the
> blues like a fuckin' puss would. Thinks he
> can just say whatever shit he wants...

INT DINER - NIGHT

5) Sitting in a booth, Jay chews on a half-eaten burger, still rambling angrily. Silent Bob stares at a cigarette in his open palm, attempting the 'Jedi Mind Trick'. The can of Yoo-Hoo still evident in his pocket.

> JAY
> Fucking guy's an asshole, I'll tell you that.
> In another minute, we were gonna stomp
> a mudhole in his ass, the bitch. Dude's got
> like zero fucking manners, man - doesn't
> know how to treat people.

6) Same shot almost, but a curvy WAITRESS walks past their table, carrying an order. Jay's head pops up, alert, as if he's just smelled something sweet.

7) Same shot almost, but now Jay cranes his neck in the direction the Waitress went.

> JAY
> HEY BABY! EVER HAVE YOUR ASSHOLE
> LICKED?!?

PAGE SIX

EXT DINER - NIGHT

1) Jay and Silent Bob are tossed out by the big Greek owner. They tumble down
the few steps.

                         JAY
            WHAT?!? IT WAS AN HONEST QUESTION!!!

EXT WALT FLANAGAN'S PARENTS' HOUSE - LATER

2) Jay and Silent Bob sit on a curb in front of a fenced-in suburban house. On
the gate hangs a sign that says 'Beware of Dog'. Silent Bob sips from his Yoo-
Hoo can.

                         JAY
            The whole fuckin' world's against us, dude.
            I swear. Our fucking freedoms are always
            being violated by the Man. We need to get
            some affirmative fuckin' action, man - like
            from the UCLA or something. We may not
            be black, but still...

3) Jay eyes Silent Bob sipping from the Yoo-Hoo.

4) Jay gets a tad vocal with his companion. Silent Bob looks at him sheepishly.

                         JAY
            How long are you gonna milk that thing,
            Fat-ass? Fuck!

5) Silent Bob looks down, cowed himself now. It looks as if he might cry. Jay
feels a bit guilty.

6) Jay puts his hand on the still-saddened Silent Bob's back, apologetically.
With his other hand, Jay reaches into his pocket.

                         JAY
            I'm sorry, man. I shouldn't come down
            on you - you're the only fuck with some
            sense in this berg.

PAGE SEVEN

EXT WALT FLANAGAN'S PARENTS' HOUSE - NIGHT

1) Jay hands Silent Bob a crumpled-up paper towel from his pocket. A tear is rolling down Silent Bob's face as he accepts it.

                              JAY
               Here, man - dry those eyes, big guy.

2) Silent Bob blows his nose as Jay watches, solemnly.

3) Silent Bob looks to Jay who's now smiling impishly.

4) Same exact image, but now Jay speaks.

                              JAY
               Dude - that's my spank-kerchief.

5) Jay moves to dart away, laughing hysterically. Silent Bob gives chase, angrily.

                              JAY
          NIIIIIIIIIIIIIIIIIIIIIIIIIIINNNNNNNNGGGG!!!!

6) Silent Bob tackles Jay into the fence.

                              JAY
               OOOOOOOF!

7) Silent Bob pushes Jay's face into the fence.

                              JAY
          GET OFFA ME, YOU FAT FUCK!!! UNCLE!!!
          UNCLE!!!

8) Suddenly, there's a tiny Rat Terrier on the other side of the fence, excitedly barking his head off at the wide-eyed pair, who tumble backwards in fear.

EXT WALT FLANAGAN'S PARENTS' HOUSE - NIGHT

1) Jay and Silent Bob peer through the fence at the yipping dog, who bounces around at them.

> JAY
> What the fuck is that, man? That's too
> fucking small to be a dog. You might
> as well own a cat, right? What kind of
> fuck would own a dog like that?

INT WALT FLANAGAN'S ROOM - NIGHT

2) Closeup on a pair of hands that hold a Trivial Pursuit-like question card, revealing only part of the printed question. The answer on the back is securely hid.

> STEVE-DAVE
> Alright, dude - this one's for your shirt...

3) Steve-Dave and Walt the Fan-Boy sit cross-legged across from each other in a room filled with comics and gaming card nonsense. There are pictures of wizards and shit on the wall. Both are in various states of undress: Walt wears a t-shirt and a pair of underwear; Steve-Dave is topless, wearing only jeans and sneakers. He is reading off the question card.

> STEVE-DAVE
> Who edited Matt Wagner's 'Mage' at Comico?

> WALT
> Um... Dianna Schultz.

4) Steve-Dave delights in the wrong answer. Walt appears deflated.

> STEVE-DAVE
> WRONG! Bob Schreck! Peel!

> WALT
> Fuck! I almost said 'Shreck'!

> STEVE-DAVE
> Almost doesn't mow the lawn, boy. Off
> with your shirt.

5) Walt pulls off his shirt, while Steve-Dave files away the card into a box of other question cards.

> WALT
> Steve-Dave - I don't know about this any-
> more. I'm almost naked here.

> STEVE-DAVE
> Then maybe you better bone up on your
> comics industry trivia, Walt. Look at me -

I'm still half-clad because I know my shit.

6) Walt looks a bit dismayed.   Steve goes wide-eyed.

WALT
But playing strip trivia... it doesn't make
us gay, does it?

STEVE-DAVE
No way, dude! How can you even have a thought
like that?! I told you - we're practicing for when
we convince that club-footed chick who runs the
gift shop to play with us.

INT WALT FLANAGAN'S ROOM - NIGHT

1) Walt holds his knees to his chest, puzzled.   Steve-Dave stands, explaining.

> STEVE-DAVE
> We both know that girls don't know anything
> about comics, right?   Well, when she comes
> over tomorrow night, we get her to play
> comics industry strip trivia.   She'll be
> naked in less than an hour.

> WALT
> Why don't we just play strip 'Magic - the
> Gathering' with her?

> STEVE-DAVE
> Too chancy - she might be a natural at gaming.
> Some chicks are. But comics trivia? She'll be
> in the raw before you or I even have a shoe off.

2) Walt and Steve-Dave high five each other.   In the distance, the dog can be heard barking.

> WALT
> And then...?

> STEVE-DAVE
> Then we can both probably get it on with her!

> WALT
> Sex with a girl and a Stan Lee autograph -
> both in one day!

> TOGETHER
> YES!

3) The door to Walt's room is pushed open, but the chain-lock prevents it from opening completely. Walt's Mother peers inside. On the back of the door is a poster of a Thor-like character.

> MOTHER
> WALTER! WHAT THE HELL ARE YOU TWO
> DOING IN THERE?!?

4) Walt hurls himself angrily against the door and bellows at his Mother.

> WALT
> Where the hell's the knock?! I told you,
> ma - this is my inner sanctum, and you
> can't open the door without knocking!!!

MOTHER

And I told you to keep that dog of yours
quiet! It's been outside barking up a storm
for the last fifteen goddam minutes! GO
OUTSIDE AND SHUT THAT DOG UP! NOW!

EXT WALT FLANAGAN'S PARENTS' HOUSE - NIGHT

5) Jay taunts the yipping dog from the other side of the fence. Silent Bob lights
a cigarette, disinterested.

JAY

What? What? You wanna piece of me?!
Come on, motherfucker! Come on out here
and get you some!

6) Jay shoves his ass at the yipping dog, looking over his shoulder. Silent Bob
cracks his neck by pulling it to the side with his hand.

JAY

C'MON AND GET SOME BROWN, BOY! HERE IT IS!
COME AND GET IT, YOU RAT-FUCK!

7) Walt and Steve-Dave step out of the front door, shirtless. Walt now wears
pants.

WALT

What the fuck's going on out here! Hey
kid! Get off my property!

PAGE TEN

EXT WALT FLANAGAN'S PARENTS' HOUSE - NIGHT

1) Steve-Dave and Walt are now at the fence, across from Jay and Silent Bob.

>   JAY
>   Take it easy, you topless fuck - this ain't
>   your fuckin' property.   It's the sidewalk.

>   STEVE-DAVE
>   It's *his*   sidewalk.

2) Walt now holds the dog, who snarls at Jay and Silent Bob.   Steve-Dave backs up his boy.

>   WALT
>   Damn straight.   This is Walt Flanagan's side-
>   walk, this is Walt Flanagan's house, and this
>   is Walt Flanagan's dog you're pissing off.

3) Jay grabs his crotch.   Silent Bob gives up a little smirk.

>   JAY
>   Oh yeah?   Well this is Walt Flanagan's mom's
>   lunch.

4) Steve-Dave has his arms up in a "You-wanna-throw-down?" fashion.   Walt looks a little hurt by Jay's comment.

>   STEVE-DAVE
>   Watch it, man - you talk about his mom, and
>   you talk about me.   You want me to come down
>   on you like Mjolinir?

5) Jay and Silent Bob stare blankly, confused by the comment.

6) Jay looks to Silent Bob, who shrugs his shoulders.

7) Steve-Dave points at Jay and Silent Bob from across the fence.   Walt nods in approval from behind, putting the dog back down.

>   STEVE-DAVE
>   Now quit bugging the dog and get your
>   stoner asses out of here before we call
>   the cops!   You mess with us, you're
>   messing with the Comic-Toast mob, bitch!

>   WALT
>   Tell 'em, Steve-Dave.

8) The front door of the house slams closed.

9) Jay and Silent Bob stare at the yipping dog, silently.

10) Same shot, except Jay looks at Silent Bob.

                    JAY
          'Comic-Toast Mob'? Is it me, or were those
          two of the biggest fucking dorks you ever
          met? Fuck them and their mutt. This
          situation calls for some sort of reprisal.

PAGE ELEVEN

WALT FLANAGAN'S PARENTS' HOUSE - NIGHT

1) Same shot, except Silent Bob now also looks at Jay.

2) Silent Bob dumps the Yoo-Hoo from the can.

3) He extracts a switchblade from his jacket and pops it open.

4) He dents the can slightly.

5) Using the knife, he punches holes in the dent of the can.

6) Silent Bob holds open his palm, revealing a fat ball of hashish. Jay smiles.

> JAY
> Yeah, boy - let's smoke the hash-pup.

7) Jay and Silent Bob are laying on their stomachs on the sidewalk, face-to-face with the yipping dog. Jay is lighting the hash on top of the can.

8) Jay inhales deeply, as the little ball smolders. The dog continues to bark.

9) Jay holds the smoke in as the dog jumps around at him from the other side of the fence.

10) Jay exhales the smoke into the yipping dog's face.

PAGE TWELVE

EXT WALT FLANAGAN'S PARENTS' HOUSE - NIGHT

1) The dog's head is surrounded by a cloud of smoke as it continues to yip.

2) Then, it stops - a peculiar expression filling it's face.

3) Jay and Silent Bob smile at each other.

> JAY
> And that wasn't even a big hit.

4) The dog is still dazed.

5) The dog shakes it off, and goes back to yipping.

6) Jay passes the can to Silent Bob.

> JAY
> Hit it, bro - then pass it on.

7) Silent Bob inhales deeply from the can, while lighting the hash ball on top.

8) He blows it into the yipping dog's face, while he passes the can to Jay.

9) The dog's yipping trails off as he gets that dazed look again.

10) "LATER..." Separated by the fence, Jay, Silent Bob, and the dog are on their backs, red-eyed and gone.

> JAY
> Fuck, dude - I'm stoned...

PAGE THIRTEEN

EXT WALT FLANAGAN'S PARENTS' HOUSE - NIGHT

1) Then, Jay reacts to the out of frame dog, and hits Silent Bob.

                    JAY
          Dude - look!

2) The dog's red-thing is sticking way out of it's sheath.   It's monstrous.

3) Jay and Silent Bob laugh hysterically.

                    JAY
          His fuckin' red thing is bigger than him,
          man!!! Look at that shit!!! Homeboy's got
          a fuckin' pooch-stock!!!

4) The dog lays on its back with it's tongue hanging out of its mouth.

                    JAY V.O.
          He's got a stoner-boner, man!   That shit
          is fucked up!

5) Tears in their eyes from laughing so hard, Jay hands Silent Bob a stick.

                    JAY
          Dude - touch it with the stick, man.   Not
          hard, man.   Just tap it and see if he blows
          a nut.

6) Silent Bob reaches through the fence with the stick, aiming for the dog's red thing.

7) The tip of the stick lightly grazes the tip of the red thing with a 'TAP'.

8) Suddenly, the dog goes wide-eyed with a yelp.

9) He rockets over the fence at Silent Bob, ferociously.   Jay shrieks.

                    JAY
          FLEE, FAT-ASS, FLEE!!!

PAGES FOURTEEN AND FIFTEEN

EXT WHEREVER - NIGHT

For most of the page, the dog chases after Jay and Silent Bob in various places, yipping viciously: through the streets, past Quick Stop, through traffic, over a car, past a building that says 'Y.M.C.A' where there are ambulances parked outside. Alternate shots of the terrified Jay and Silent Bob (at least one frame where Jay's in Silent Bob's arms, with the dog at Bob's heels) and the pissed off rat terrier.

EXT WALT FLANGAN'S PARENTS' HOUSE - DAWN

1) Finally, they wind up back at Walt Flanagan's pad. Jay and Silent Bob race into the yard, followed by the dog.

2) They hop the fence, and slam the gate shut behind them.

3) The dog continues to yip, as Jay and Silent Bob collapse near the fence, breathless.

>   JAY
>   Fuck, dude - that's one fast dog.

4) Walt leans out of the front door, wearing pajamas. Groggy-eyed, he yells.

>   WALT
>   KRYPTO! GET IN HERE!

5) The dog runs into the house past his master.

6) Jay and Silent Bob continue to pant.

7) Jay leans up, looking at Silent Bob.

>   JAY
>   I'm parched, bro. The mall opens in an
>   hour. Let's go get an Orange Julius.

8) Jay and Silent Bob stumble down the street - their backs to us.

>   JAY
>   I'll tell you what, Silent Bob - you can never
>   get stoned with a fuckin' dog. Especially one
>   of those small ones. Fuckers can't handle
>   their high. But a monkey, man - that'd be
>   the shit.

END

Check out www.AboutComics.com to

- order copies of the comics based on these scripts!
- tell us what you thought of this book!
- learn about our other books for comics fans and creators!